IMAGES
of America

MEXICO BEACH

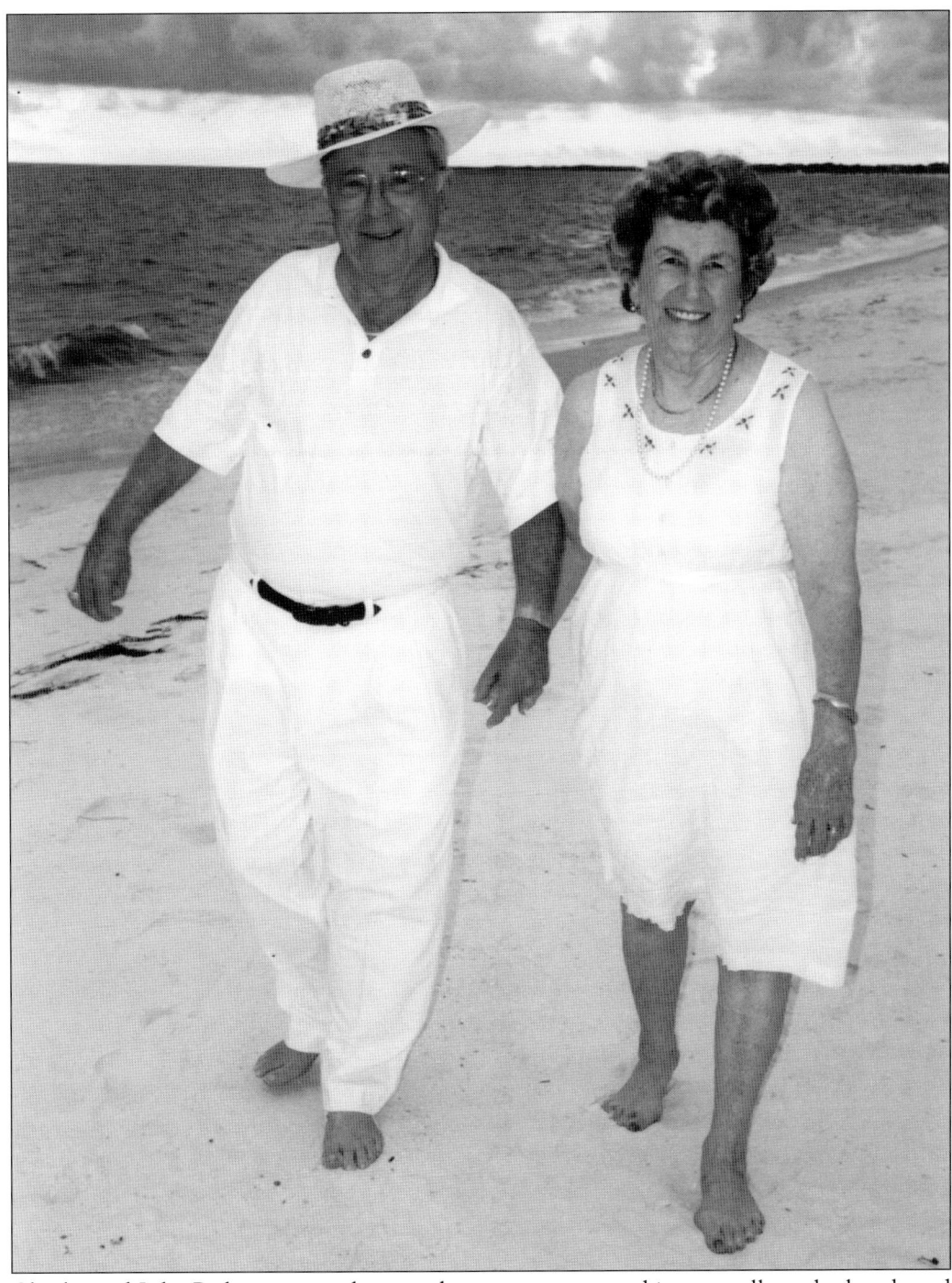

Charlie and Inky Parker are seen here in their sunset years, taking a stroll on the beach and reminiscing about a great life during the summer of 2001. (Courtesy of Dana Palmer.)

On the Cover: A typical summer day of fishing and fun in the sun is seen in this view of the Mexico Beach jetties in 1965. (Courtesy of Florida State Archives.)

IMAGES
of America
MEXICO BEACH

Al Cathey and Cathey Parker Hobbs

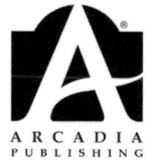

Copyright © 2014 by Al Cathey and Cathey Parker Hobbs
ISBN 978-1-4671-1160-7

Published by Arcadia Publishing
Charleston, South Carolina

Printed in the United States of America

Library of Congress Control Number: 2013949111

For all general information, please contact Arcadia Publishing:
Telephone 843-853-2070
Fax 843-853-0044
E-mail sales@arcadiapublishing.com
For customer service and orders:
Toll-Free 1-888-313-2665

Visit us on the Internet at www.arcadiapublishing.com

*Above all, we would like to show our appreciation to our parents,
Charlie and Inky Parker and Bubba and Marion Cathey,
for all they did to make Mexico Beach a wonderful place to
call home. It is an honor to dedicate this book to them.*

Contents

Acknowledgments		6
Introduction		7
1.	A Place to Remember	9
2.	Fun in Paradise	23
3.	Let's Go Fishing	37
4.	Mom-and-Pop Businesses	53
5.	Pioneer Families	67
6.	Making Memories	81
7.	Early Beach Cottages	89
8.	Past and Present	95
9.	Hurricane Season	107
10.	Beacon Hill and Overstreet	115

ACKNOWLEDGMENTS

The authors would like to thank Beverly Mount Douds for her knowledge and guidance in helping make this book a reality. Beverly has written three pictorial history books about area towns and is an avid researcher. Thank you to Judy Carrell for providing the information on Marianna Hill for the introduction. Also to be thanked are all the people who love Mexico Beach and helped by sharing their photographs and stories with us.

Introduction

Accounts of Mexico Beach's past are vague before the early 1900s. As French interests in the Americas dwindled, records indicate very little activity in the area until rumors of buried riches and sunken ships brought treasure hunters to the coast. Businessman Felix du Pont purchased the land now occupied by the city of Mexico Beach in the early 1900s. Native pine trees were harvested to produce turpentine, and the area gained a bit of exposure to public eyes. Fishermen were the first to embrace the newly discovered and newly accessible beaches. The allure of amazing spring and fall runs of migratory fish were as difficult to resist then as they are today. In 1918, Gordon Parker moved his wife and family from Brewton, Alabama, to a small town on the banks of the Apalachicola River to go into the lumber and veneer business. From then on, the Parker name would forever be linked to the area.

The 1930s saw the completion of Highway 98, which vastly increased the number of visitors to the area. In early 1941, Tyndall Field was constructed and became the training site for pilots in the Air Force. Livestock and wildlife still roamed freely along the new road and accommodations were very limited. Growth was slow, and the sleepy community remained quiet.

In April 1946, a picturesque parcel of property on the north side of Highway 98, from Route 386 west to Sea Street, was purchased by L.C. Tucker of Blountstown, through O.O. Miller, from Felix du Pont for $5,148. In that same year, Marianna native Floie Packard, the wife of John C. Packard, negotiated with Tucker to purchase a portion of the property. Due to the size of the property, Packard contacted friends and associates in hopes of finding prospective buyers. With the majority of the buyers coming from Packard's hometown, Marianna Hill was born. On March 7, 1947, the Tuckers deeded the 1,350 feet of Gulf-front property to the State of Florida for its preservation and perpetual public use. The original owners shown on the deeds were Virginia Brownlee (Marianna), Julia Criglar (Marianna), Floie Packard (Marianna), Clara Farley (Marianna), Slade West (Marianna), Annie West (Marianna), Reva Greening (Springfield, Illinois), Margarite Finlayson (Marianna), Dexter McCaskill (Marianna), Bruce Singletary (Marianna), Margarite Cooper (Prattville, Alabama), H.V. Milton (Marianna), W.F. Fite (Marianna), Anna and Constance Dozier (Columbus, Georgia) Lawrence Dozier (Columbus, Georgia), Mr. and Mrs. William Johnston (Columbus, Georgia), L.L. MacKinnon (Marianna), and Margaret and Henry Hanson (Jacksonville).

In late 1946, a group of farsighted businessmen led by Gordon Parker, W.T. McGowan, and J.W. Wainwright purchased 1,850 acres along the beach for $65,000. Shortly thereafter, development began in earnest. Parker's youngest son, Charlie, soon took over development responsibilities for his father's company, the Mexico Beach Corporation. His determination, effort, and vision shaped the area into the Mexico Beach of today. Charlie Parker and his wife, Inky, moved their lives and their two daughters to the Unforgettable Coast in 1949. Through their strong belief in God and their dedication to family values, hard work, and sacrifice, they made Mexico Beach home.

The little community suffered growing pains, with many plans for development realized and others shelved. The challenges were many, but slow growth ensued, and Mexico Beach boasted several hundred residents by 1955. Landmark accomplishments by the Mexico Beach Corporation under the guidance of Charlie Parker remain as footprints in the sand today. A beautiful, more-than-one-mile-long unobstructed view of the Gulf of Mexico is a result of all Gulf-front property from Seventh Street to Sea Street being platted and recorded for public use in 1949. In 1953, the water plant and a 100,000-gallon elevated storage tank were constructed, and in 1955, the Mexico Beach Canal became a reality. In 1957, the First United Methodist Church of Mexico Beach was organized.

By 1967, the little town was ready to incorporate, and the City of Mexico Beach was formed. Residents elected Charlie Parker as their first mayor. Since then, the beach town has kept growing steadily. Over 1,000 residents currently call Mexico Beach home. City officials have embraced Parker's vision, preserved Mexico Beach's reputation as a family-friendly vacation spot, and attracted quality mom-and-pop businesses to the Unforgettable Coast. Mexico Beach has undeniable appeal. Residents love it, and out-of-town visitors happily return year after year. Some 60 years ago, Mexico Beach was a nameless rainbow curve of white sand beaches with blue water and sloping dunes speckled with sea oats the color of weathered gold. There were no piers, no roadhouses, no motels, and no gas stations. Only Route 98, within a snapshot of the water, laid a track across the sand so fine it was compared to sugar. Those fortunate enough to visit and those blessed enough to call it home are grateful to the early families of Mexico Beach who worked tirelessly to preserve this "special little place on earth."

The authors were raised by pioneer families, and their childhood days were filled with some lasting "beach kid" memories. Shell hunting on the beach without worries, scooping buckets of blue crabs from the Gulf, and fishing from the surf or the pier were all part of the daily routine. Exploring sand dunes and enjoying private beach cabanas were common events. Fireworks were the display of phosphorus from splashing hands and feet in the Gulf on a moonlit night. A beach social was a game of putt-putt golf or a gathering of friends and family around a bonfire enjoying hot dogs and marshmallows. A daring and exciting evening at the skating rink was punctuated by jumping Coca-Cola crates or finding oneself on the end of "the whip." Beach life was good, and that has not changed.

Much beloved by his community and dearly missed by his family, Charlie Parker passed away in 2003. His beloved wife, Inky, reunited with him in 2007.

One
A Place to Remember

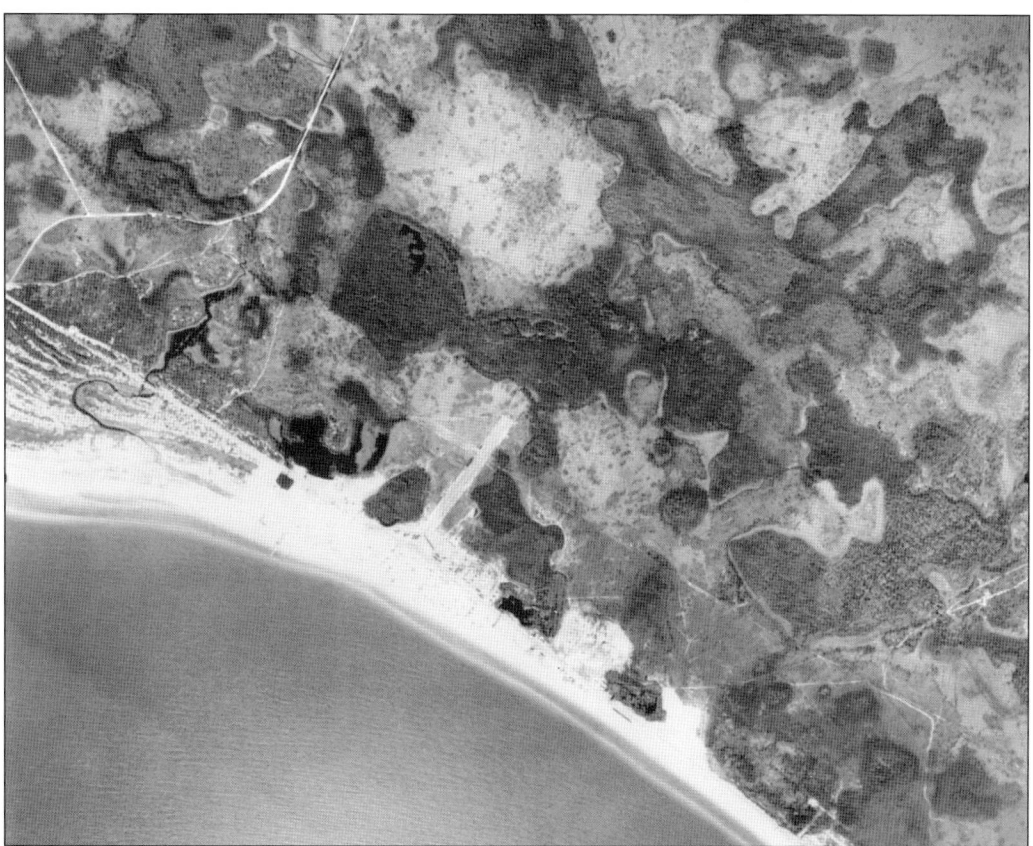

In 1953, a grass airstrip (center) was built behind Mexico Beach Shopping Center on North Thirty-first Street. The airstrip was developed and maintained by the Mexico Beach Corporation and was used by home owners and fishermen. This photograph shows the original lay of the land before the canal system was dug, when Salt Creek (far left) meandered toward the Gulf. The airfield was operational from the late 1940s through the early 1960s. (Courtesy of Al Cathey.)

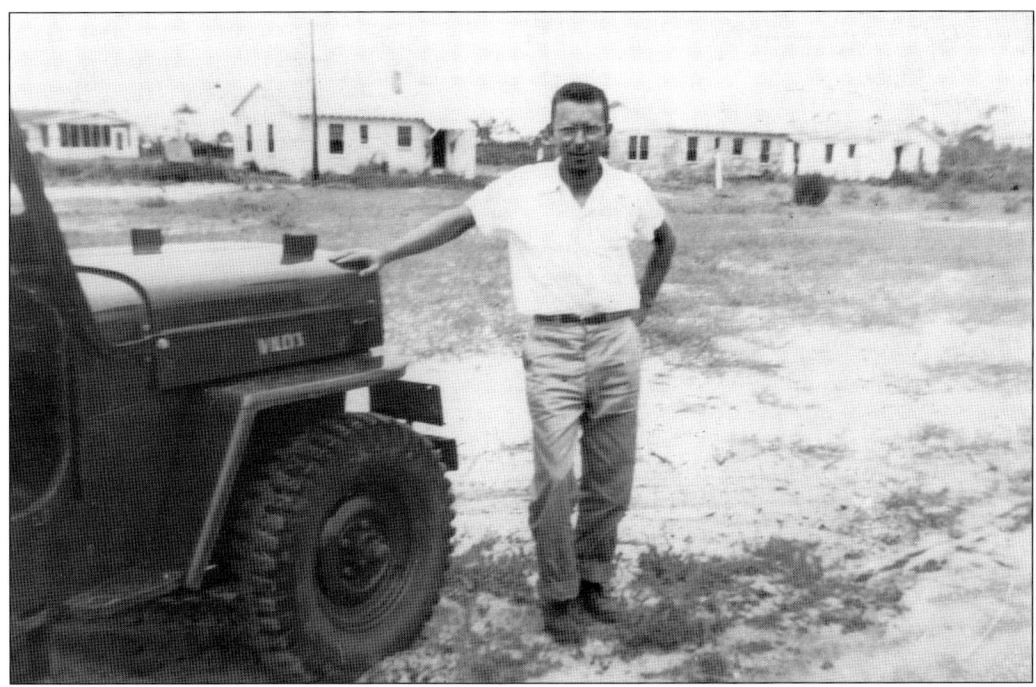

Throughout the 1950s, Charlie Parker traveled from job site to job site in his Willis Jeep. (Courtesy of the Parker family.)

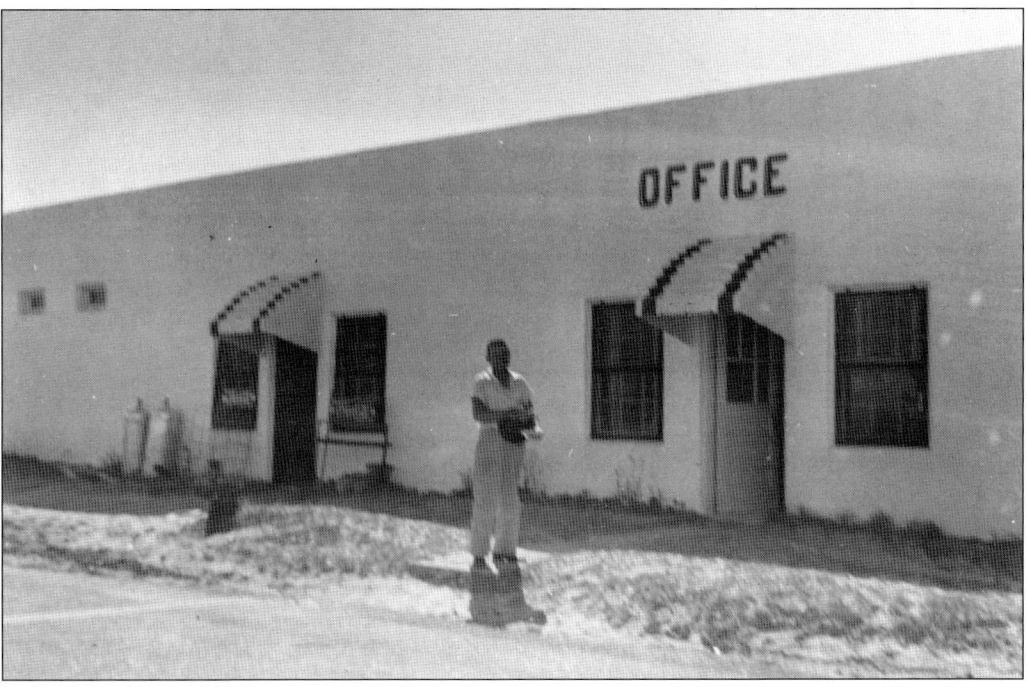

Charlie Parker stands in front of his first office in Mexico Beach, which was located in the rear of the first grocery store. A launderette was located in the middle section of the store. (Courtesy of the Parker family.)

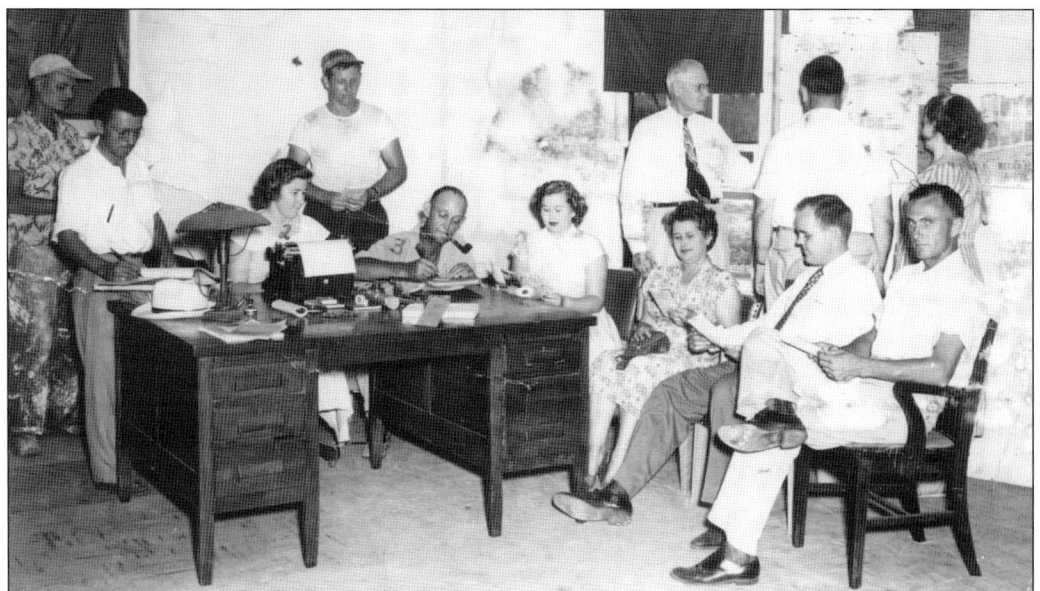

This photograph offers a glimpse into a Mexico Beach planning meeting in the early 1950s. Identified are the following: Inky Parker, sitting at desk; Charlie Parker, to her left; Richard L. Fortner, seated with pipe; W.D. McGowin, standing wearing a tie; and J.D. Fleming, seated in the last chair on the right. J.D. Fleming and his wife, Beulah, and children Bill, Jadine, Donna, and Dewey lived in Mexico Beach in the early 1950s when J.D. worked on the early development of the town. (Courtesy of Sonny Fortner.)

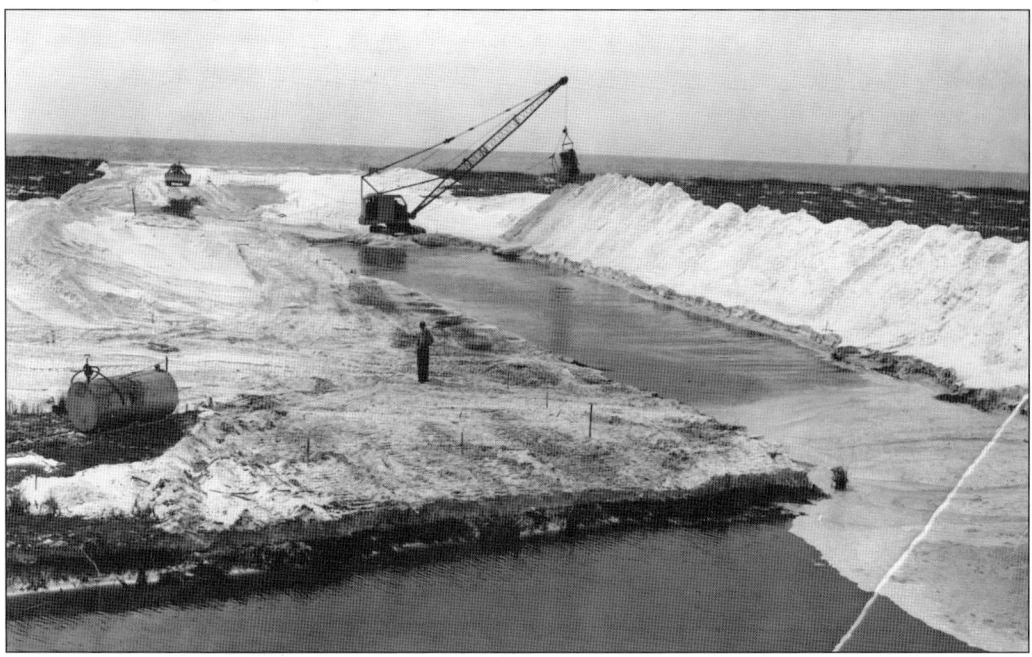

The dream of Mexico Beach founder Charles M. Parker to have easy and safe access for boaters to and from the Gulf of Mexico became a reality in 1955. As the town grew, the Mexico Beach Canal became an integral part of the community's economy, which it still is today. (Courtesy of Brenda Ward.)

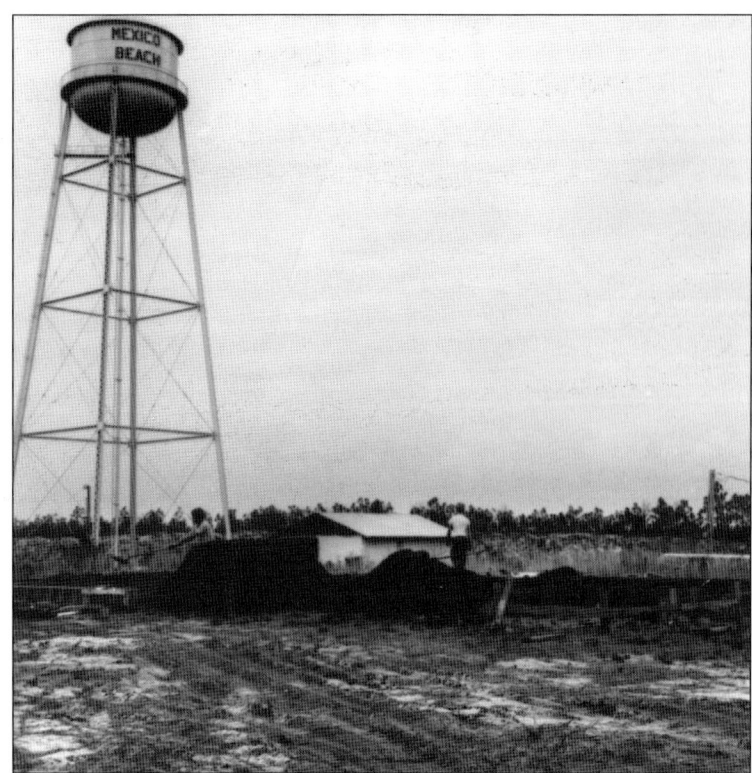

The Mexico Beach water tank and pump house are seen here being built. The water for the town was supplied from an 18-foot, 625-foot-deep well. The 100,000-gallon water tower and water plant were constructed in 1953. The facility was purchased by the City of Mexico Beach from the Mexico Beach Corporation in 1979 for $557,000. (Courtesy of Cathey Parker Hobbs.)

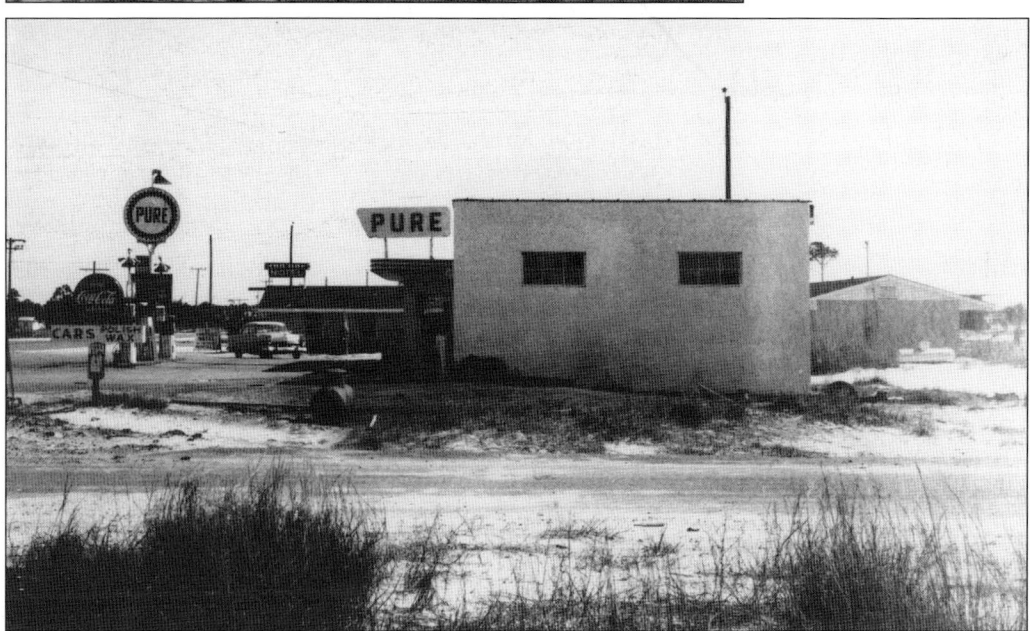

The Pure Oil station and the Ebb Tide Motel (background) were located between Fortieth and Forty-first Streets on Highway 98. After being built in the mid-1950s, both businesses were sold in 1959 by owner Zack Brookins to George and Louise Holland. Later that year, the Hollands became partners with the Earley family—Barney and Mary and sons Chris and Phil. (Courtesy of Al Cathey.)

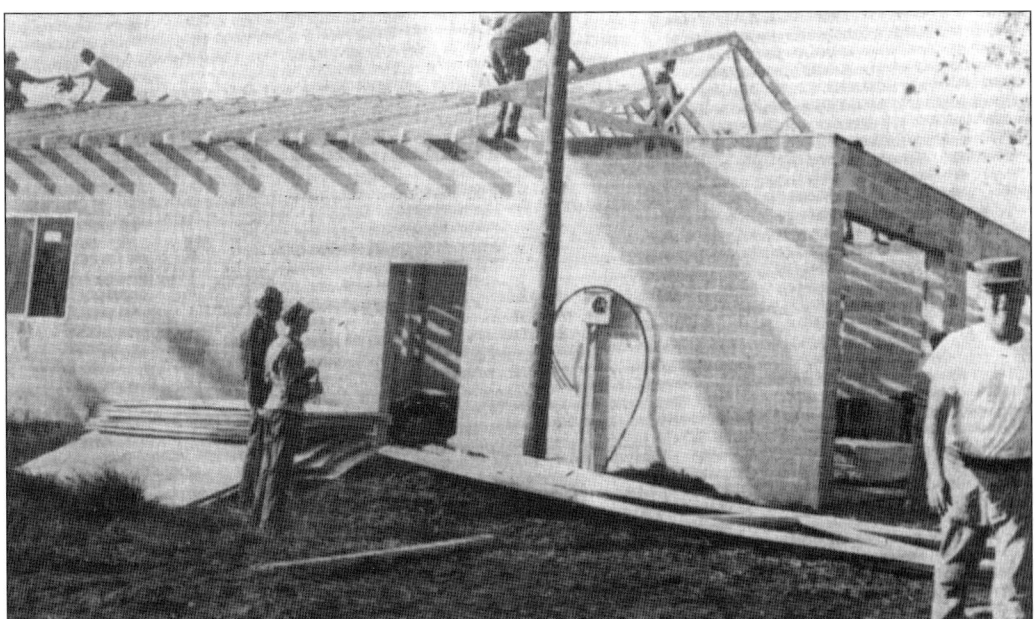

Mexico Beach residents literally "raised the roof" on a Saturday in the early 1970s when they gathered to finish the community's new firehouse. With additions and renovations, the building, located at the end of Fourteenth Street, remains today as the city's fire and police station. (Courtesy of the Mexico Beach Volunteer Fire Department.)

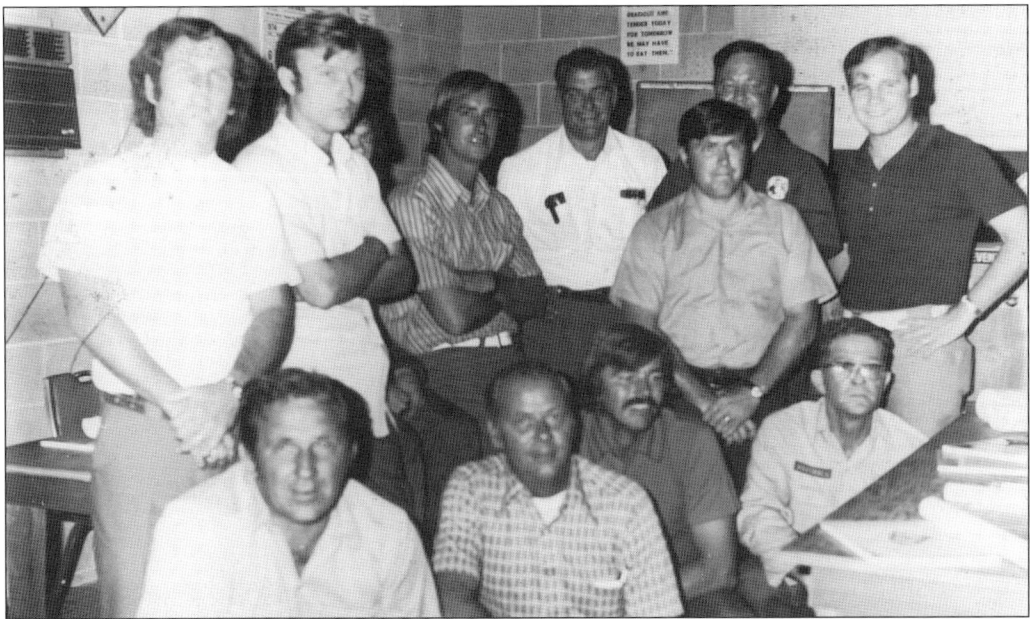

Mexico Beach welcomed their first volunteer firefighters in November 1970. The newly formed fire department served St. Joe Beach, Beacon Hill, Overstreet, and Mexico Beach. Seen here in February 1974, the volunteers were, from left to right, (first row) assistant fire chief George Hunter, fire chief Ken Keiser, Larry Brooks, and ranger Archie Marshall; (second row) Ernest Thursbay, Jim Leckie, Jerry Cozart, Jim Middleton, Ralph Kimmell, ranger Gene Hanlon, Ralph Kimmell, and Bernie Diesler. (Courtesy of the Mexico Beach Volunteer Fire Department.)

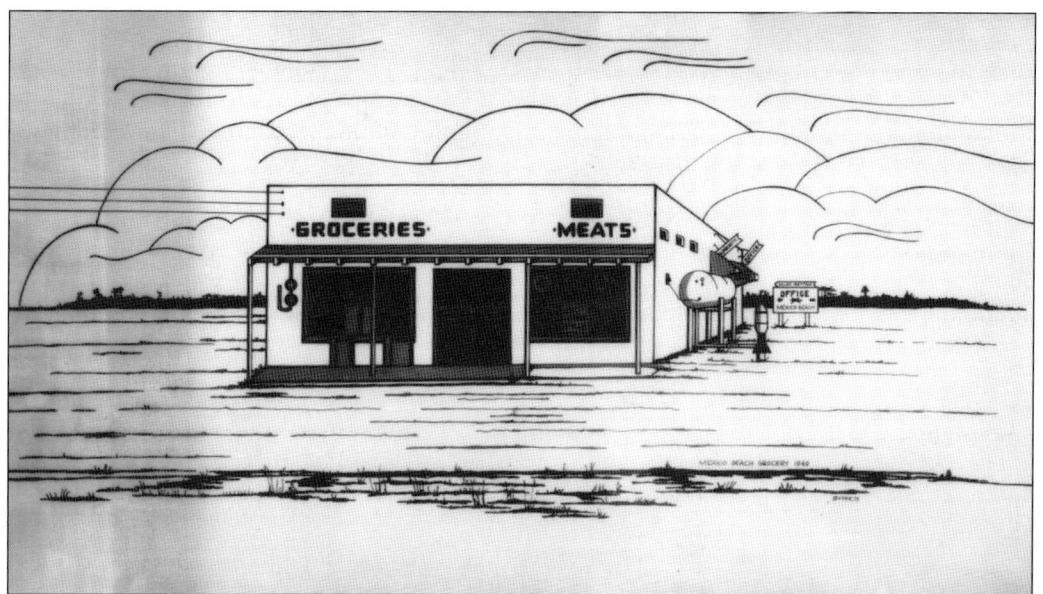

Mexico Beach Grocery was built in 1949 by Gordon Parker. In August 1949, Charlie and Inky Parker; their two daughters Cathey and Sue; Inky's mother, Estelle "Mom" Cathey; and her son Val all moved to Mexico Beach. Estelle Cathey, whose husband, Othal Cathey, had recently passed away, purchased and operated the grocery. The back of the store was the Parkers' first real estate office, and a small space in between was the first launderette. (Courtesy of George Boyer.)

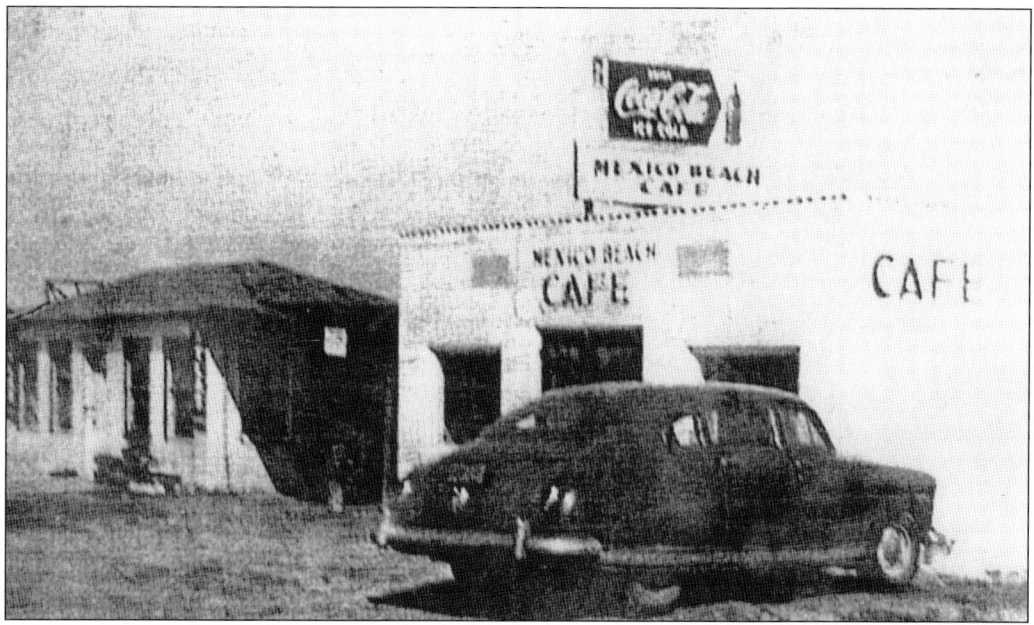

The Mexico Beach Café was the first restaurant in Mexico Beach. Built by the Hendricks family in 1949, it truly was a family-run business. The father tended the gas pumps, the mother cooked, and their daughter waited tables. Because of health problems, Hendricks felt that the café was too much of a burden on his family and sold the business to Roy Conoley in the early 1950s. (Courtesy of Cathey Parker Hobbs.)

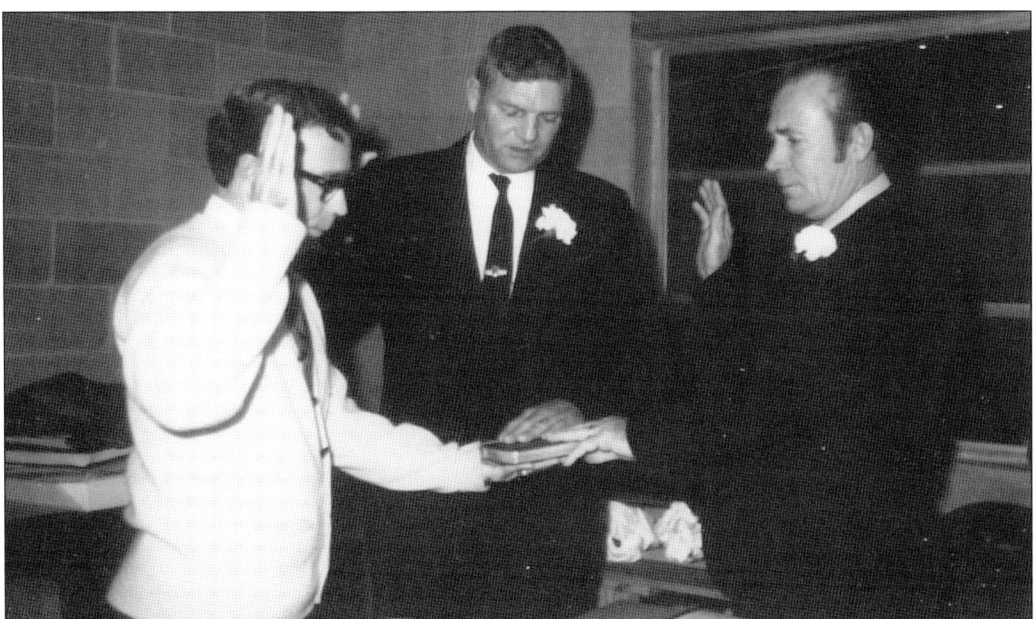

Mayor Charlie Parker swears in new councilmen Jim Long and Ed Crooms in November 1969. Long later became the town's first policeman. From left to right are Charlie Parker, Jim Long, and Ed Crooms. (Courtesy of the Parker family.)

This ballot shows the vote count for the incorporation of the Town of Mexico Beach (63-61 favoring incorporation) as well as the election results for the first mayor and town council. (Courtesy of Al Cathey.)

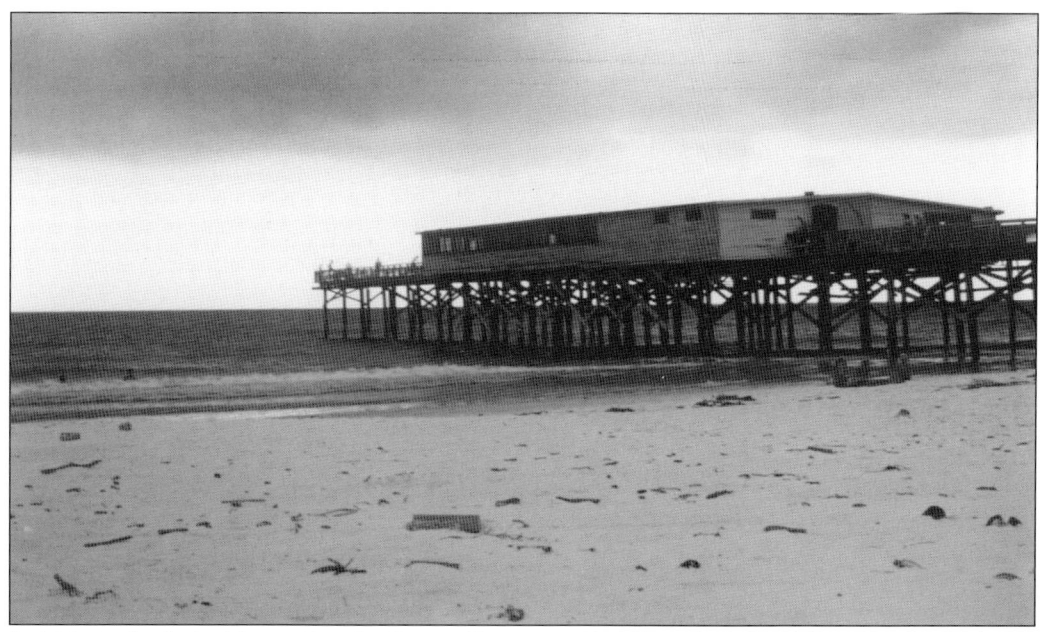

Jack Taylor built the Tapper Pier for George Tapper in 1949. It included bathhouses, a bar, a dance floor, a kitchen, and a dining hall, with the last 100 feet open for fishing. Doc Gillespie managed the fishing pier, while the Greek-style restaurant was leased and run by the Vathis family. The pier was severely damaged on September 24, 1956, by Hurricane Flossy. Currently, the location is home to the Mexico Beach Pier. (Courtesy of Al Cathey and Cathey Parker Hobbs.)

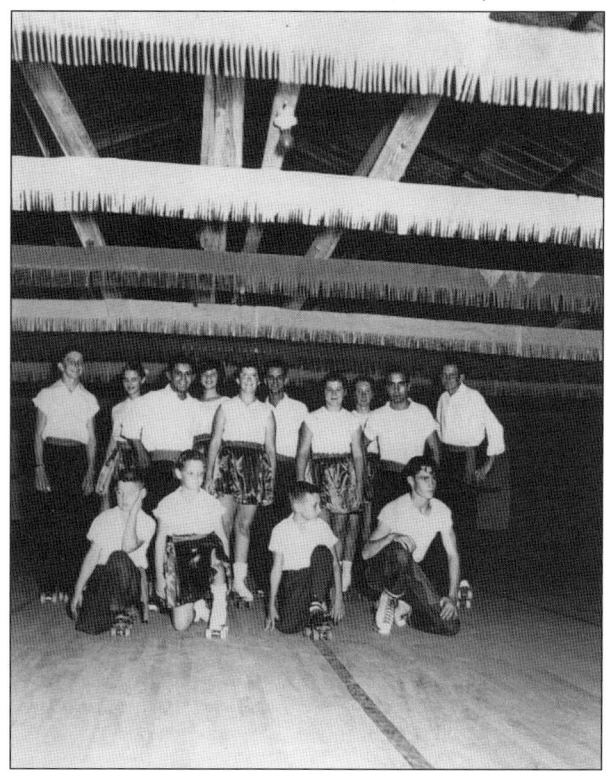

Pictured here is the old skating rink owned by Lee Williams during the late 1940s and 1950s. It was enjoyed by locals and later was turned into a mini mall with shops and food places until it was torn down. The Paradise Shores Condos at 800 Highway 98 were later built in the same location. From left to right are (kneeling) Robbie Costin, Brenda Ward, Richard Thompson, and unidentified; (standing) Binky Kilbourn, Skip Scission, two unidentified, Bobbie Ward, unidentified, Delores Chism, Carol Thompson, and two unidentified. (Courtesy of Mary Agnes Stephens.)

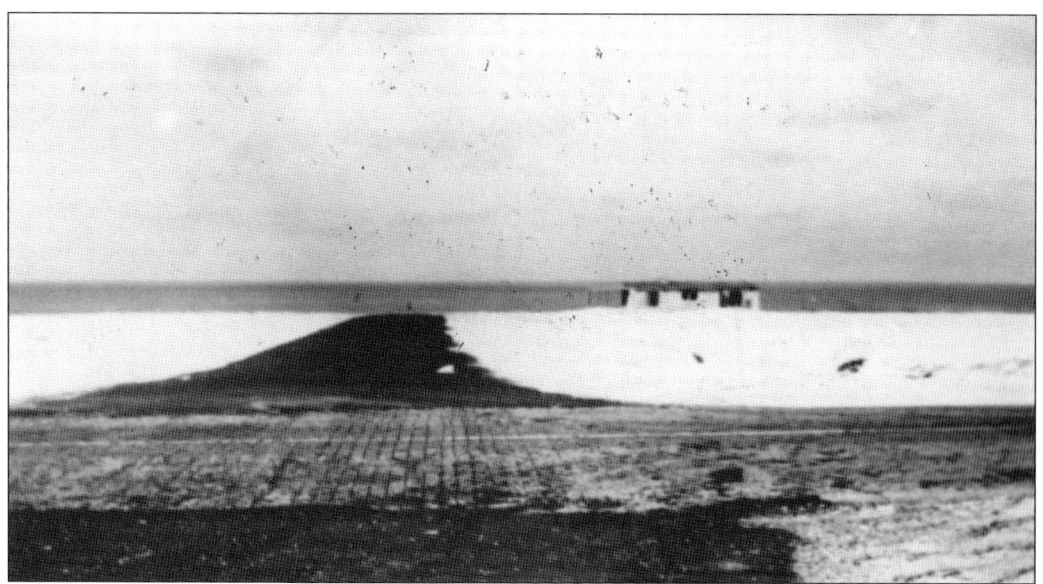

In 1949, a lonely waterfront beach cottage sits at the end of Thirty-second Street, south of Highway 98. (Courtesy of the Parker family.)

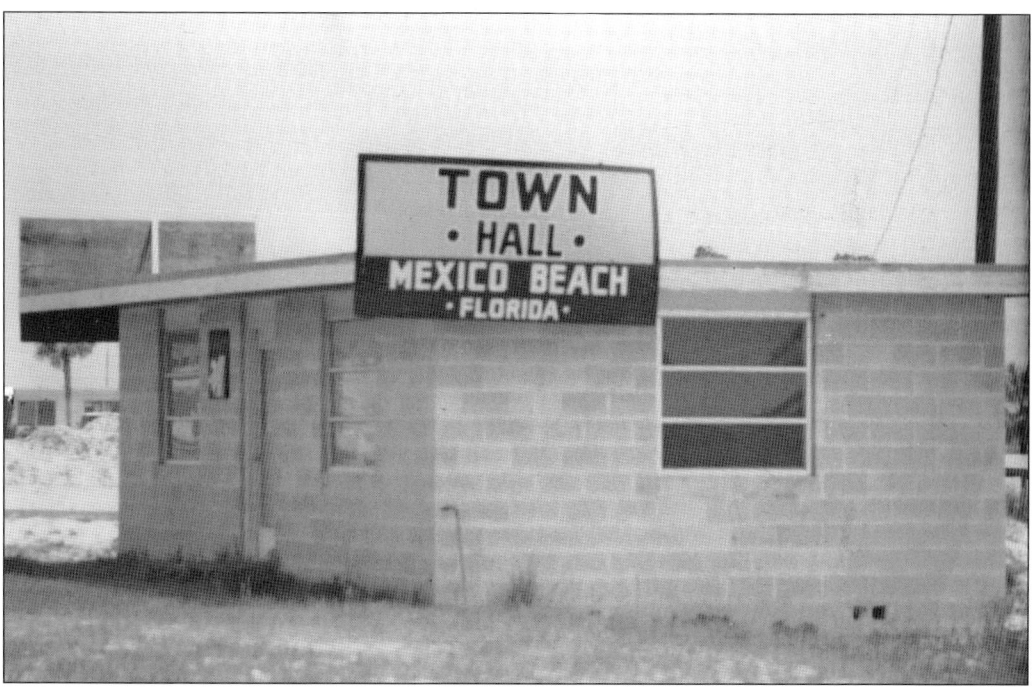

From 1967 to 1971, the first town hall was located in a building originally constructed by James Gaddis in 1964. After a state inspection found the building had no plumbing, it was vacated in 1971. The first town clerk was Harry Cook, while the first assistant town clerk was Tracie Middleton (Gaddis). Town hall moved in 1971 to the location of the current public safety building at the end of Fourteenth Street. (Courtesy of Doris Watson.)

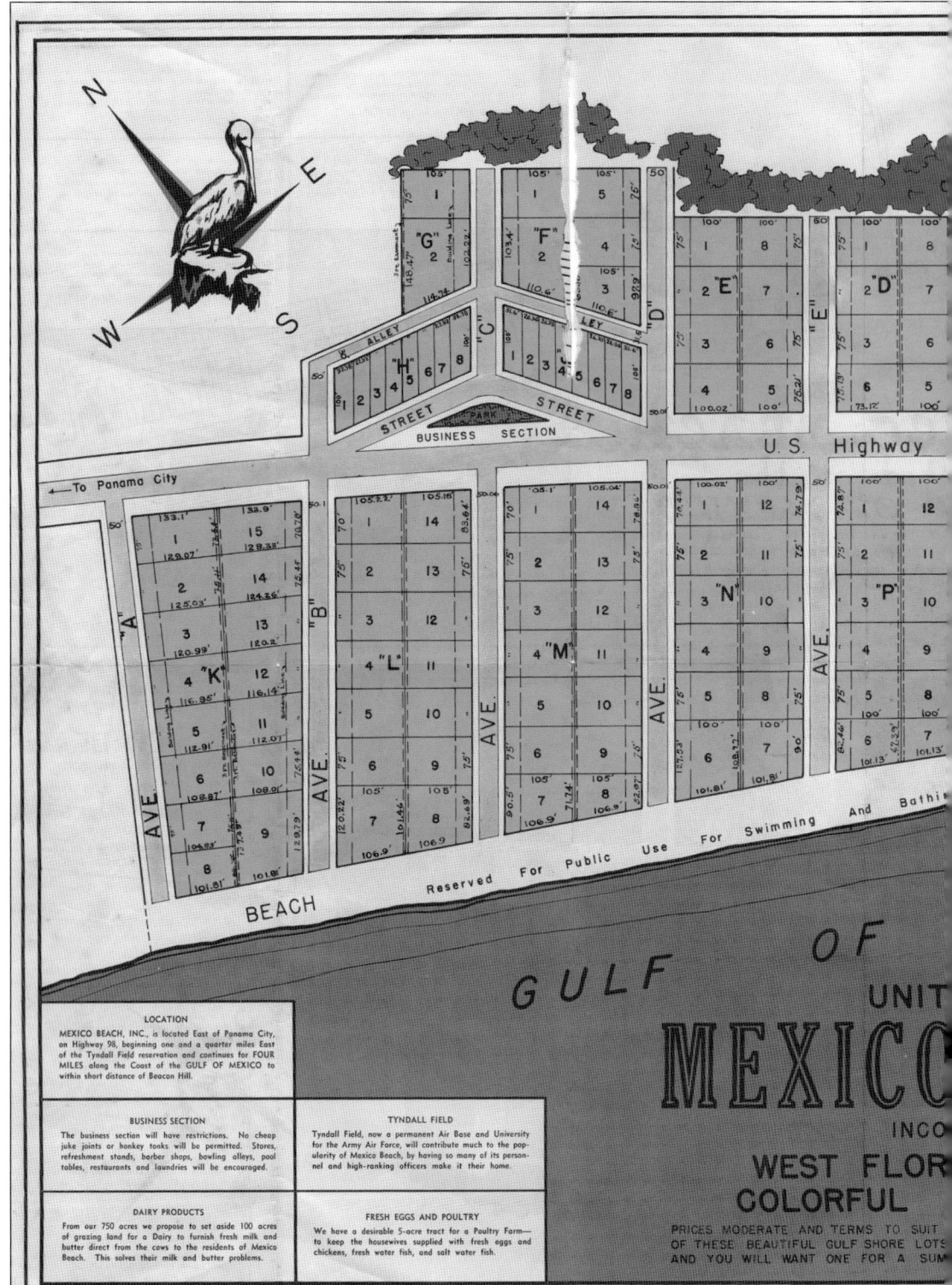

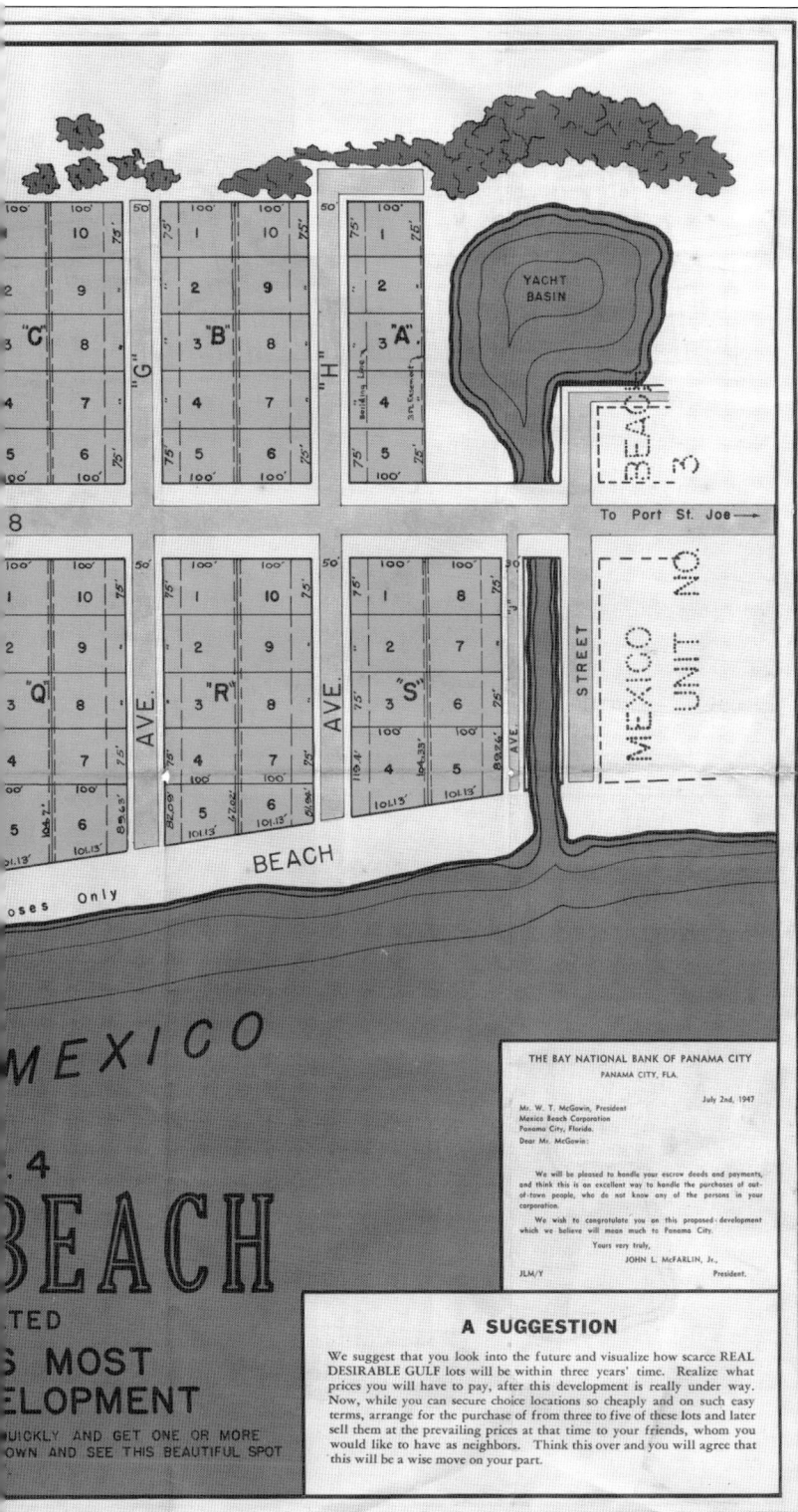

A 1948 Mexico Beach Unit 4 plat map is seen here in a local advertisement from the early 1950s. (Courtesy of Cathey Parker Hobbs.)

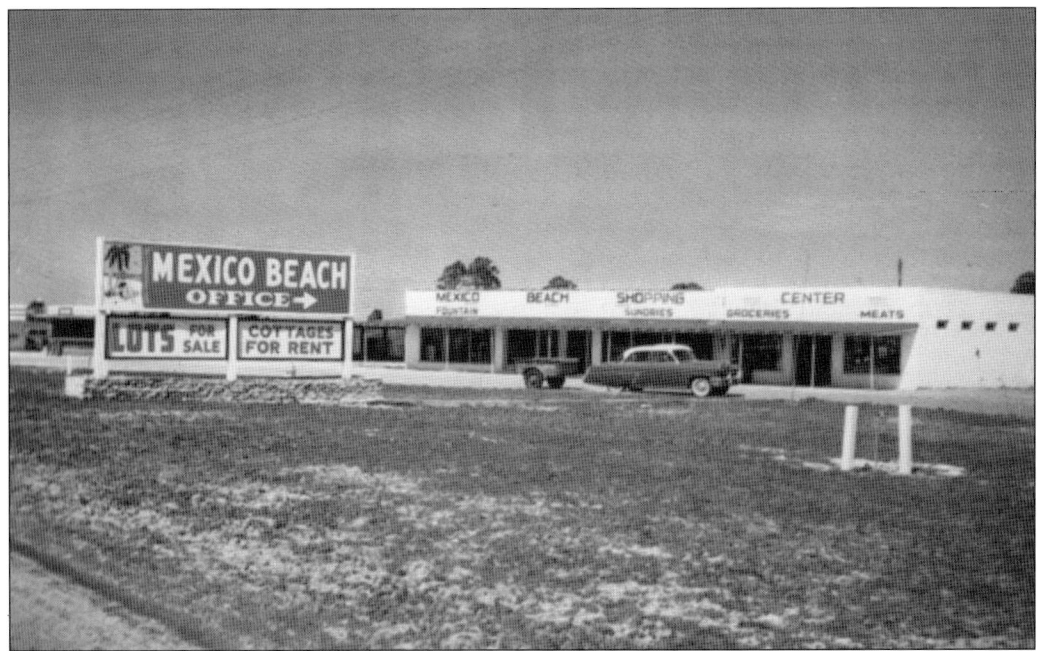

In 1953, the original Mexico Beach Grocery building was expanded to include a sundries store and post office. After this addition, the newly named Mexico Beach Shopping Center became the hub of business activity for the growing community. (Courtesy of the Parker family.)

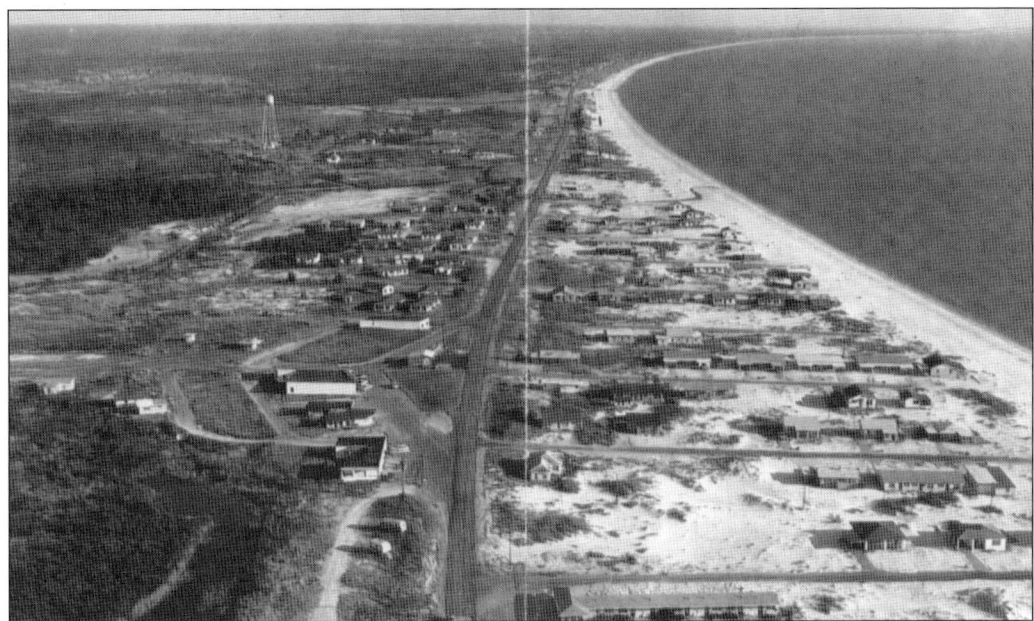

Mexico Beach is a long strip of beautifully curved beach on the Gulf of Mexico; the sand is so white it is sometimes called "Florida Snow." This 1959 aerial view starts at Thirty-third Street looking east. Note the business center, including the grass airfield and the T-hanger, the Mexico Beach Shopping Center, the Patio, Roy's Club, the launderette, the putt-putt golf, and Parker Realty. (Courtesy of the Parker family.)

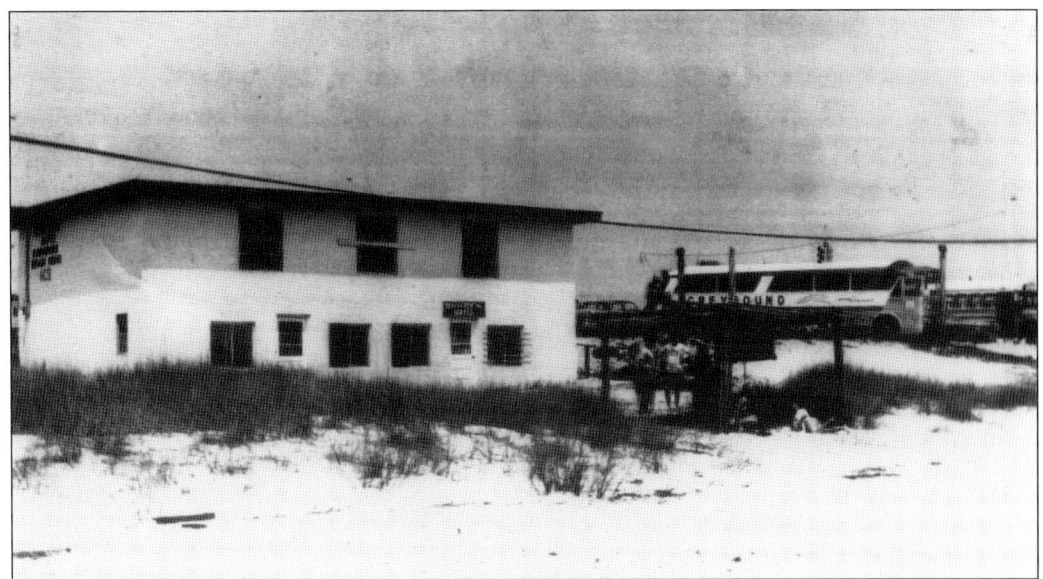

James and Lucille Gaddis and their children Terresa, Garry, and Allen moved to Mexico Beach in 1968. They owned Wayside Beach Supply, which was built in 1969 and then modified several times before being badly damaged during Hurricane Eloise in 1975. In 1989, it was sold and became Toucan's Restaurant, which is still in business at that site today. (Courtesy of Allen Gaddis.)

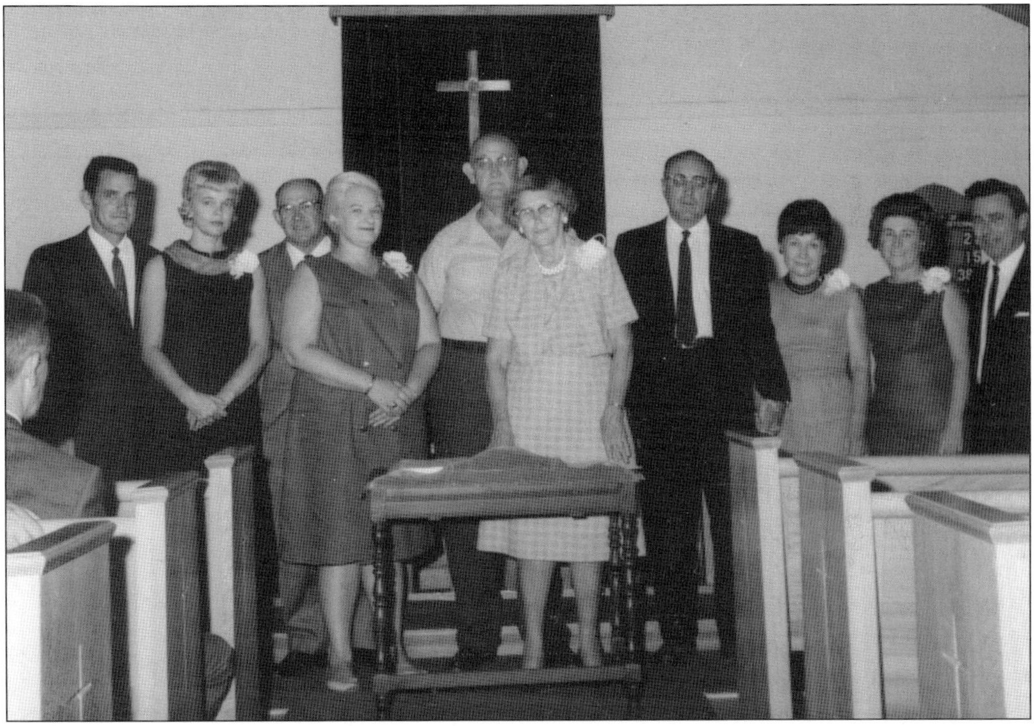

The first city council meeting was held on September 11, 1967, at the Methodist church in Mexico Beach. From left to right are George and Louise Holland, Ed and Inez Austin, Richard L. and Tommie Fortner, Sam and Mary Harmon, and Inky and Charles Parker. (Courtesy of the Parker family.)

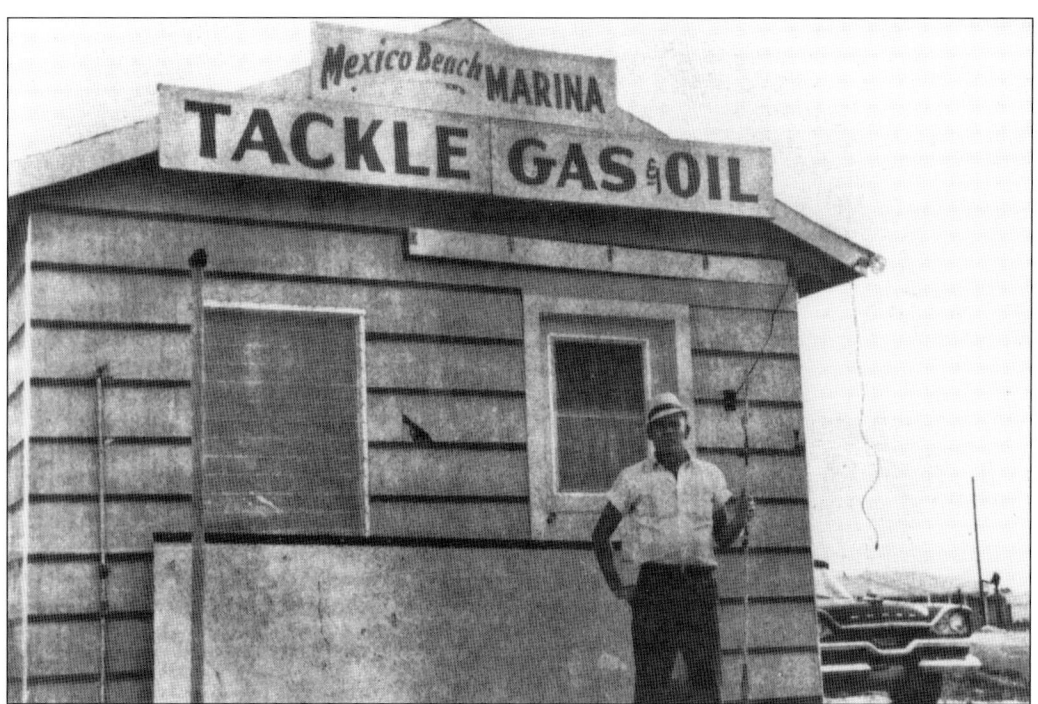
Wandell Butler, the owner of the renowned Butler's By the Bay Restaurant, stands in front of Mexico Beach Marina in the 1950s. (Courtesy of Ronnie Butler.)

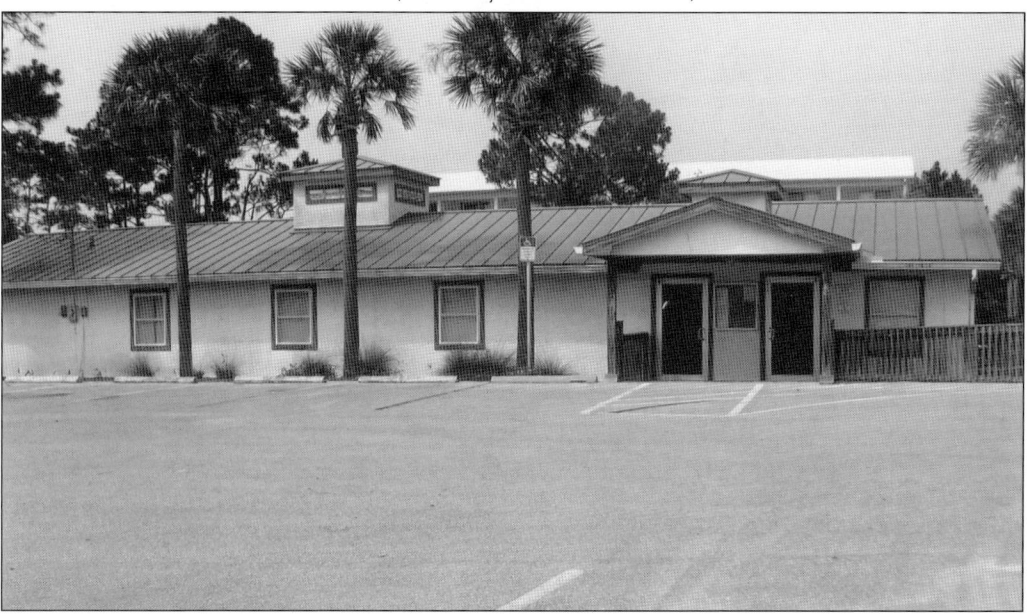
The Mexico Beach Civic Center was originally built in the early 1960s by the Mexico Beach Corporation. In 1972, a group of 32 local residents and businesspeople borrowed approximately $40,000 to purchase the land and the building. Soon, the chamber of commerce was formed, and the building was transformed into a meeting hall for chamber activities, senior citizens gatherings, town dinners, and Wednesday night bingo. In the mid-1990s, the property was deeded to the city. (Courtesy of Cathey Parker Hobbs.)

Two
FUN IN PARADISE

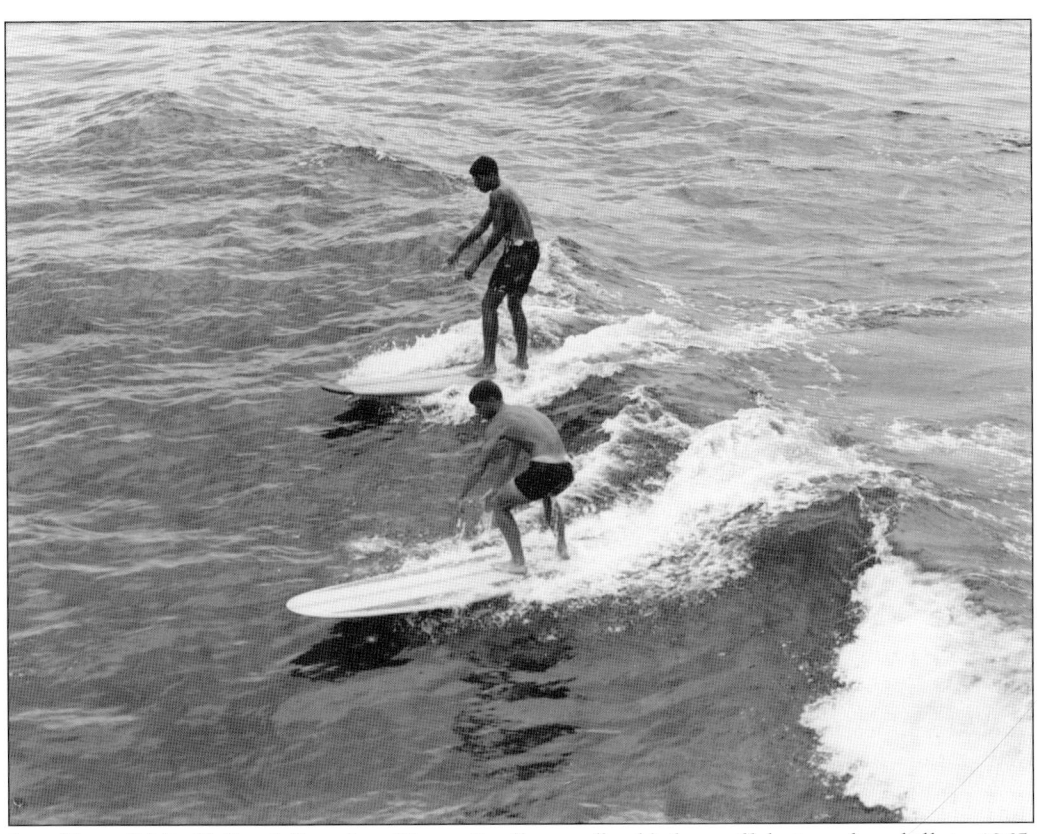

Local boys Eddie Holland (front) and Larry Snellgrove (back) show off their surfing skills in 1965. (Courtesy of the Parker family.)

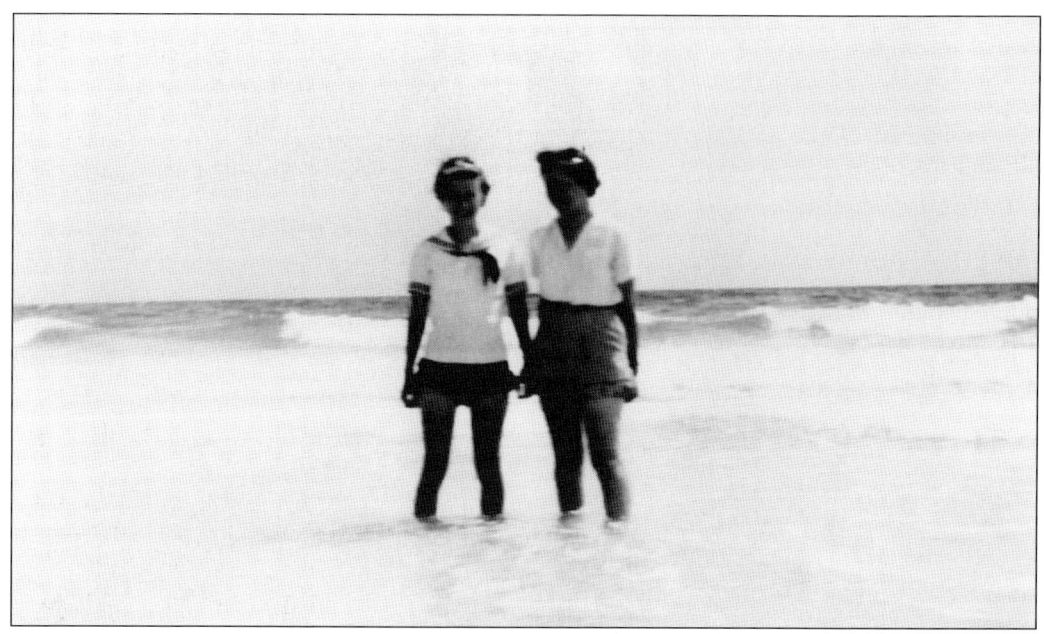

Pioneers Inky Parker (left) and Marion Cathey (right) stand in the waves of the Gulf of Mexico at the end of Thirty-first Street in the early 1950s. (Courtesy of the Parker family.)

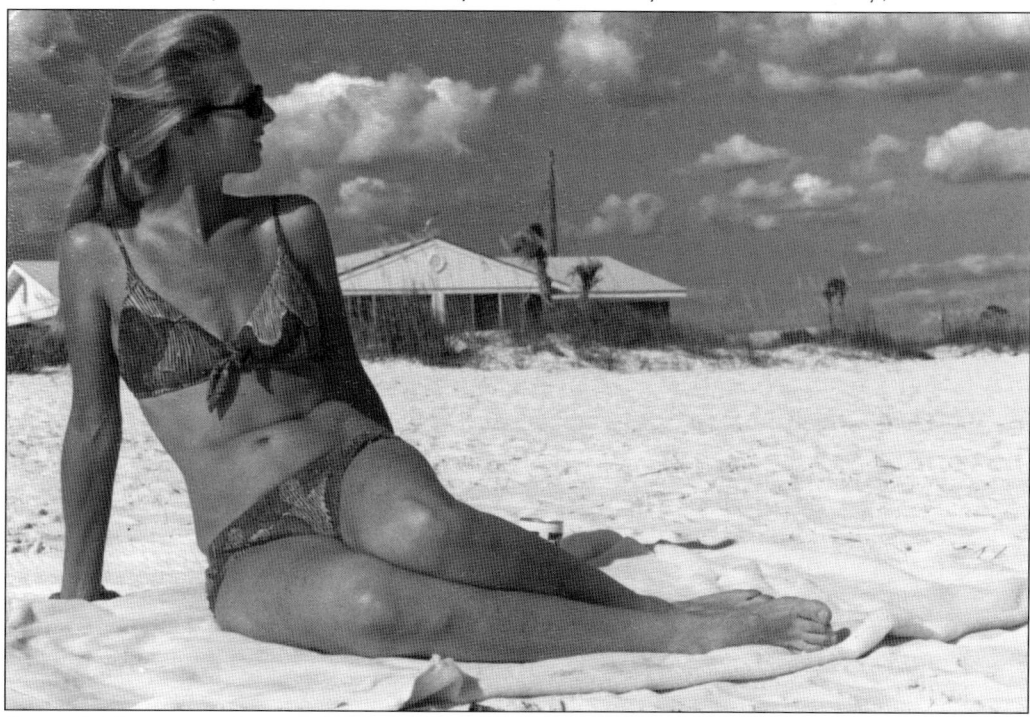

Orena Miller is seen here on the beach in the 1970s at Forty-second Street in Mexico Beach, where she and her husband, Frank, have lived since 1969. When asked why they chose Mexico Beach as their home, Frank said that he had traveled the world and that Mexico Beach was the most beautiful place he had ever seen. He said the people are the friendliest and the beaches are the nicest and cleanest. (Courtesy of Frank Miller.)

From left to right, Cathey and Sue Parker ride the merry-go-round in the 1950s. Other attractions that came to Mexico Beach in the early days were an outdoor skating rink, a train ride, elephant rides, and other carnival rides. (Courtesy of the Parker family.)

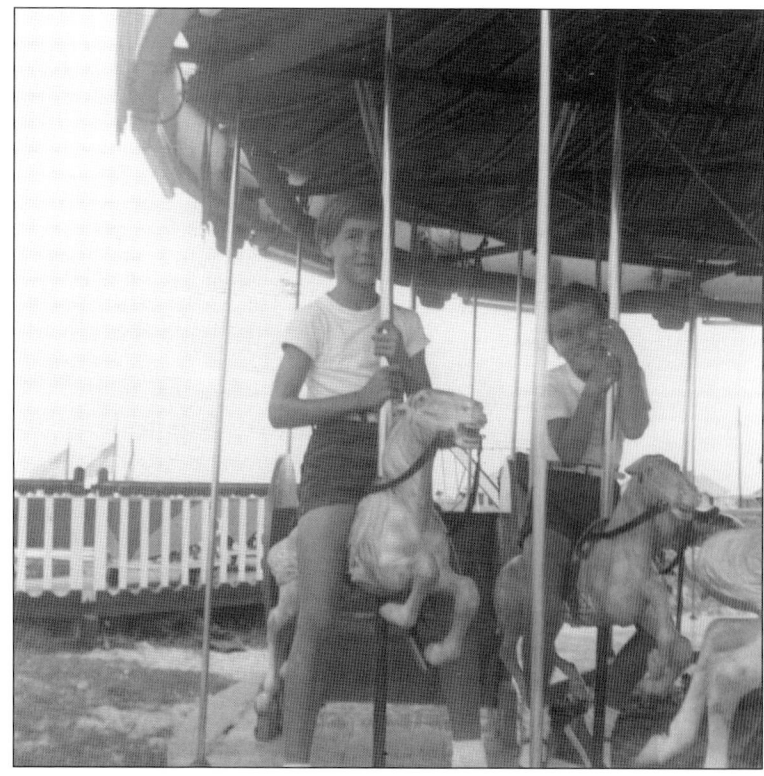

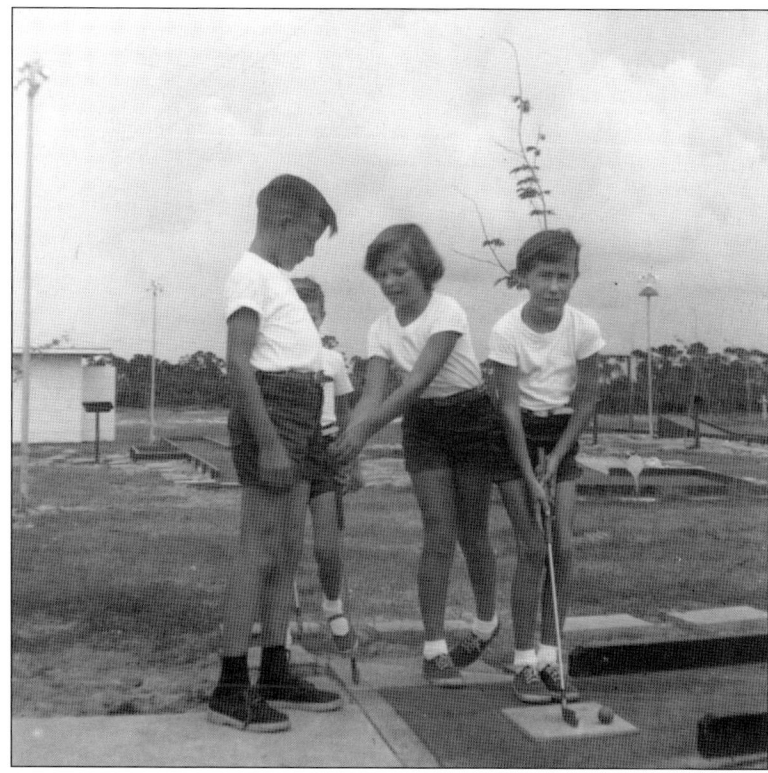

In the mid-1950s, from left to right, Barney Barrett, Sue Parker, Linda Barrett and Cathey Parker play a round of miniature golf at the putt-putt golf course behind what are now the Fish House Restaurant and Cathey's Ace Hardware. (Courtesy of the Parker family.)

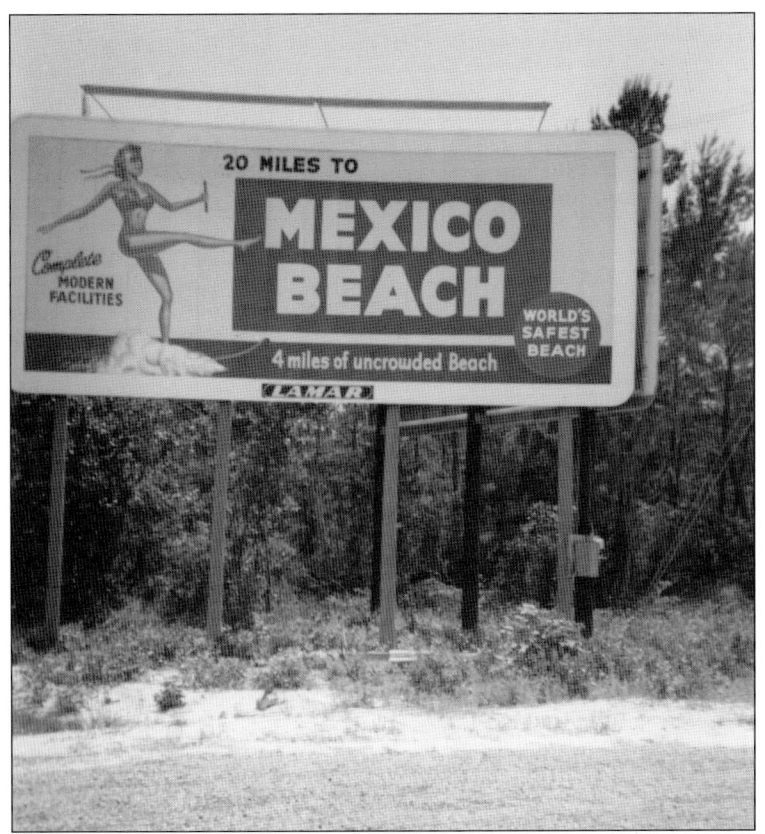

This was the first billboard advertising Mexico Beach. It appeared in the early 1960s and was located in Panama City near the intersection of Transmitter Road and Highway 231. (Courtesy of Al Cathey.)

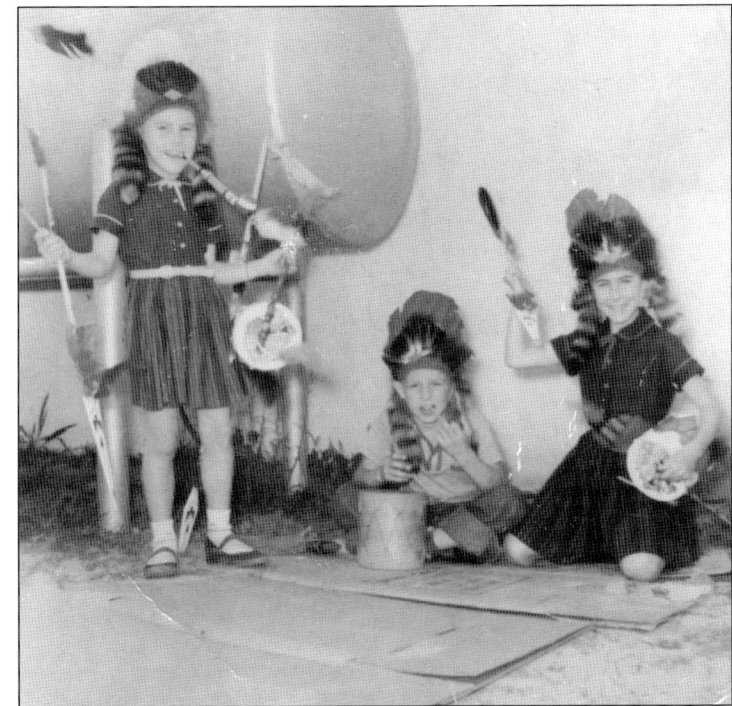

"Three Little Indians" play on the side of Mexico Beach Grocery in 1954. They are, from left to right, Sue Parker, Al Cathey, and Cathey Parker. (Courtesy of the Parker family.)

When the local carnival came to town, Roy Conoley would put a sheet on his head so that he looked like an Arab sheik, and then he would ride the elephant around town to delight all the local children. Margaret Buckloh is the girl riding with him in this photograph. (Courtesy of Roy Conoley Jr.)

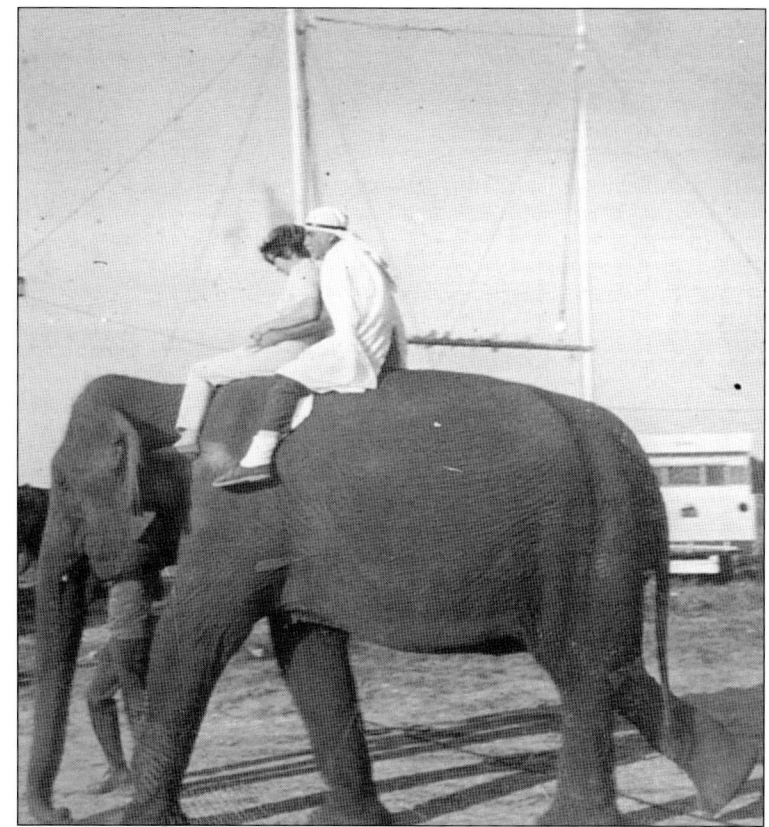

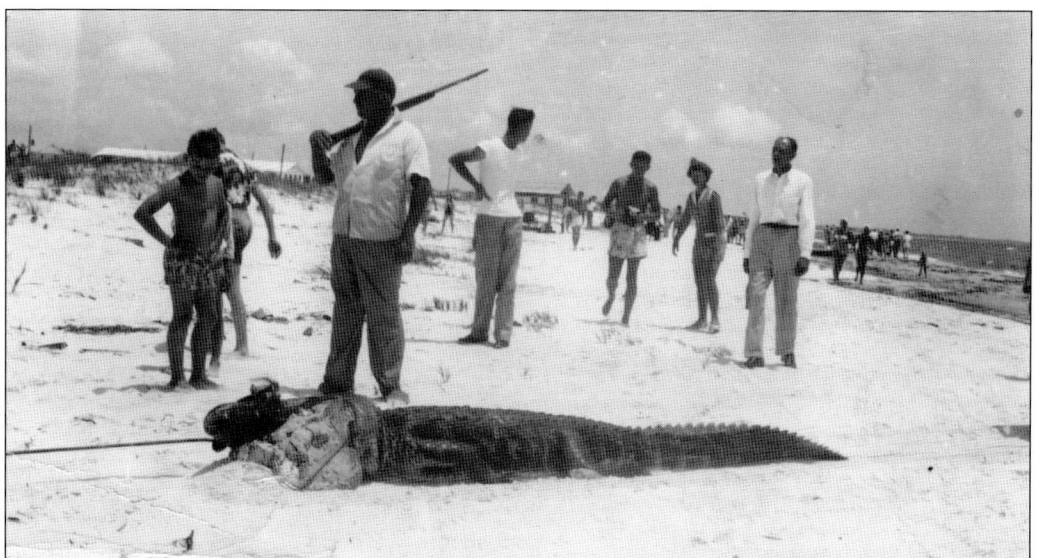

A 12-foot alligator was killed in the surf at the end of Thirty-second Street in May 1954 by Roy Conoley and Walter Howerton. Conoley had the gator stuffed and displayed at his Gulf station. He was sure people would come from all around to see the giant reptile, and they did. Later, a stuffed timber wolf was added to the collection. Big Gator Trailer Park was named after the beast. (Courtesy of Al Cathey.)

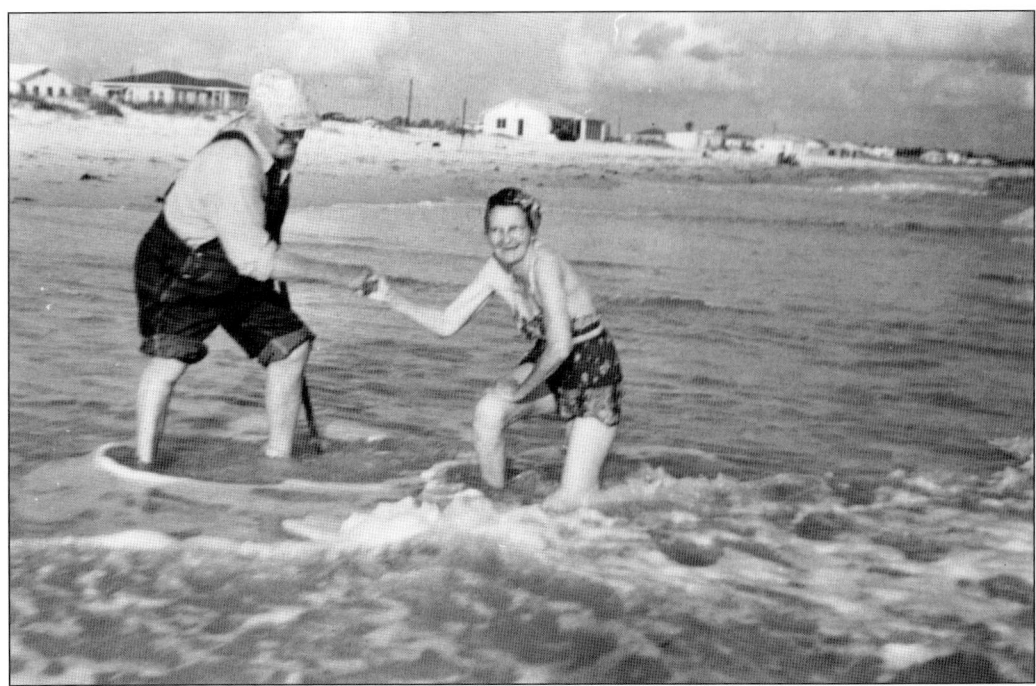

Jim Dodd and wife Margie, of Kosciusko, Mississippi, enjoy the surf at Mexico Beach in the 1950s. Margie was the sister of Estelle "Mom" Cathey. (Courtesy of the Parker family.)

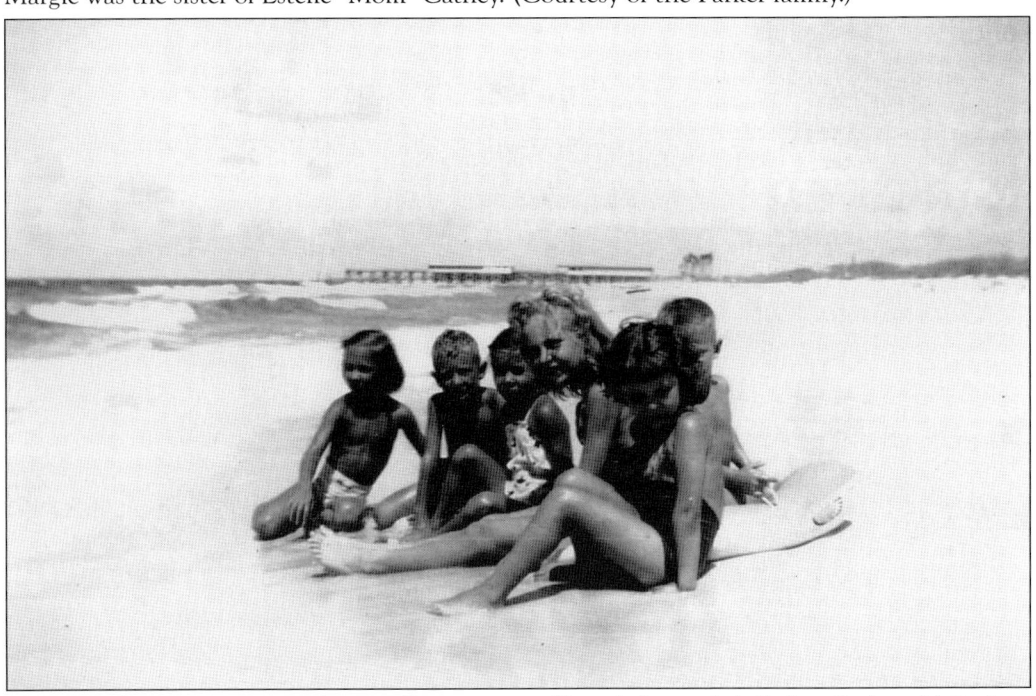

Sharing a day in Mexico Beach in 1953 are cousins (from left to right) Cathey Parker, Al Cathey, Sue Parker, Barbara Barrett, Charlie Barrett, and Nancy Barrett. The Barretts were the children of Voyne and Mildred Barrett of West Frankford, Illinois. Voyne was Estelle Cathey's brother. Note the Tapper Pier in the background. (Courtesy of Charlie Barrett.)

Sitting under a cabana on the beach east of Sea Street in the summer of 1952, Alma Wandeck and John Milton of Marianna enjoy a holiday at the Wandeck beach house. They later married and still enjoy coming to the beach house on Marianna Hill in Mexico Beach. (Courtesy of Joann Wandeck Wynn.)

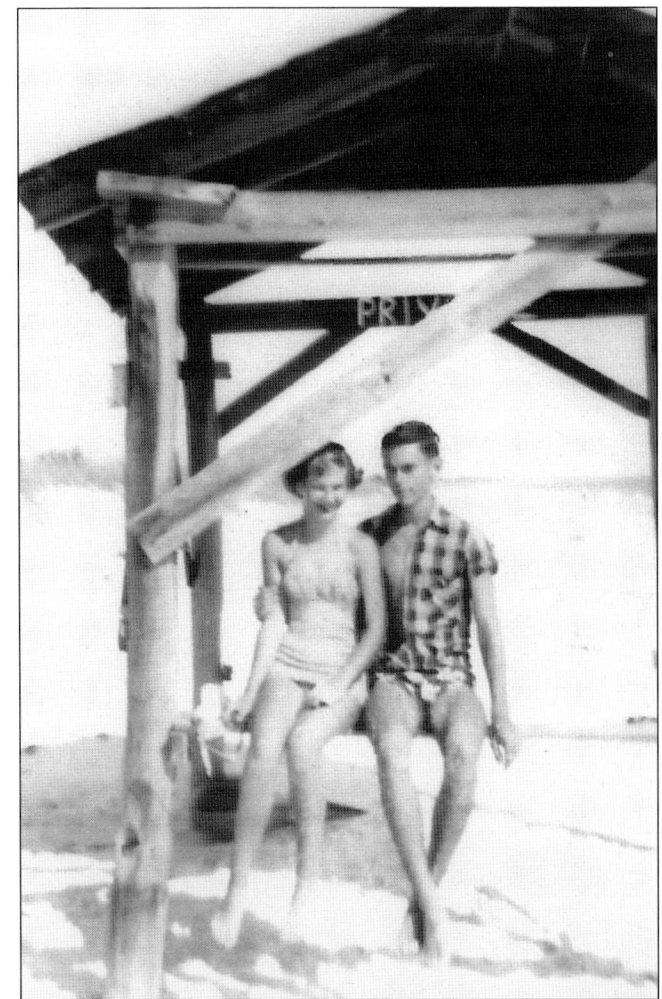

Joanne Wandeck Wynn and Charles Wynn of Marianna stand in front of their beach house in the mid-1950s. The house is on Marianna Hill facing the Gulf of Mexico. (Courtesy of Joann Wandeck Wynn.)

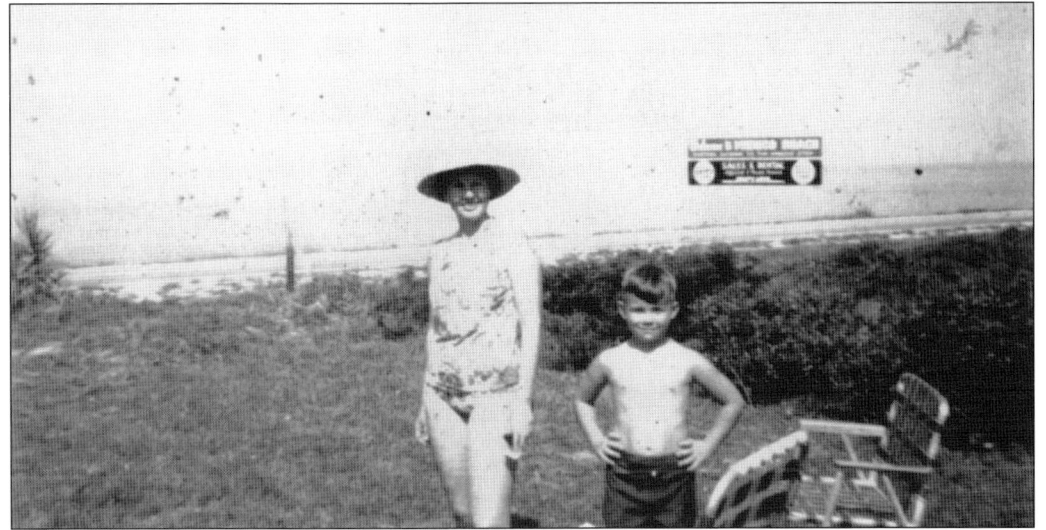

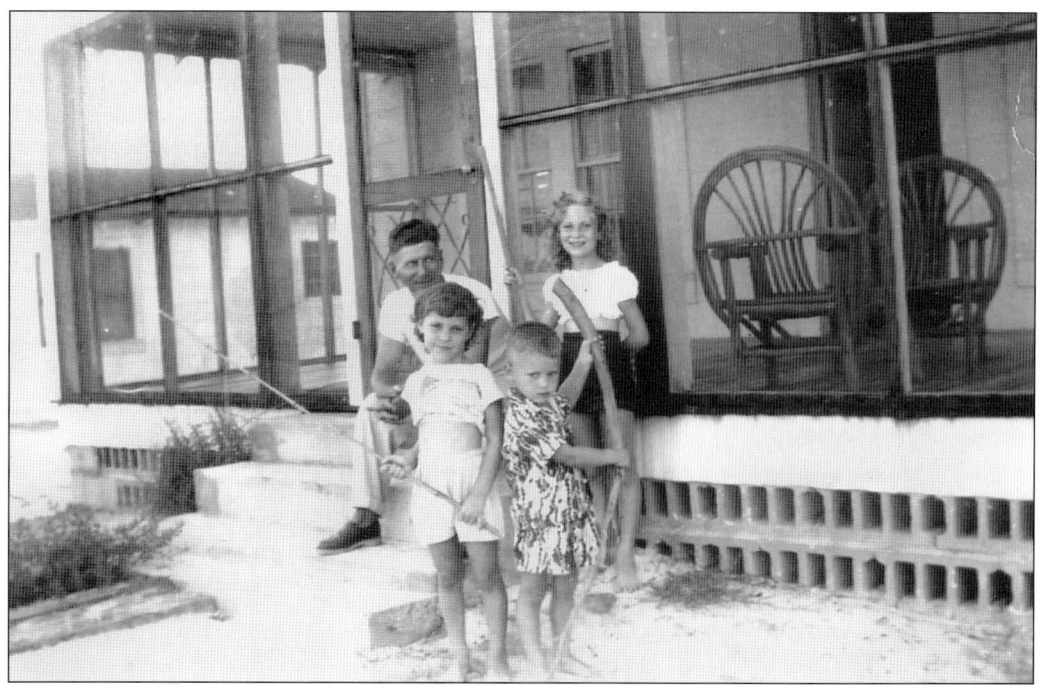

Voyne "Pete" Barrett and his children sit on the steps of their beach cottage while vacationing in Mexico Beach. The child standing in the rear beside her father is Barbara (with blonde hair). In front are Nancy (with short dark hair) and Charles. (Courtesy of Charlie Barrett.)

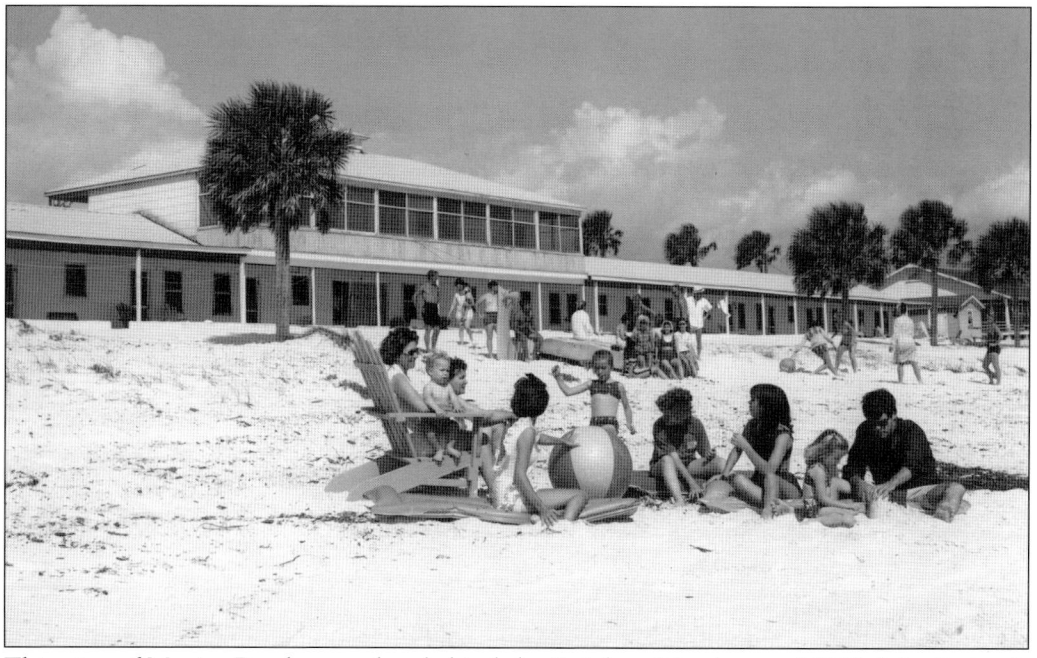

This view of Mexico Beach was taken behind the Rainbow Motel around 1965. Inky Parker is sitting in a chair with her grandson Charles and her granddaughter Kim. Playing in the sand are Cathey Parker, Nan Parker, and Janie Cathey. The Rainbow Motel was built in the 1950s by Edward Parker. (Courtesy of the Parker family.)

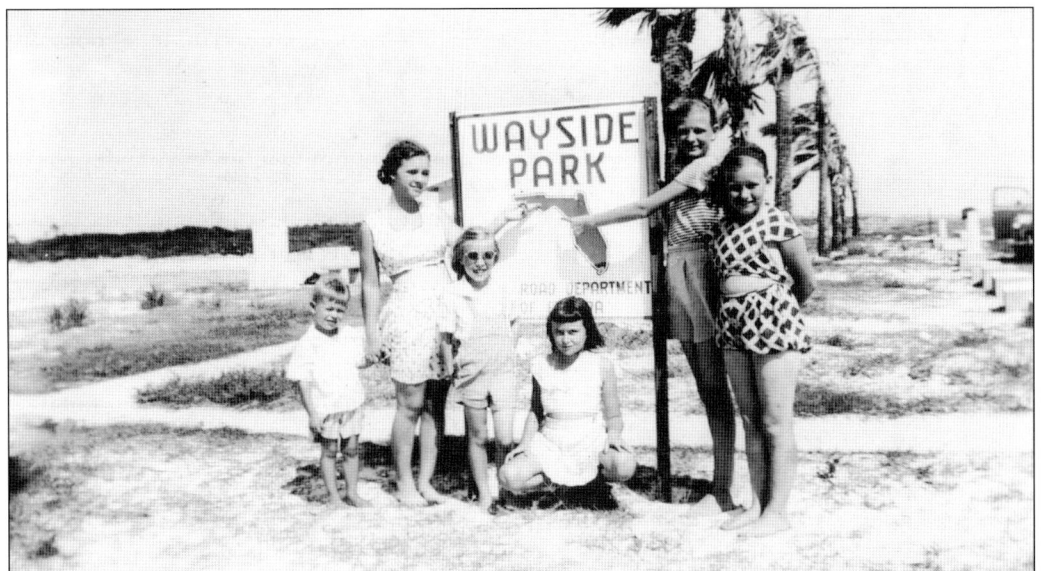

From left to right, Gordon Parker, unidentified, Terry Parker, Joan Parker, and Marion and Norma Mills stand in front of the Wayside Park sign in the late 1940s. Wayside Park was located across the highway from the beach between Seventh and Eighth Streets. (Courtesy of Terry Parker Pope.)

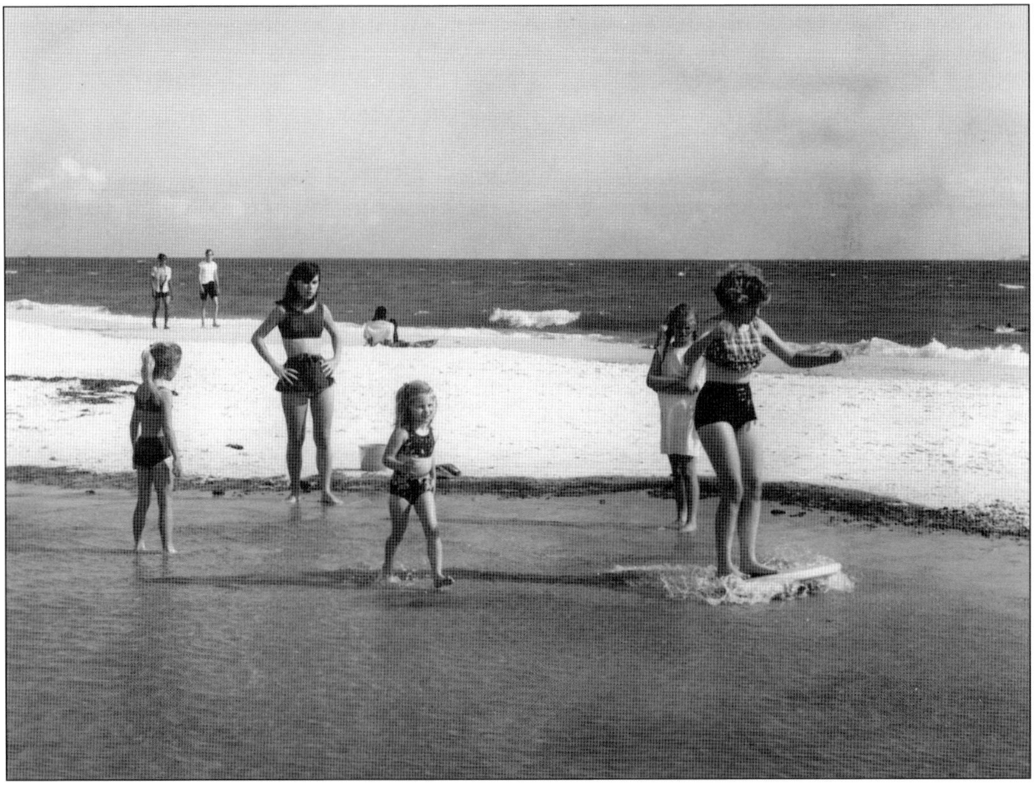

These folks are enjoying some beach fun. From left to right, locals Nan, Sue, and Kim Parker, along with Vicky Richards and Janie Cathey, take turns trying their skills at skim boarding in 1965. (Courtesy of the Parker family.)

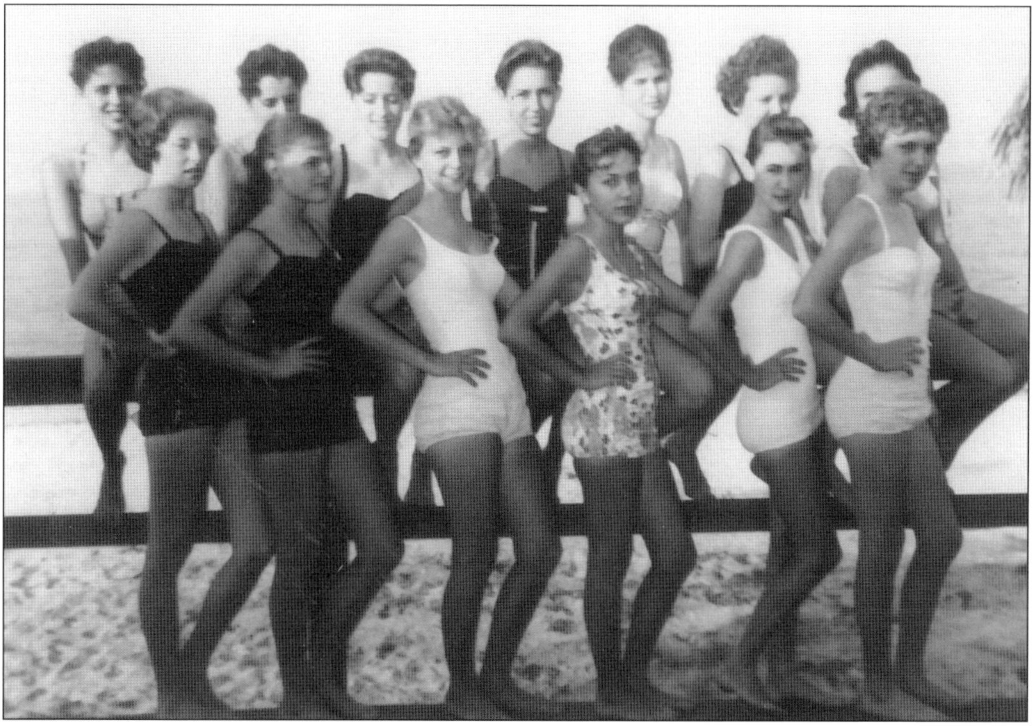

This group of Mexico Beach bathing beauties is seen in 1959 at Cathey Parker's birthday party at the family beach cottage on Twelfth Street. They are, from left to right, (first row) Sandra Brown, Pat Kerrigan, Connie Munn, Alice Land, Cathey Parker, and Dianne Hannon; (second row) Judy Bateman, Kay Creech, Peggy Pyle, Mary Dell Ramsey, Jan Rawls, Brenda Ward, and Catherine Duren. (Courtesy of Cathey Parker Hobbs.)

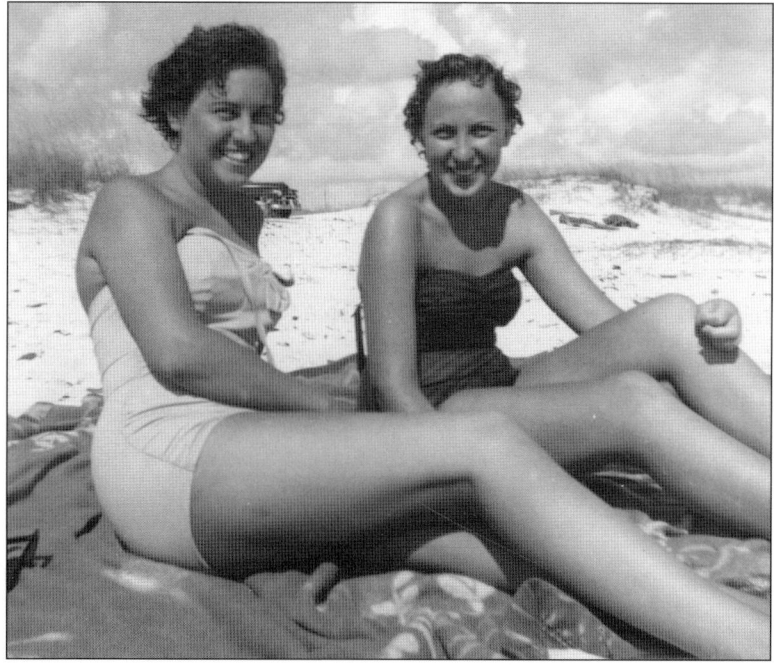

Elizabeth Cerny (left) and Lynn (Ramsey) Kerigan (right) were college roommates and are seen here enjoying the sun and surf at Mexico Beach during a school break around 1958. (Courtesy of Lynn Kerigan.)

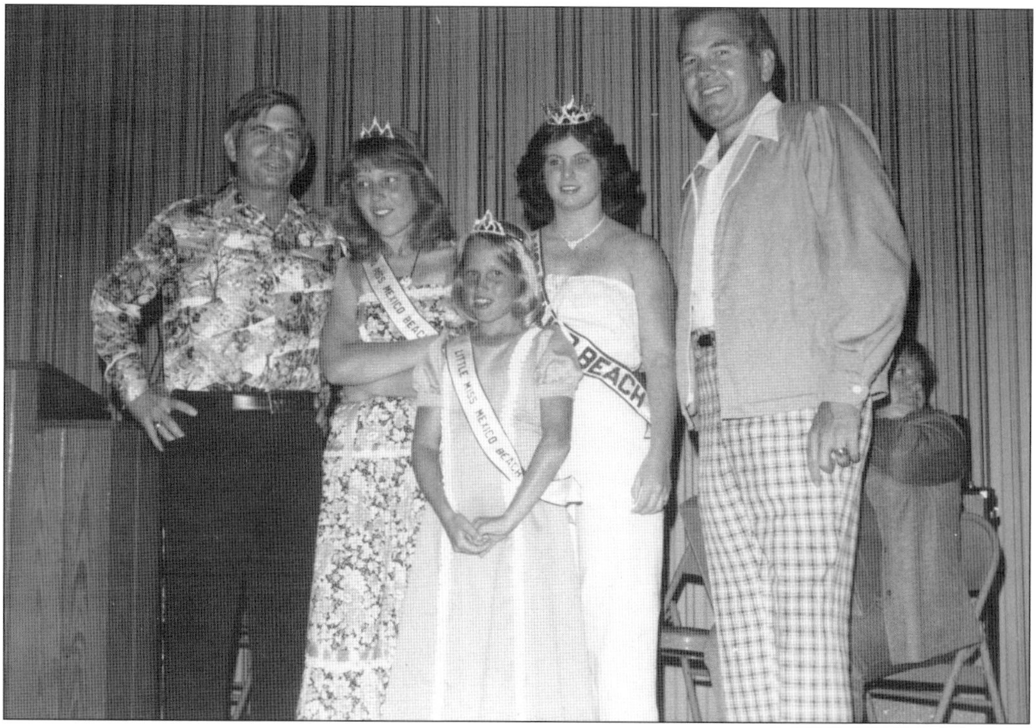

Seen here at the 1978 Miss Mexico Beach competition are, from left to right, state representative Billy Joe Rish, Shawna Wood (Young Miss Mexico Beach), Christy Angerer (Little Miss Mexico Beach), Kim Parker (Miss Mexico Beach), and state senator Pat Thomas. (Courtesy of Cathey Parker Hobbs.)

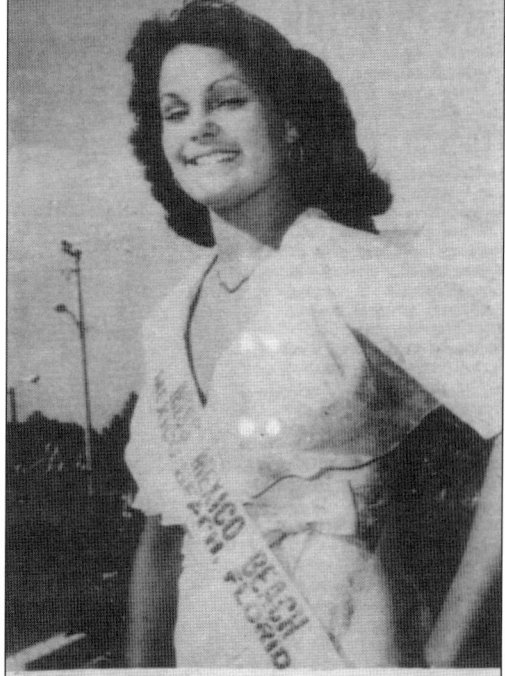

Terresa Gaddis, the 17-year-old daughter of James and Lucille Gaddis, was crowned Miss Mexico Beach in 1976. She still resides in Mexico Beach and is the owner of Forgotten Coast Property Management and Rentals, located at 710 Highway 98. (Courtesy of Allen Gaddis.)

PRETTY MISS--Terresa Ann Gaddis 17-year old daughter of Mr. and Mrs. James Edward Gaddis is the present "Miss Mexico Beach." She will relinquish her crown to a new Miss Mexico Beach this summer. She will preside at the Ling

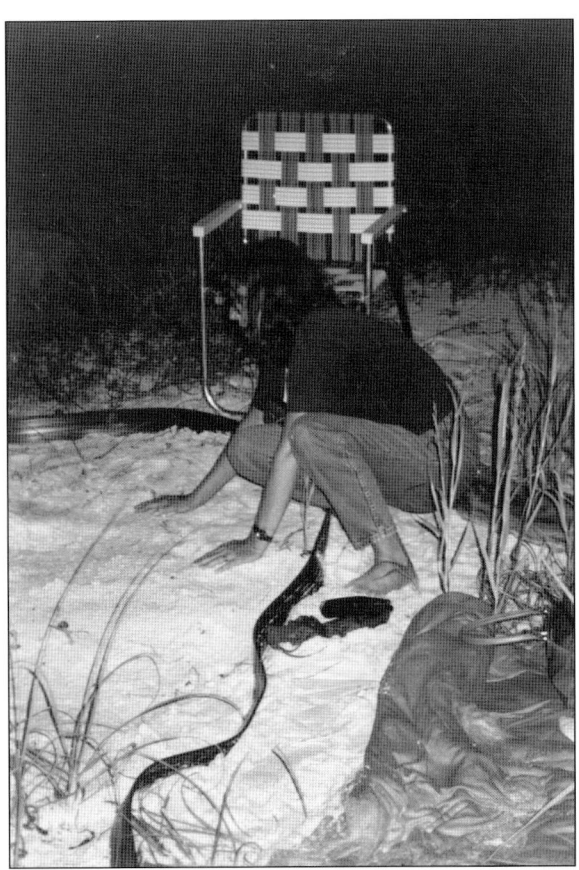

Paula Boone is seen here helping with sea turtle hatchings on Mexico Beach. Boone is a member of the local turtle patrol on the Gulf beaches. (Courtesy of Cathey Parker Hobbs.)

Local turtle lady Barbara Eells is seen here in August 1991 at a sea turtle hatching on Mexico Beach between Twenty-fourth and Twenty-fifth Streets. (Courtesy of Cathey Parker Hobbs.)

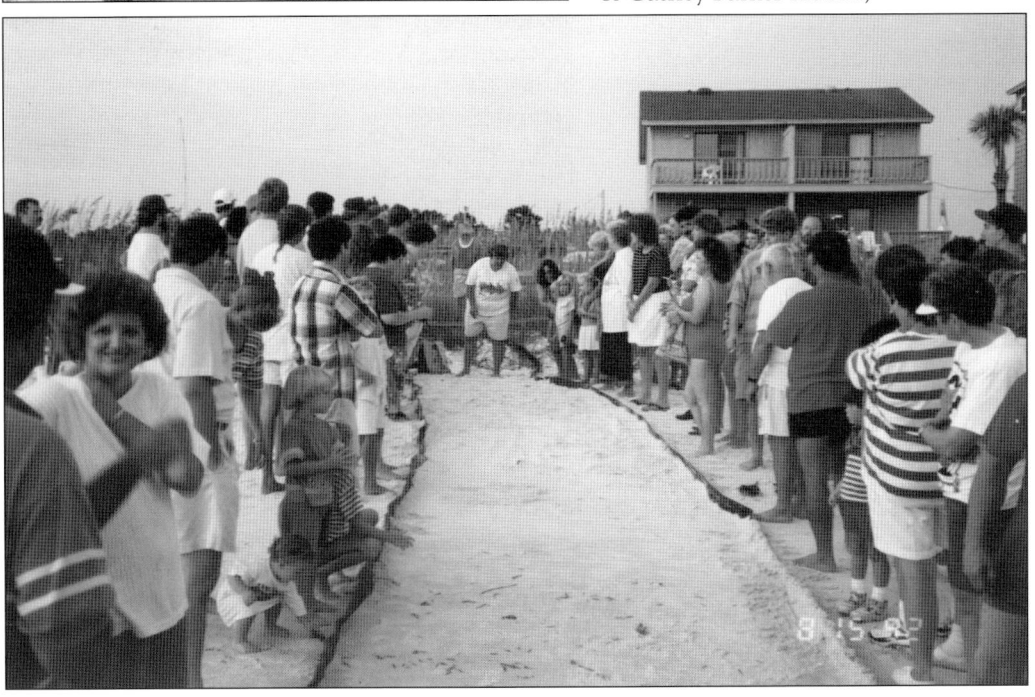

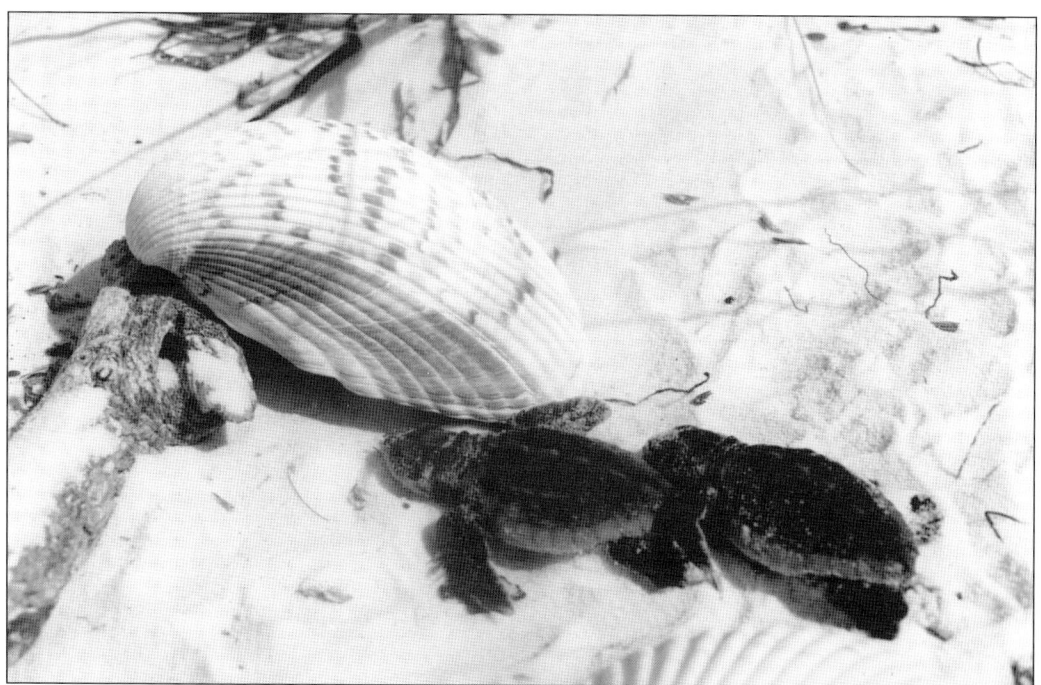

Two little baby turtles, just after being hatched, try to make their way to the water. (Courtesy of Cathey Parker Hobbs.)

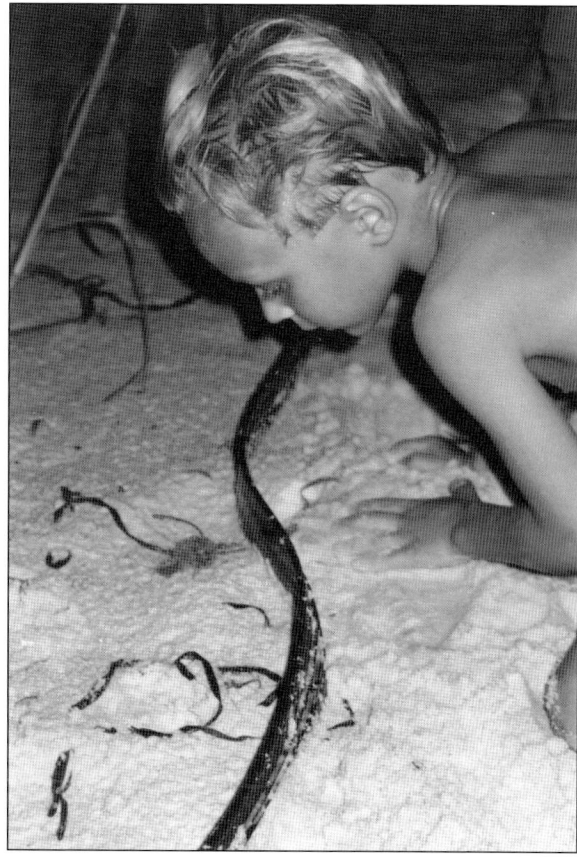

Ben Hobbs, the son of Cathey and Ralph Hobbs, watches baby turtles make their way to the water at a turtle hatching in the mid-1990s. (Courtesy of Cathey Parker Hobbs.)

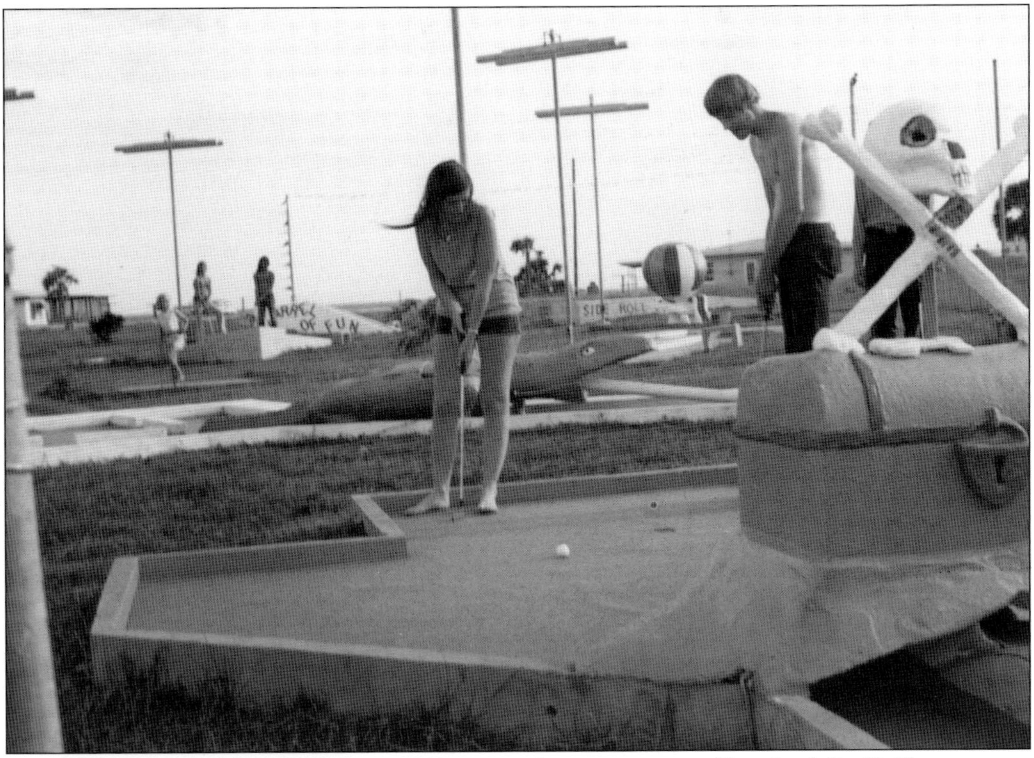

Teenagers play miniature golf at the Jolly Golf on Fourteenth Street in Mexico Beach. The Jolly Golf was built in the 1960s by Betty and Morris Missler. It was purchased in the early 1970s by Al and Hedy Garcia. (Courtesy of Cathey Parker Hobbs.)

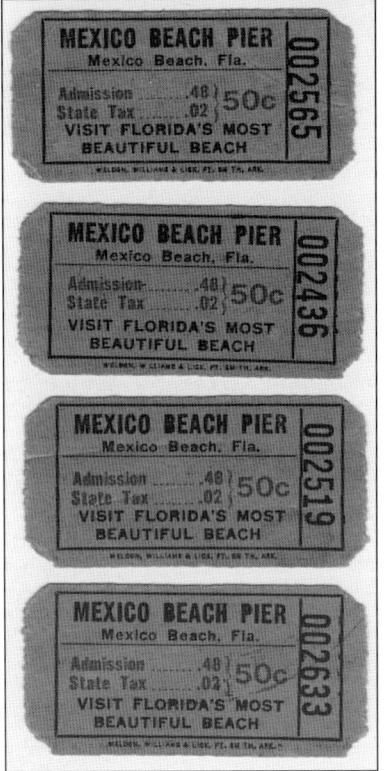

In the 1950s and early 1960s, pier pass tickets were sold by pier manager Doc Gillispie. (Courtesy of Cathey Parker Hobbs.)

Three
LET'S GO FISHING

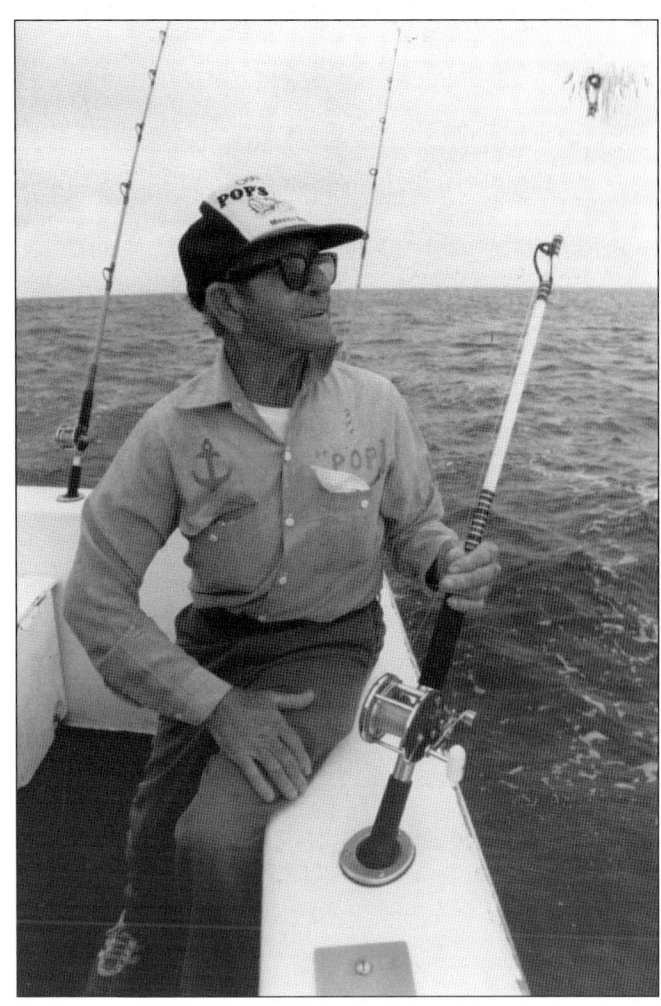

James "Pop" Guilford patiently waits for a king mackerel to take his bait in 1982. In his later years, Guilford helped out as a deckhand on his son Chuck's charter boat, the *Charisma*. He was an avid fisherman and loved being on the water. He passed away in 1985. (Courtesy of Chuck Guilford.)

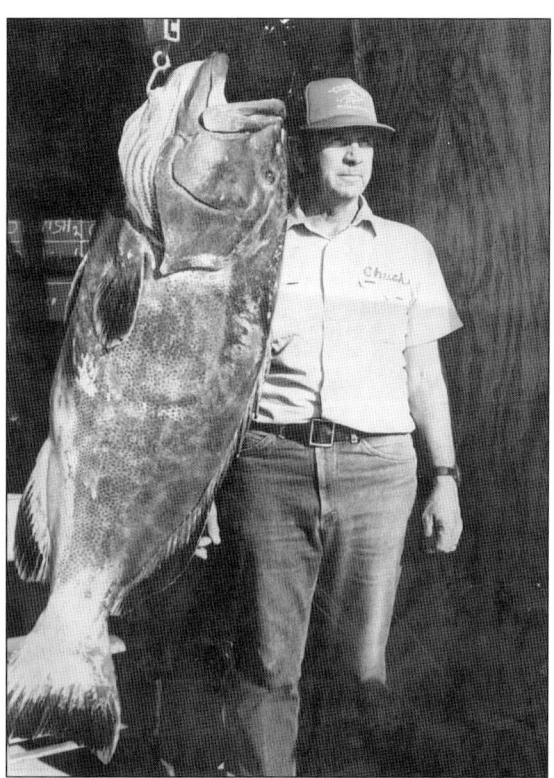

Capt. Chuck Guilford poses with a 75-pound rare true black grouper in 1974. (Courtesy of Bobby Guilford.)

Betty and Earl Harrington are seen here with their ling catch in the mid-1970s. They were devoted workers for the Mexico Beach Chamber of Commerce and regularly oversaw bingo nights at the community center. (Courtesy of Chuck Guilford.)

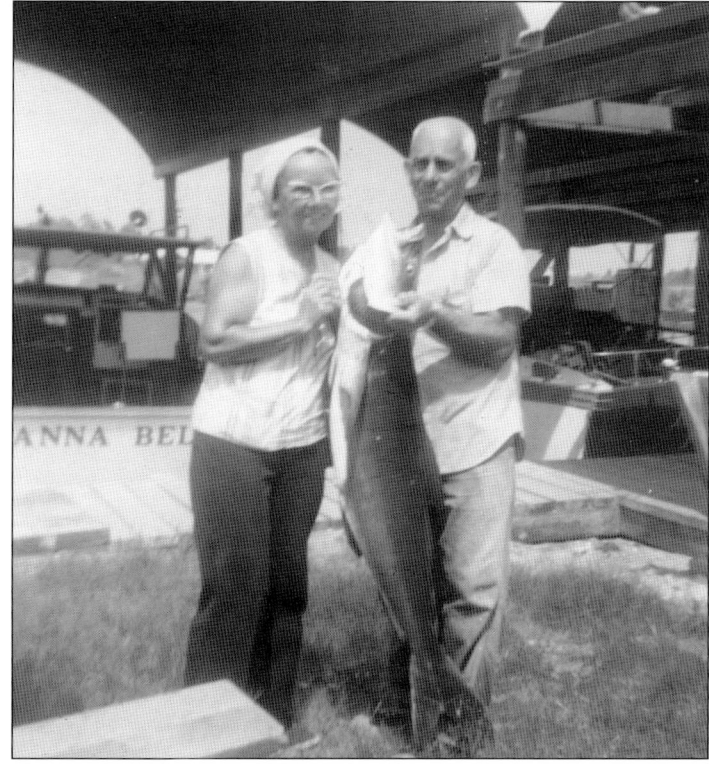

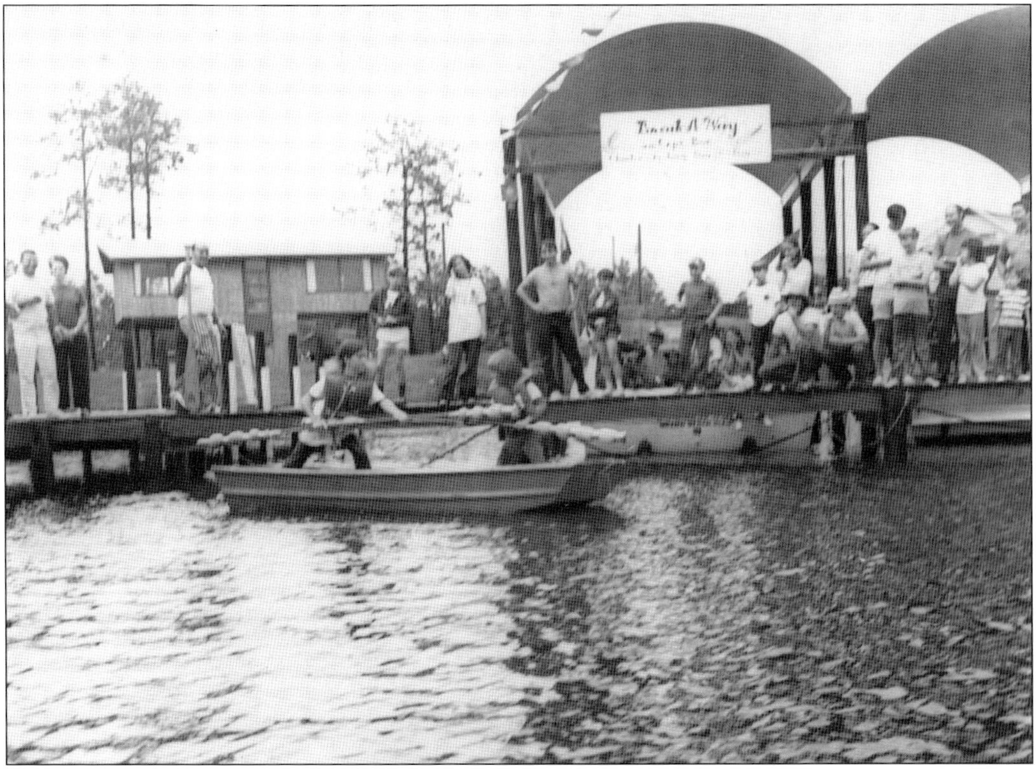

This jousting contest was held across from Capt. Joe's Marina during the 1974 Ling Ding Fishing Tournament. (Courtesy of Cathey Parker Hobbs.)

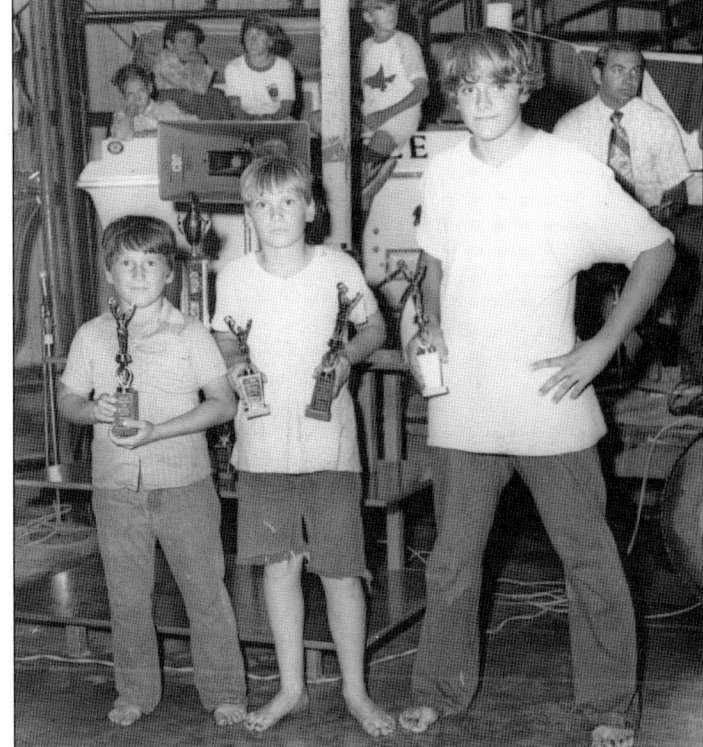

The 1974 Ling Ding Fishing Tournament jousting contest winners are seen here. They are, from left to right, Fred Hunter, unidentified, and Allen Gaddis. (Courtesy of Bennie Hunter.)

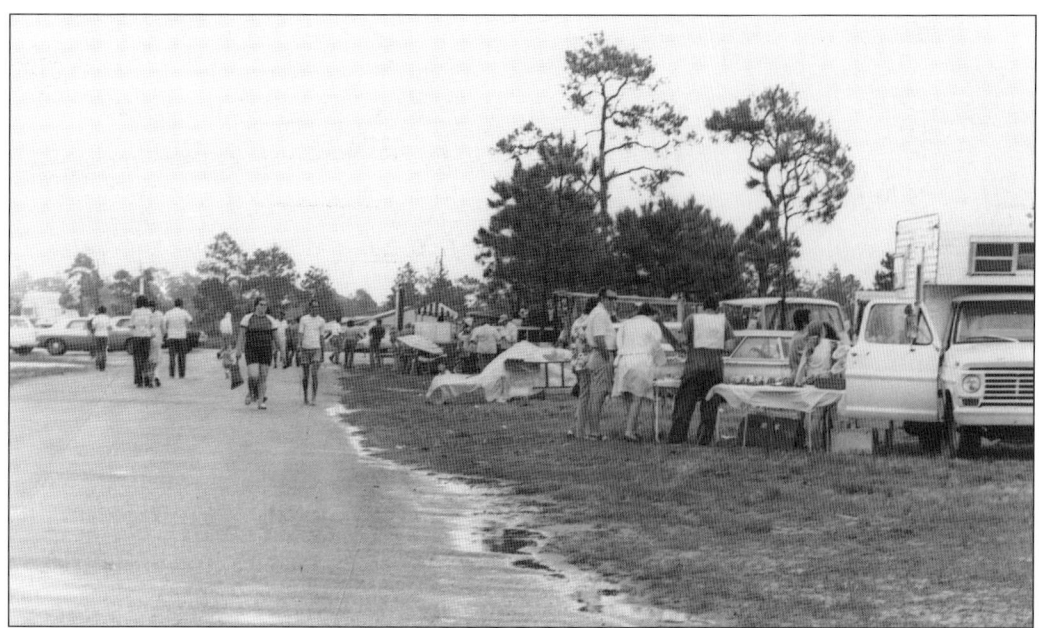

Beginning in the early 1970s, the Ling Ding Fishing Tournament took place on the pier road (Thirty-seventh Street), prior to construction of the current townhomes. Every weekend in April and May, fishermen competed for trophies and prizes based on the largest catches of ling (cobia), Spanish mackerel, and amberjack. The event also included a beauty pageant, food venders, jousting games, arts and crafts, a parade, and a street dance. (Courtesy of Cathey Parker Hobbs.)

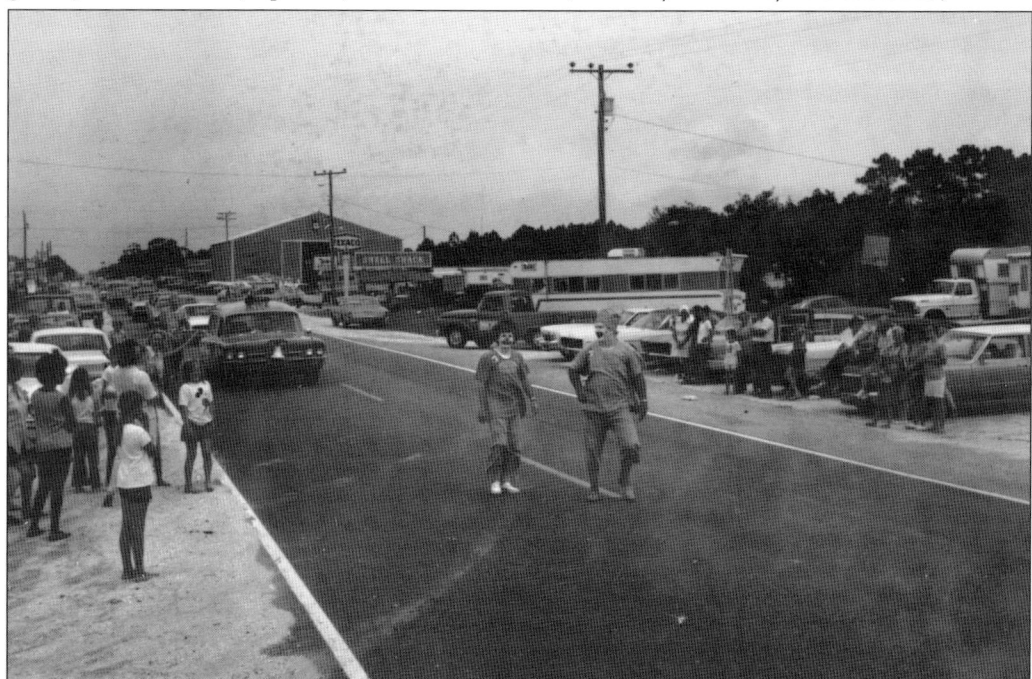

This 1973 Ling Ding parade was part of the fishing tournament's closing festivities. The event included over $5,000 in prizes, a fish fry, a presentation of awards, and a grand fiesta dance. (Courtesy of Cathey Parker Hobbs.)

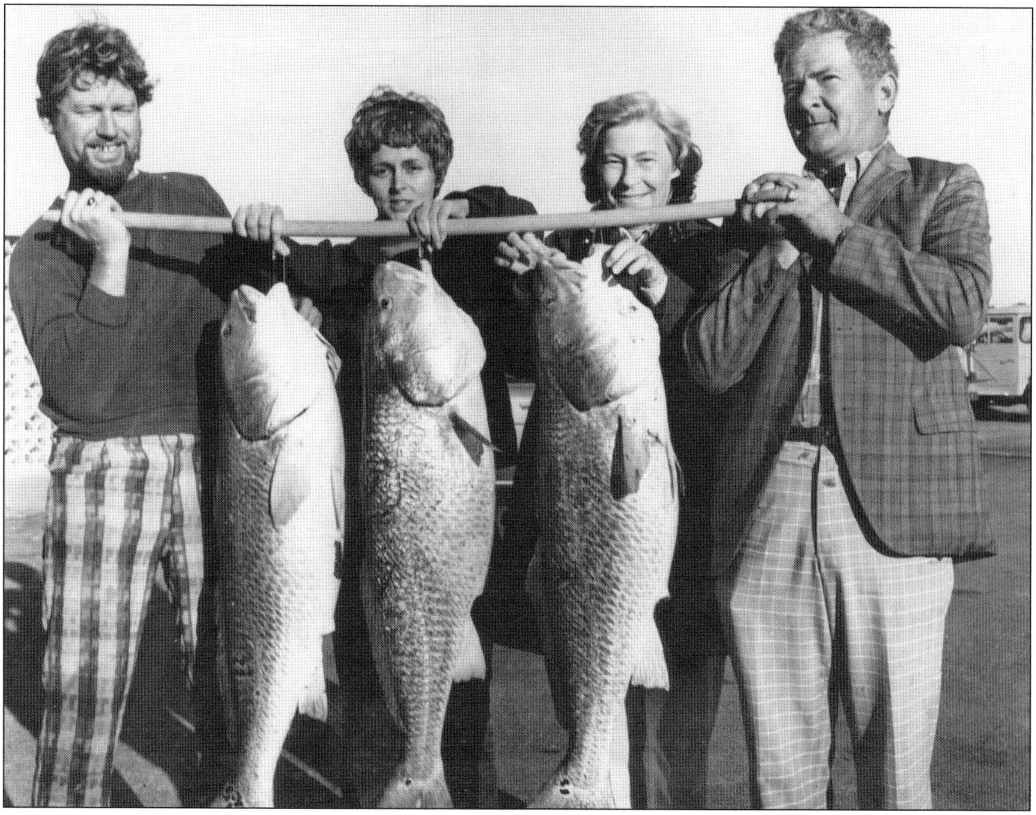

From left to right, Mr. and Mrs. Doc Holliday and Tom and Susie Hudson show off their catch of monster red fish in the 1970s. (Courtesy of Al Cathey.)

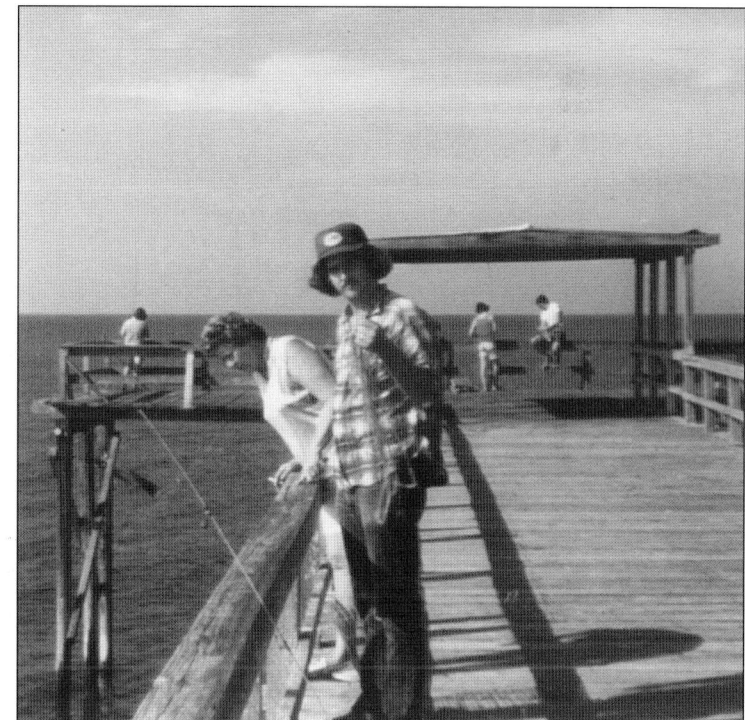

Steve Hebb (right) of Marianna and Jess Parker, the wife of James Parker of Blountstown and the sister-in-law of Charlie Parker, enjoy a day of crabbing and fishing in August 1974 from the pier behind the Surf Restaurant. (Courtesy of Terry Travis Hebb.)

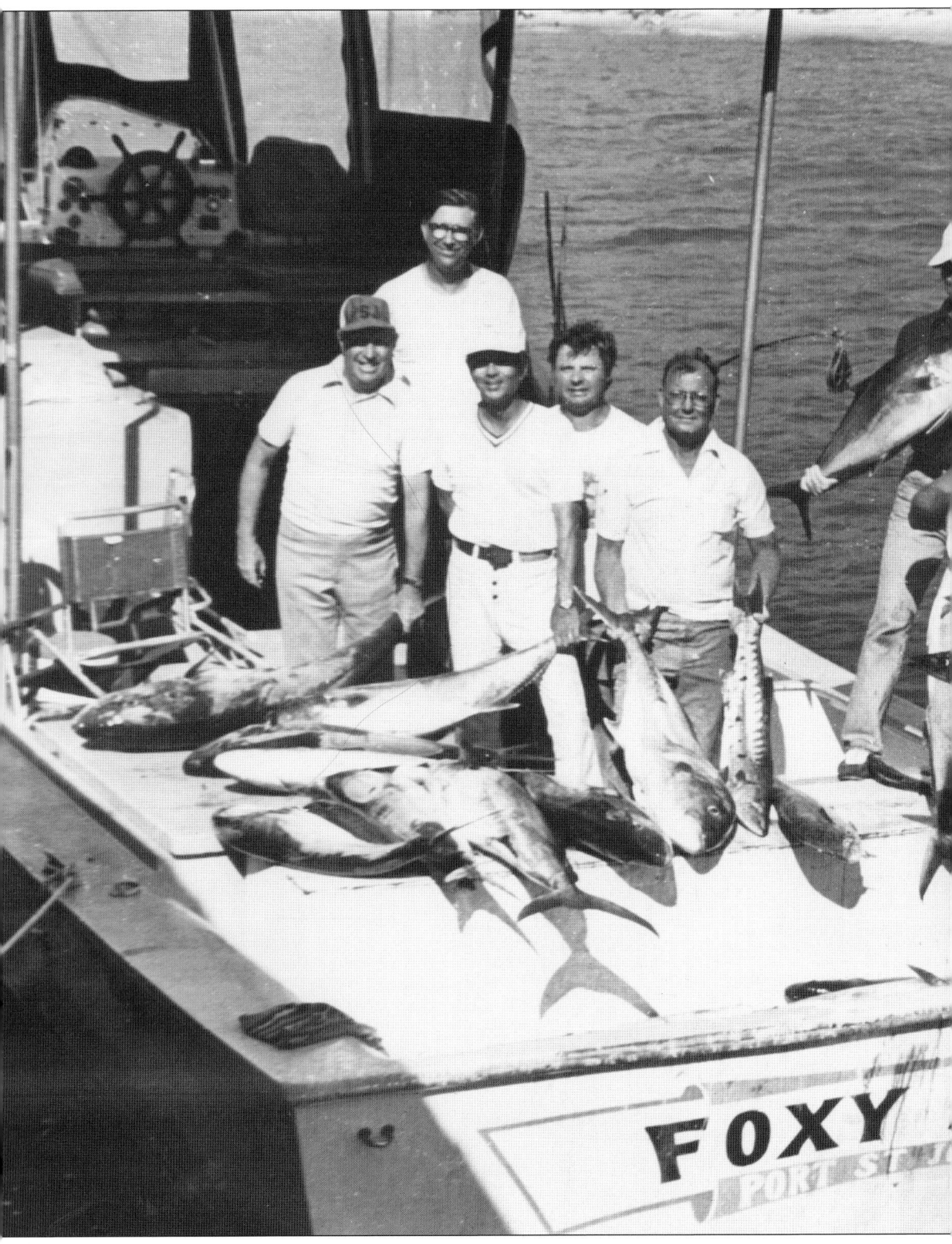

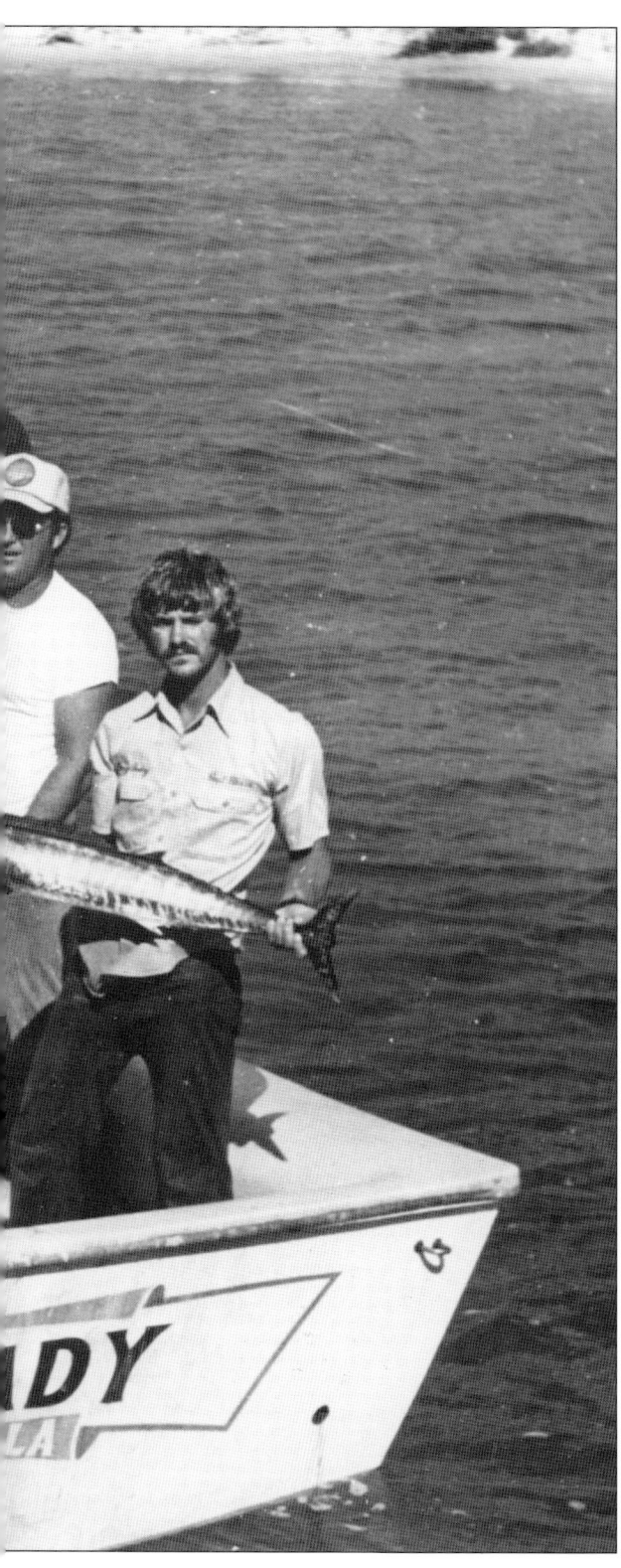

This group of happy anglers returned to port after trolling the Empire Mica in 1976. The *Foxy Lady*, owned and operated by Capt. Chris King, had an exceptionally good catch of amberjack, wahoo, dolphin, snapper, and bonita. From left to right are Tom Coldeway, Dr. Bob King, Dr. Joe Hendrix, Hume Coleman, Bill Cannon, John Miller, Ted Cannon, and Capt. Chris King. (Courtesy of Chris King.)

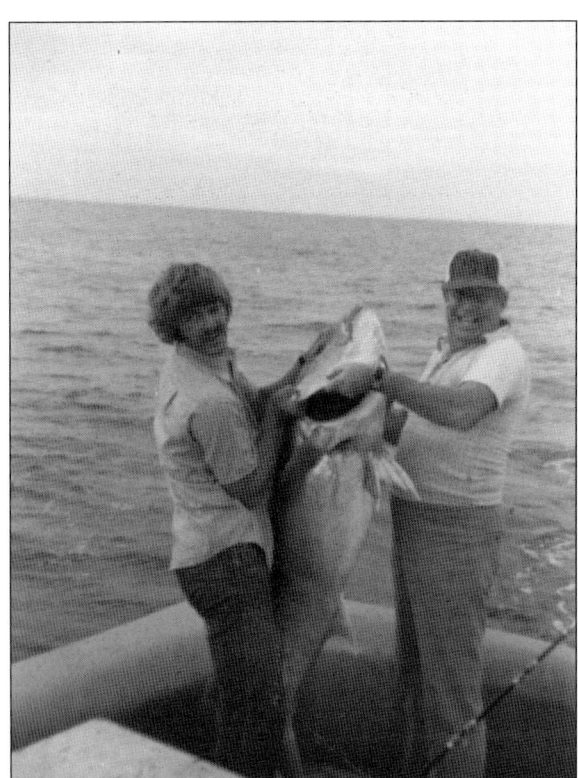

Chris King (left) and Tom Coldeway (right) display a 100-pound amberjack caught on the Empire Mica in 1976. (Courtesy of Chris King.)

From left to right in this 1974 photograph taken at Capt. Joe's Marina, Chris King, Charles Britt, and Mike Wimberly show off their catch, which included a 10-foot hammerhead shark. (Courtesy of Chris King.)

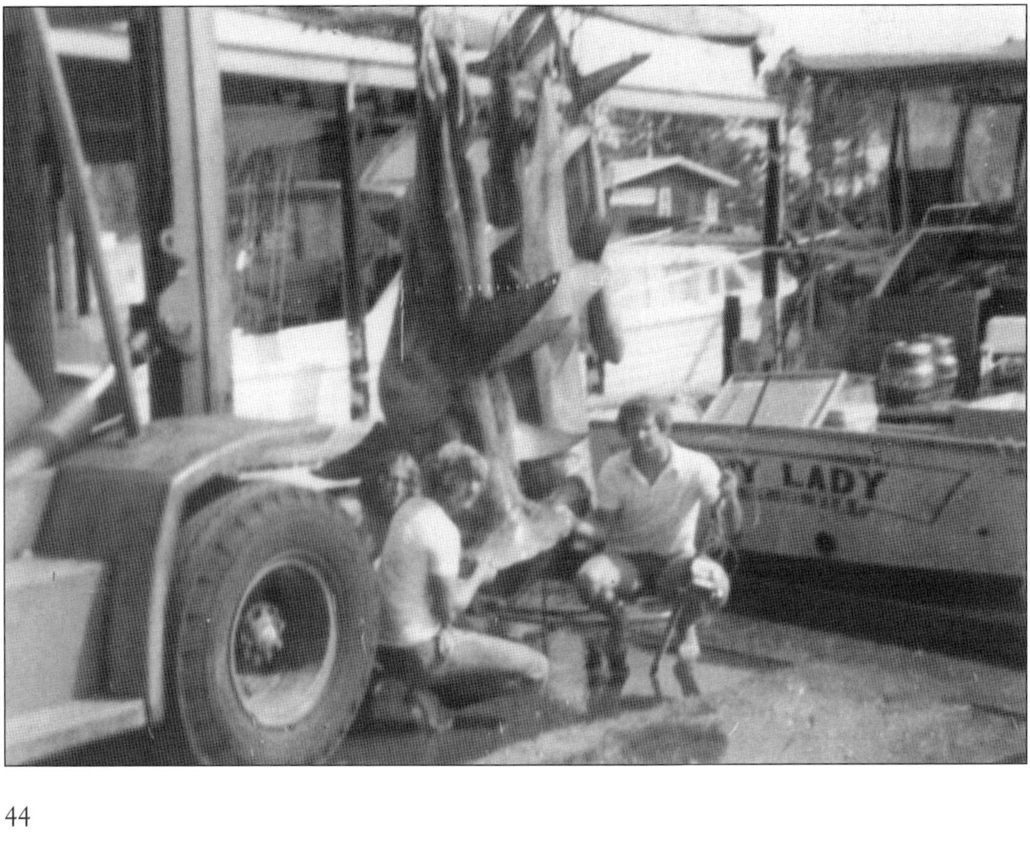

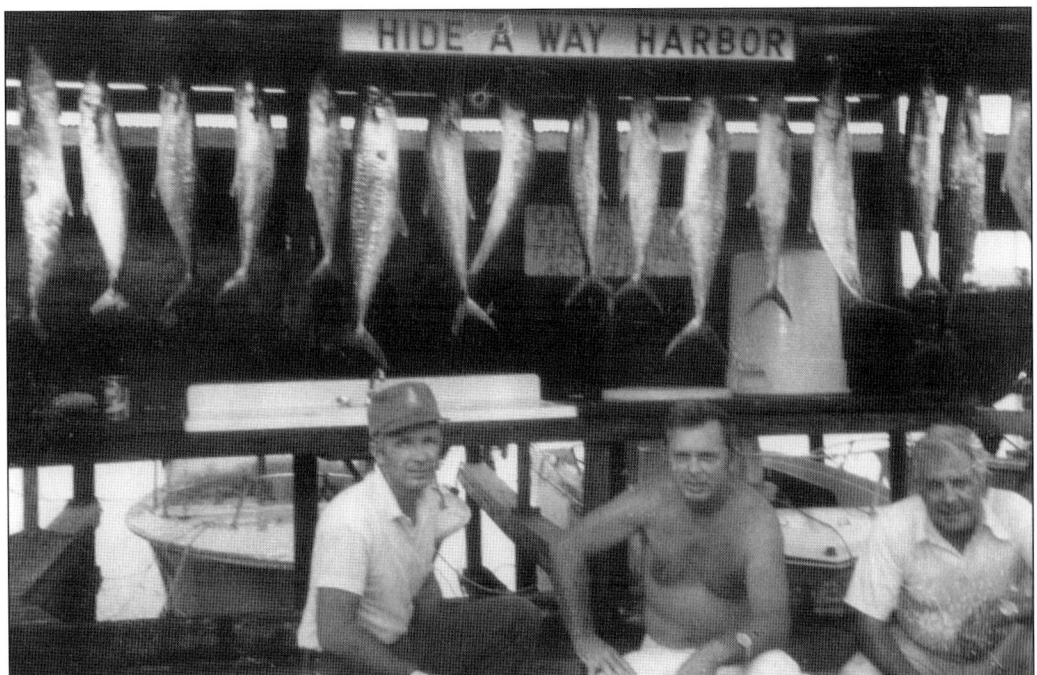

Fishing off the *Phantom Clipper*, home-based in Hide-A-Way Harbor Marina, are, from left to right, Bill Hughes, Don Waddell, and Ralph Morang. During this trip, in November 1975, they caught 17 kings. (Courtesy of Bill Hughes.)

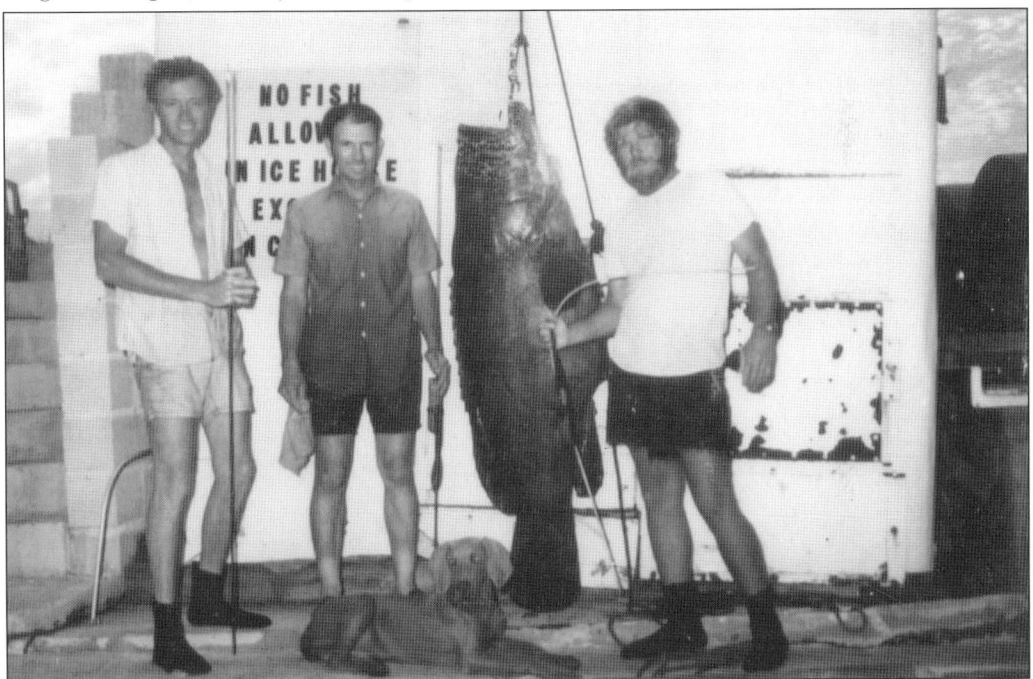

In 1972, from left to right, Gains "Red" Stanton and Chuck and Bobby Guilford, with Bobby's beloved dog Grey Dog, show off a 317-pound Goliath grouper. The huge fish was shot through the driver's-side window of the old school bus on the Car Body Reef. (Courtesy of Bobby Guilford.)

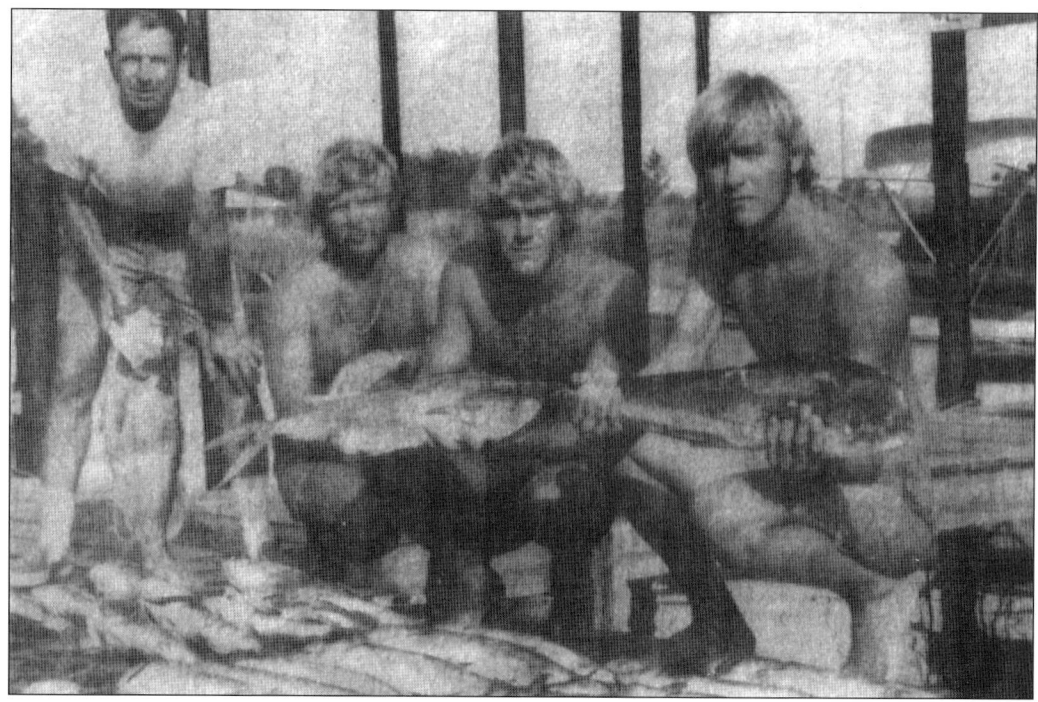

From left to right, Chuck and Bobby Guilford, Charles Britt, and Henry Boone enjoy a great fishing day in October 1973. (Courtesy of Bobby Guilford.)

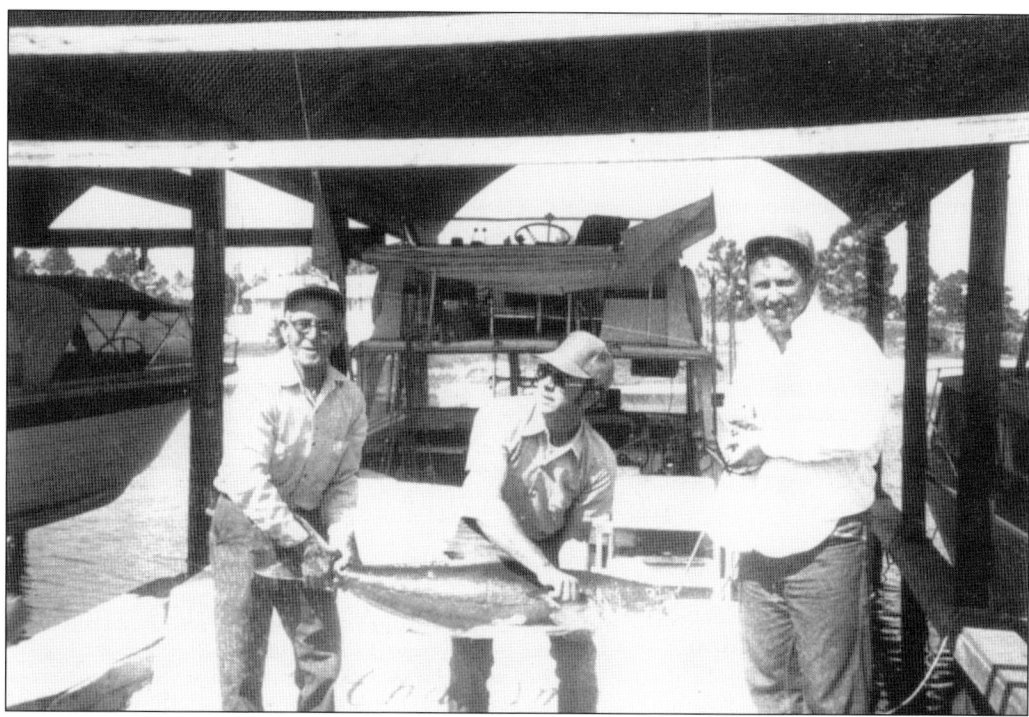

In 1978, from left to right, Pop and Chuck Guilford and James Padgett stand at the rear of the *Charisma*, a local charter boat, with a 50-pound ling. (Courtesy of Chuck Guilford.)

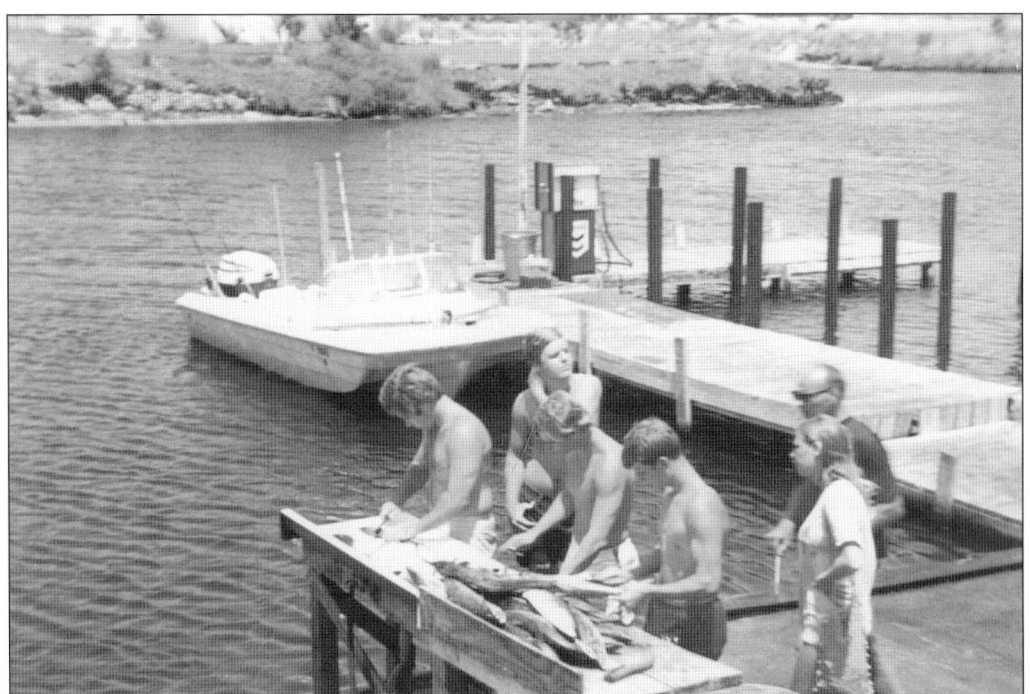

Boys clean fish in the early 1970s at the fuel dock of the Hide-A-Way Harbor Marina. Dr. Joe Hendrix's Thunderbird tri-hull design boat, in the background, was one of the first of its kind in the area. In the photograph are, from left to right, Dr. Hendrix's two sons, Joe and Bill; Knapp Smith; and unidentified out-of-town guests. (Courtesy of Joe Hendrix Jr.)

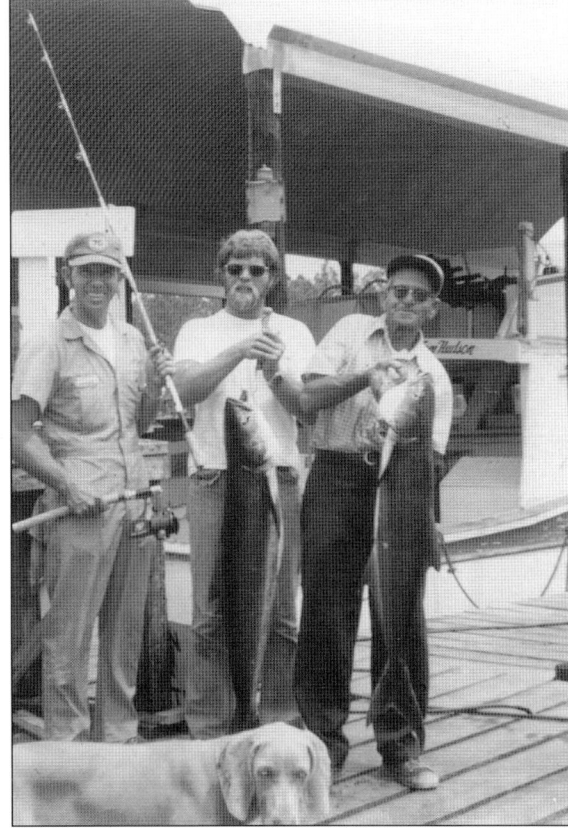

From left to right, Chuck, Bobby, and Pop Guilford show off their catch of ling in the 1978 Ling Ding Fishing Tournament. Also posing is Bobby's traveling companion Grey Dog. (Courtesy of Chuck Guilford.)

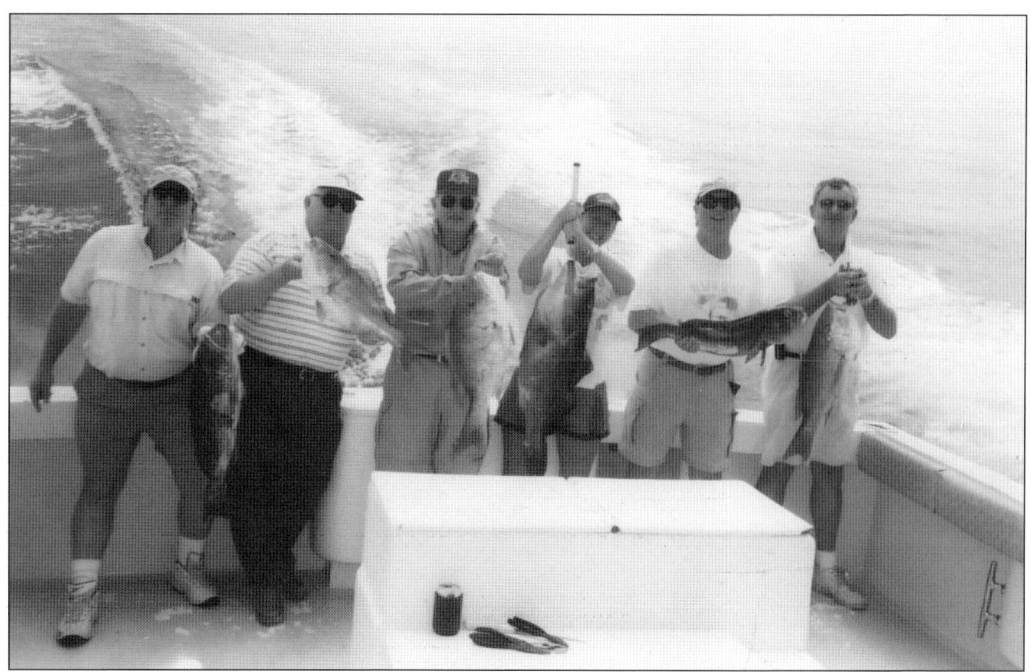

A day on the water for guys and gals was a lot of fun aboard the *Charisma* in the late 1970s. Seen here from left to right are Bill Lee, J.W. "Dub" Vinson, Bill Bass, Rhonda Vise, Monty Ferrell, and Donnie Brogdon. (Courtesy of Al Cathey.)

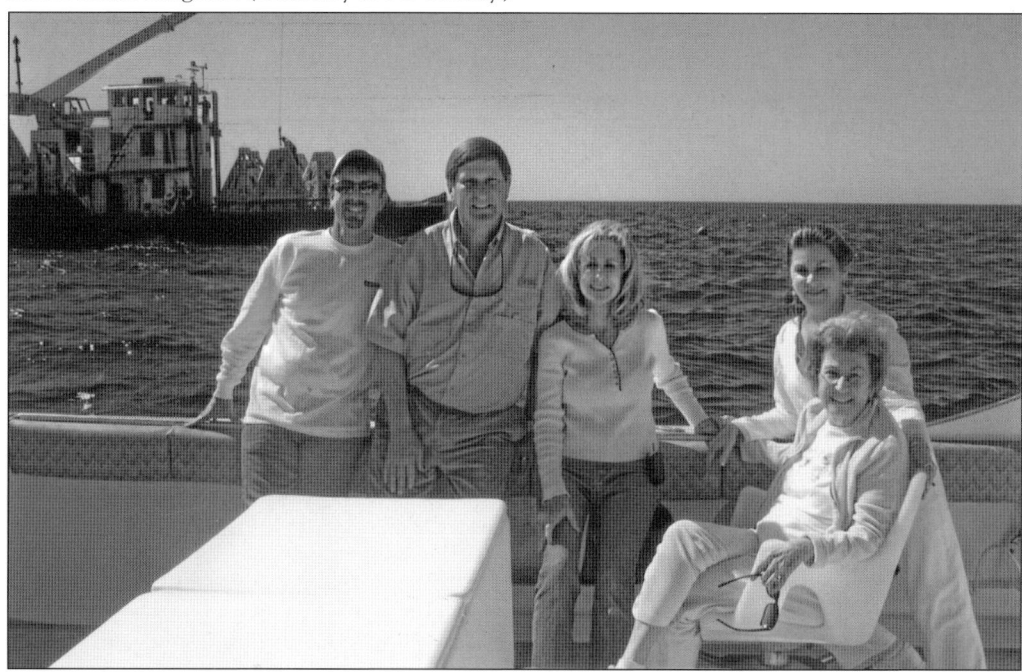

When Charlie Parker passed away in 2003, the Mexico Beach Artificial Reef Association named a fishing reef in his memory. Family members on hand to watch the placing of the reef included, from left to right, William Thursbay, Ralph Hobbs, Cathey Parker Hobbs, Sue Parker Thomas, and Inky Parker. (Courtesy of the Parker family.)

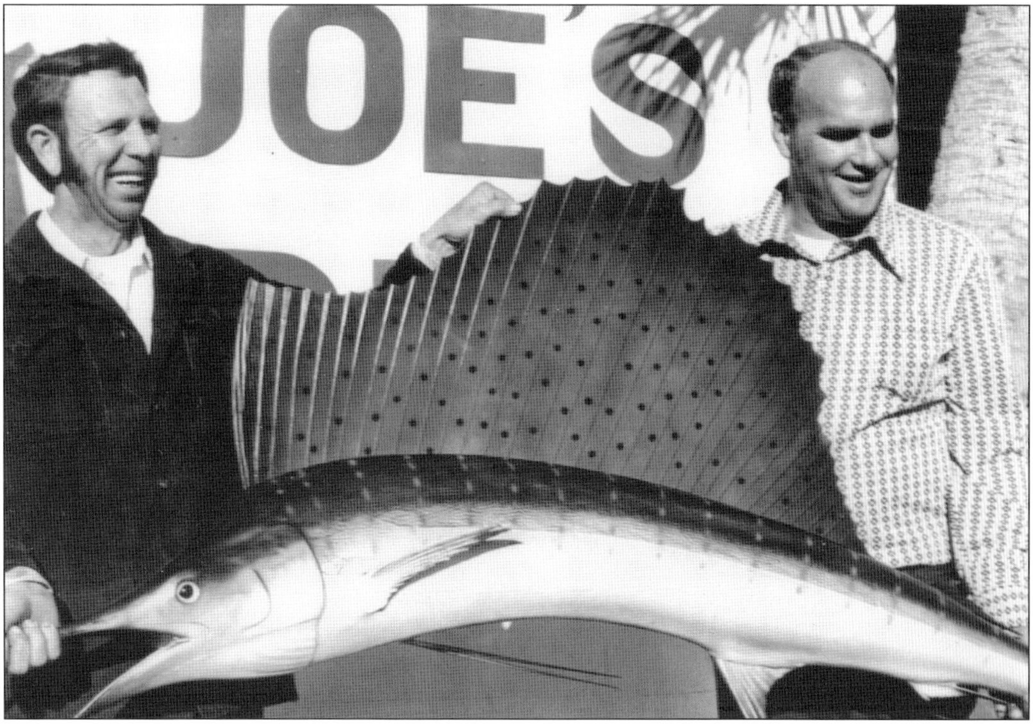

Chuck Guilford (left) and Joe Large (right) display a sailfish at the grand opening of Capt. Joe's Marina in 1972. (Courtesy of Chuck Guilford.)

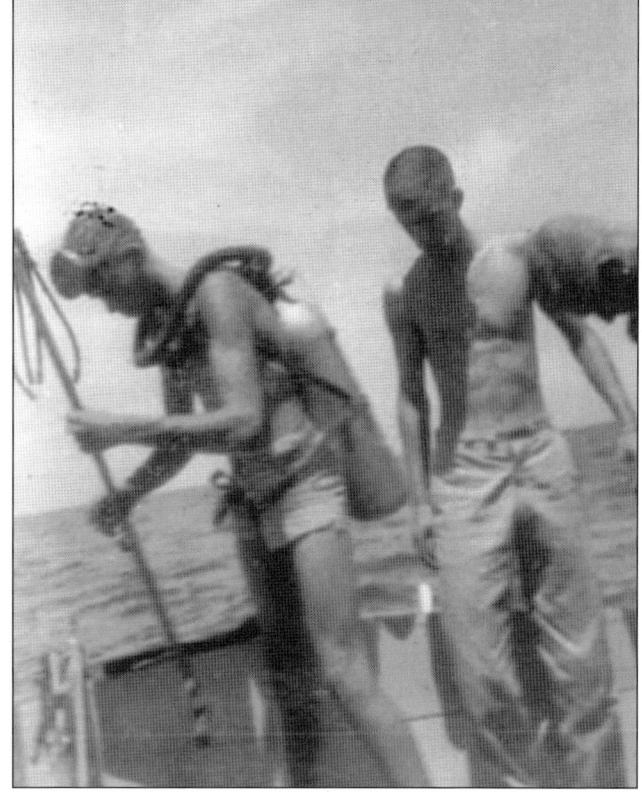

Jim Hines of Bainbridge, Georgia, is seen here with a speargun and tank. He, along with Stuart McKenzie (center) and Bobby Wheat (right), went diving on the lumber ship off Mexico Beach in August 1957. The divers reported that the ship was in pretty good shape but that the prize, the ship's bell, had already been taken. (Courtesy of Jim Hines.)

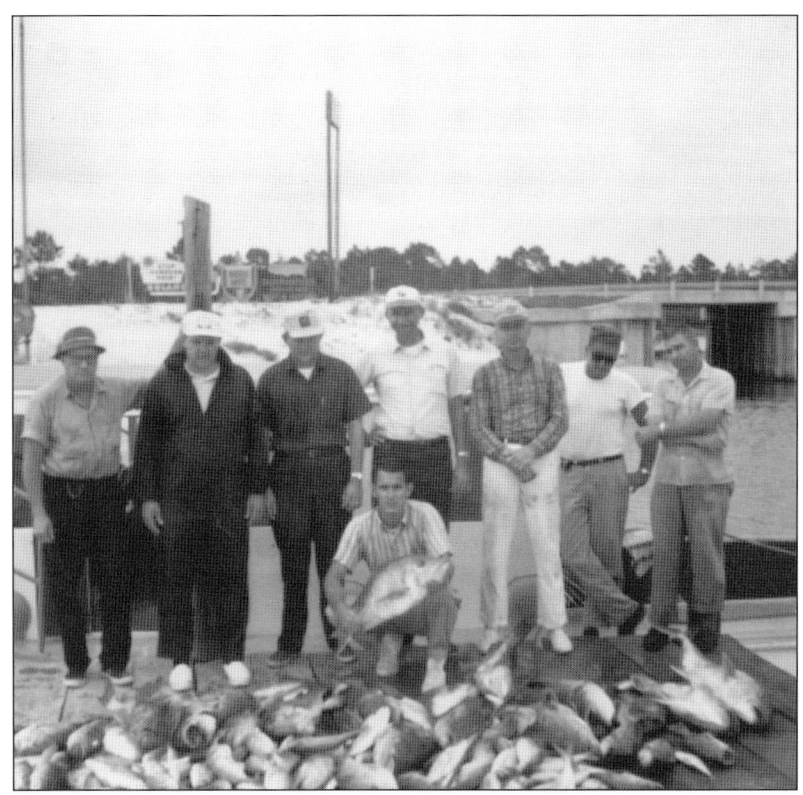

Capt. George Holland (center, with fish) is seen here in the late 1960s showing the catch from a day fishing on the *Miss Louise*. With him, from left to right are P.B. Prowse, Walter Dodson, Blake Tominlson, Dr. Bob King, Dr. Joe Hendrix, Bob Holland, and Billy Joe Rish. This photograph was taken at the old loading dock on the north side of Highway 98 on the Mexico Beach Canal. (Courtesy of George Holland.)

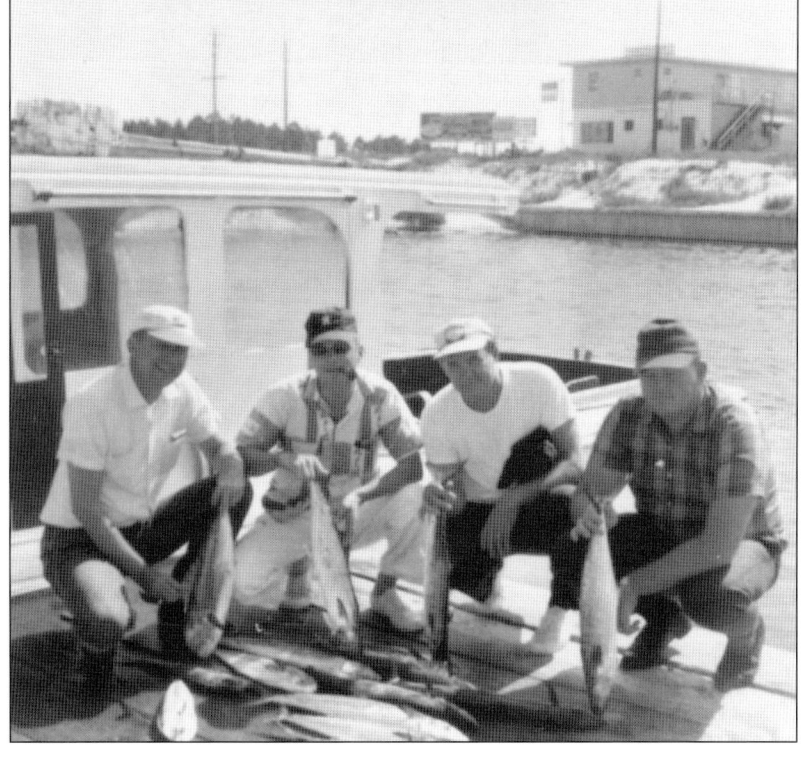

After a good day on the water fishing off the *Miss Louise* with Capt. George Holland in the late 1960s, from left to right, local dentist Dr. Bob King, local physician Dr. Joe Hendrix, banker Walter Dodson, and commercial fisherman Gene Raffield posed for this shot. (Courtesy of Chris King.)

Richard "R.L." Fortner (left) and Lee Williams (right) show off their shark in front of the skating rink at Highway 98 and Eighth Street in the mid-1950s. (Courtesy of Sonny Fortner.)

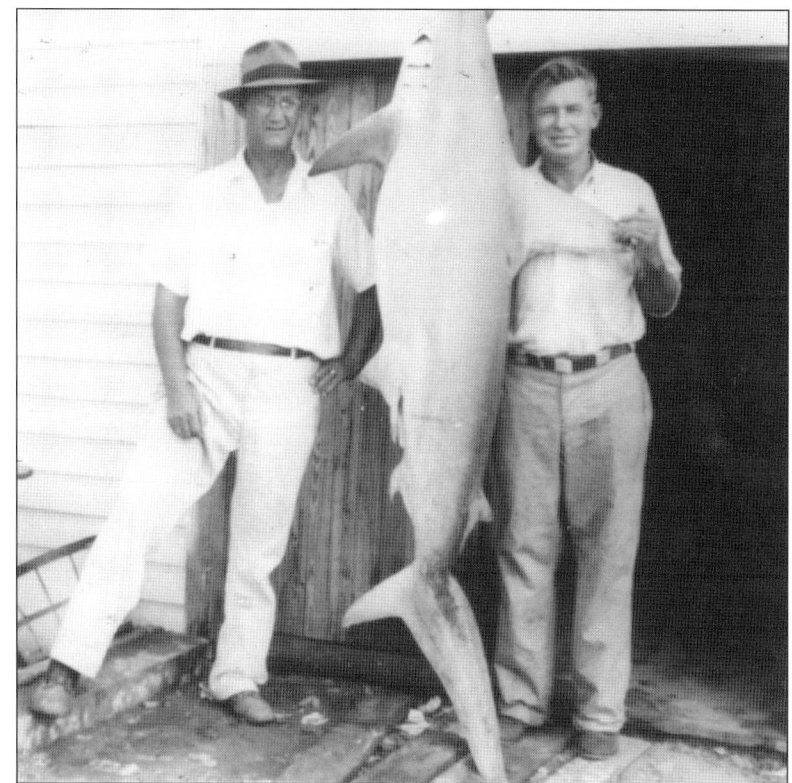

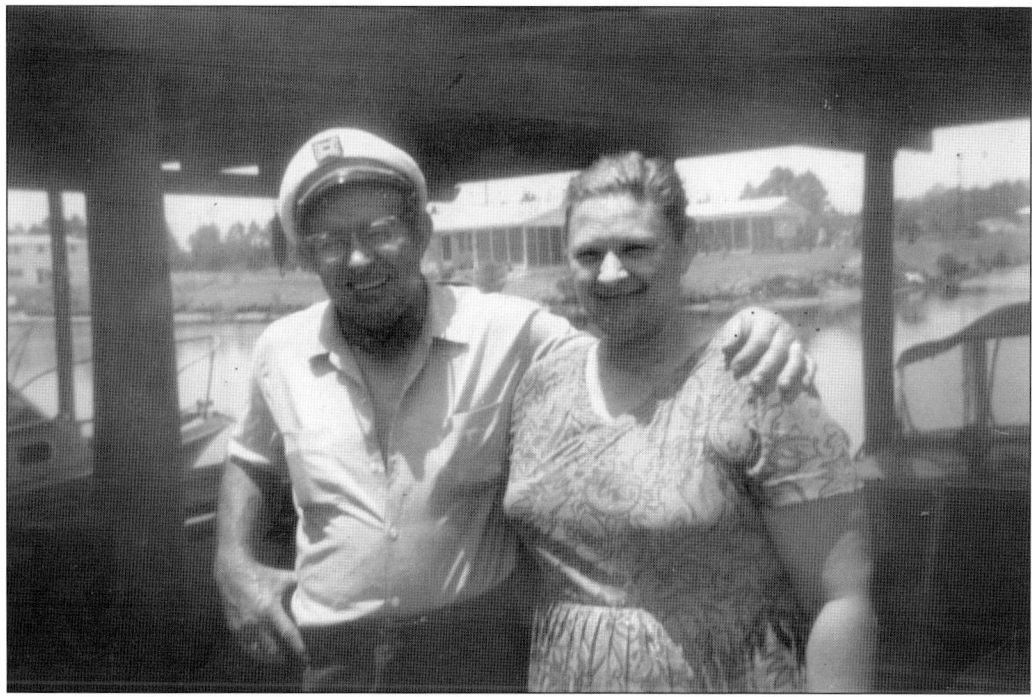

Inez and Ed Austin managed the Hide-A-Way Harbor Marina during the time owner Bill Hughes was in the Air Force, from 1967 to 1973. (Courtesy of Bill Hughes.)

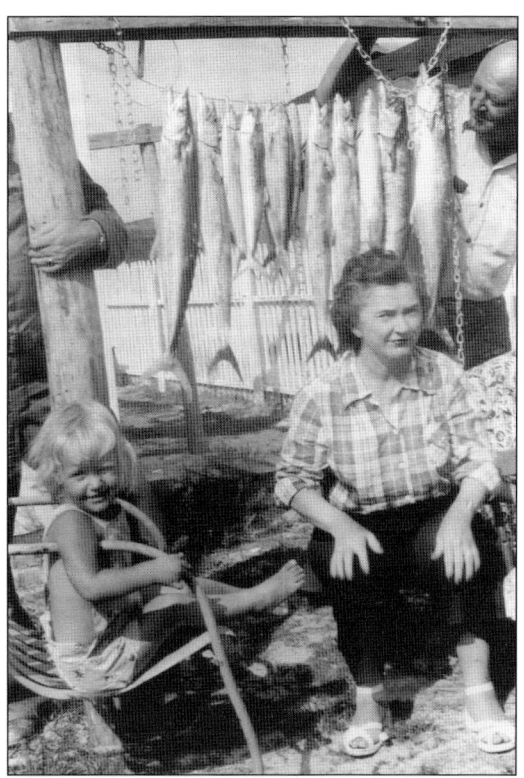

Around 1950, Rhoda McFalls and Jack Prince show off their nice catch of king mackerel while little Ronnie Prince sits in the chair. (Courtesy of Ronnie Prince McDonald.)

Joe and Mildred Rycroft hold a string of king mackerel. On Mildred's left is her uncle Allie, who was 86 when this photograph was taken in 1967. That same year, Joe and Mildred built their home at 124 Miramar Drive, where Mildred still lives today. Joe passed away in 2001. (Courtesy of Mildred Rycroft.)

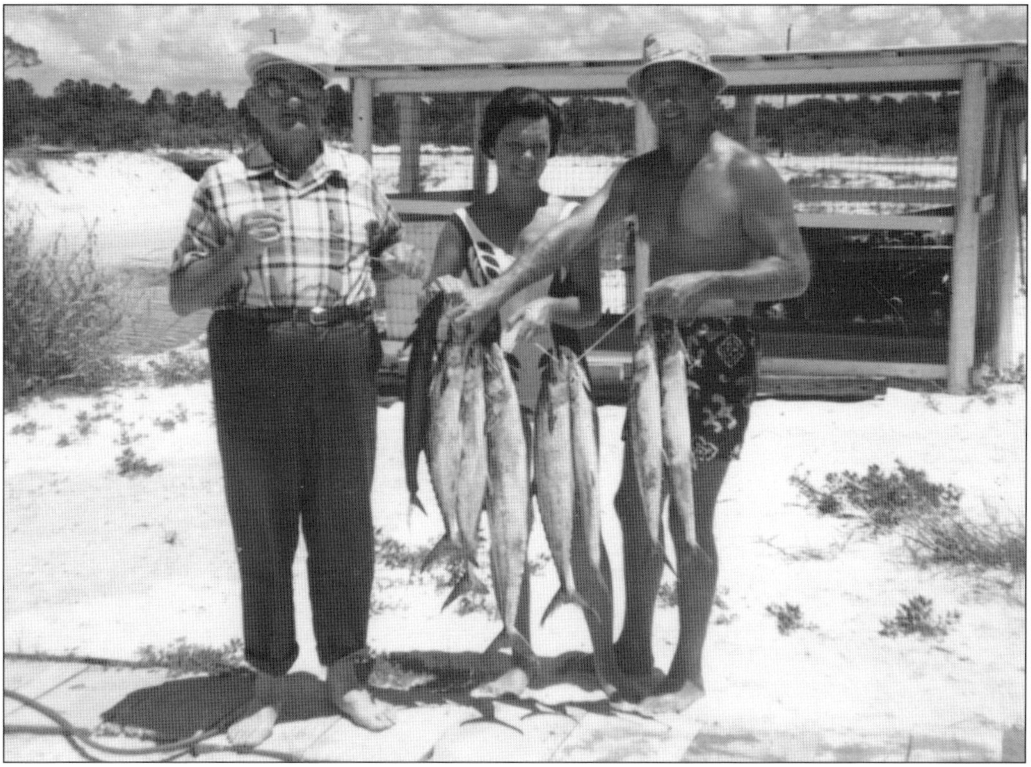

Four
MOM-AND-POP BUSINESSES

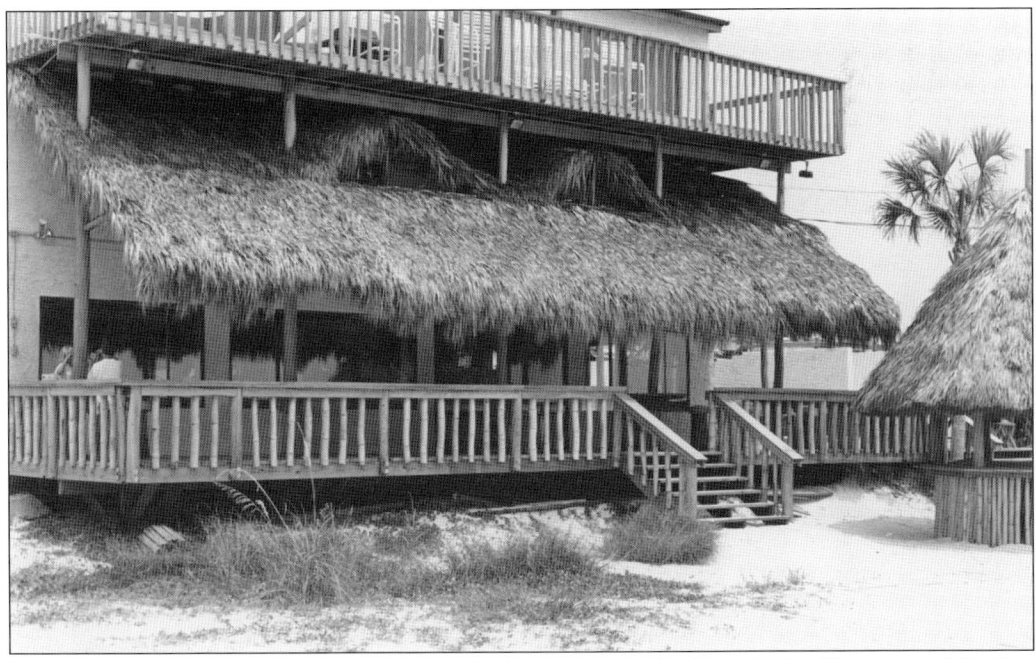

This beach view shows the iconic Toucan's Restaurant in the late 1990s. (Courtesy of Cathey Parker Hobbs.)

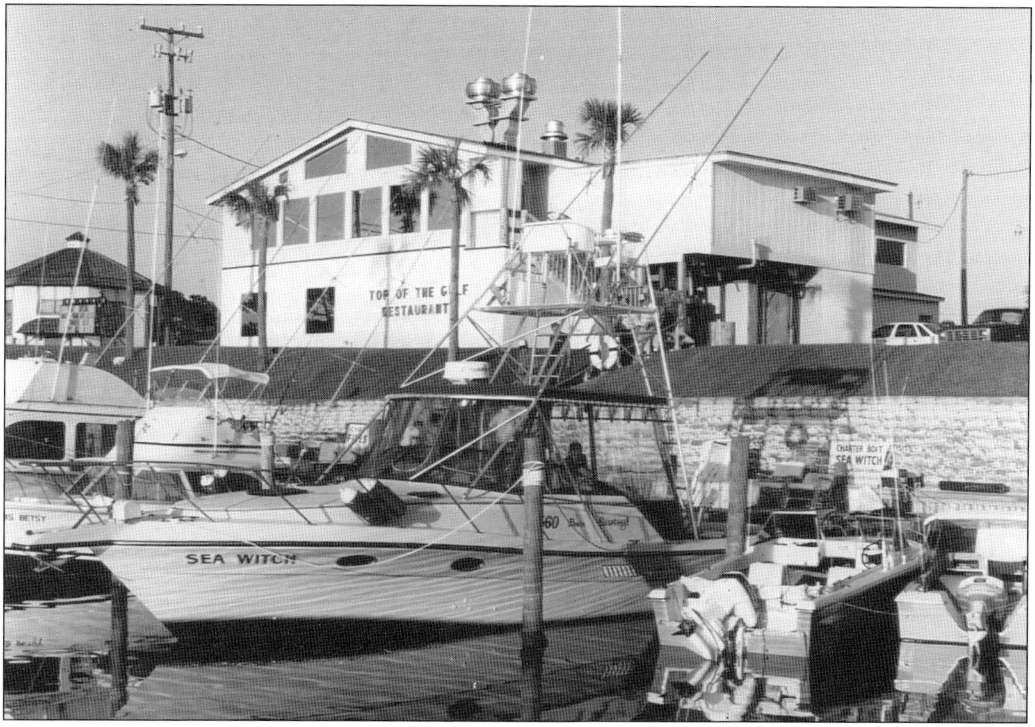

This photograph shows the Top of the Gulf Restaurant with the *Sea Witch* at the dock. Ralph Bush and Jim Heathcock purchased the restaurant from Sparkie Raffield in the early 1970s. In the late 1970s, Jim and his wife, Jean Heathcock, took over. They then sold it to Don Baxter, Inc., in 1983. The restaurant was located on the corner of Forty-second Street and Highway 98. The *Sea Witch* was a 36-foot Sportcraft fishing boat owned by Art and Sylvia Dillard. (Courtesy of Cathey Parker Hobbs.)

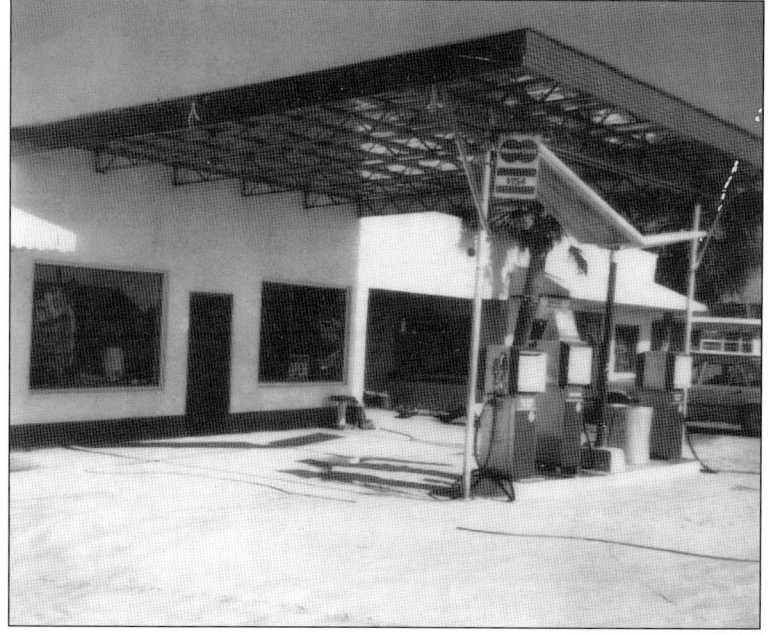

On March 19, 1952, the Mexico Beach Café and Gulf Oil station opened for business with Roy Conoley at the helm. He and his family had opened a small café in Port St. Joe, but Conoley was not satisfied with just one business—he had sand in his shoes and headed to Mexico Beach because it was time to make a move. (Courtesy of Roy Conoley Jr.)

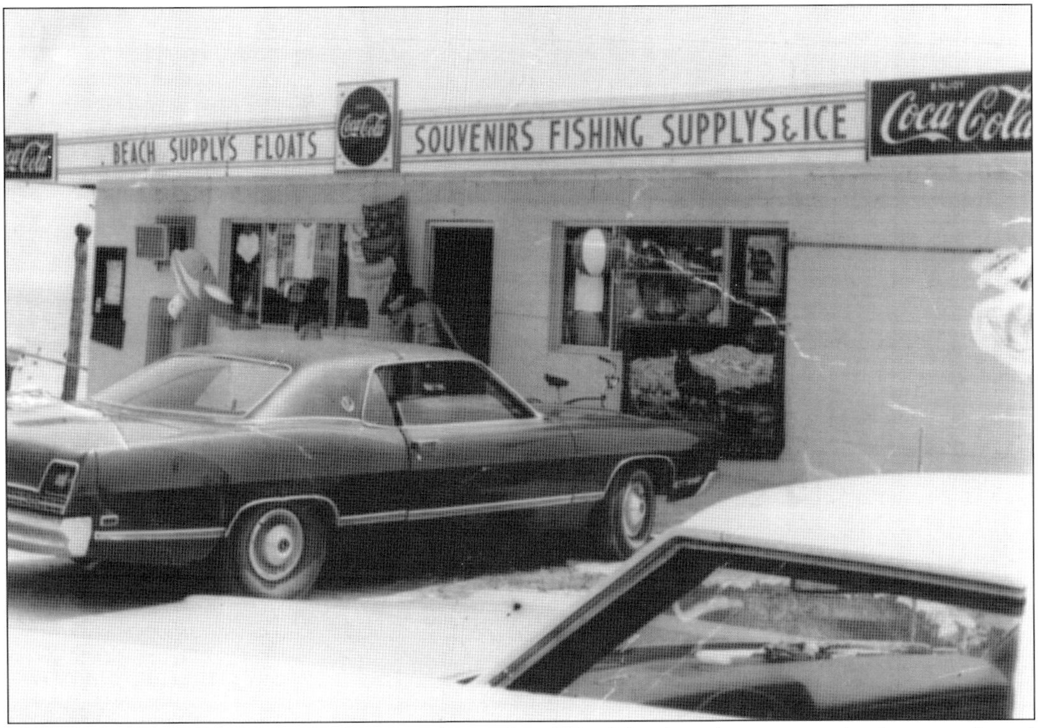

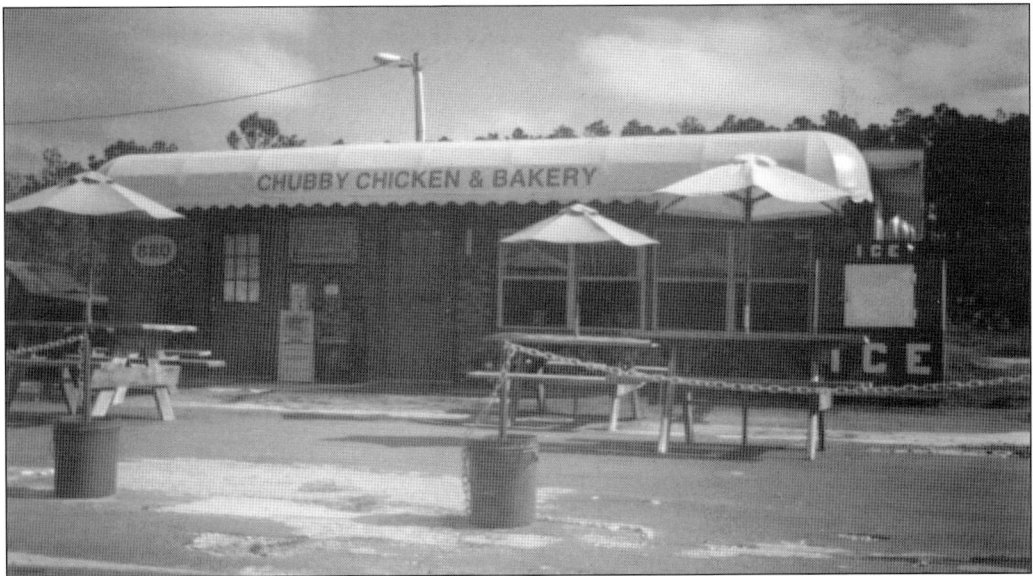

Wayside Beach Supply is seen here in the early 1970s. The beach store was built, owned, and operated by James and Lucille Gaddis. In 1989, the property was sold to Paul Francis and it became Toucan's Restaurant. (Courtesy of Allen Gaddis.)

In the early 1990s, the business address of 820 Highway 98 was home to Gulfaire Realty and the Mexico Beach Post Office. In 1997, Ike Duren sold the property to Betty Harwood and Carol Bonanno, who opened Chubby Chicken & Bakery there in April 1998. In July 2003, the property became the home of Killer Seafood, owned and operated by Michael Scoggins, Kim Halverson, and Kevin Crouse. (Courtesy of Cathey Parker Hobbs.)

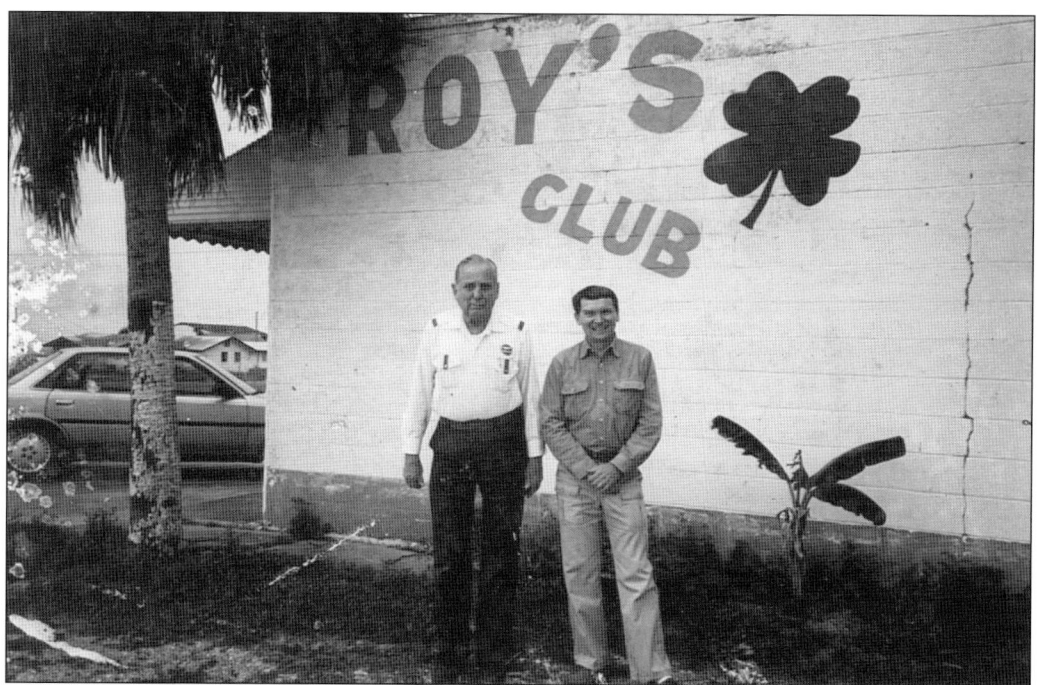

At some point in time, the Mexico Beach Café changed names, after which it was forever known as Roy's Club. Here, Roy Conoley (left) and an unidentified man are standing outside his club. (Courtesy of Roy Conoley Jr.)

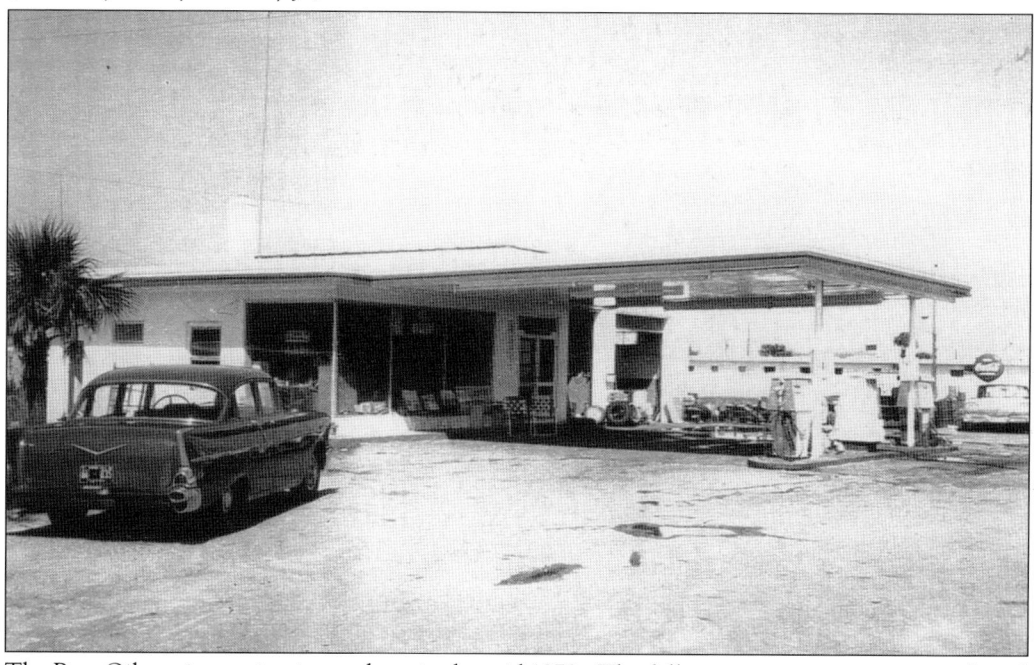

The Pure Oil service station is seen here in the mid-1970s. The full-service gas station was purchased by Chuck Guilford in 1971 from Barney Earley. Arlene and Jim McCollough then purchased the station in 1976 and were joined shortly after by partners Beverly and Leroy Sherman. (Courtesy of Chuck Guilford.)

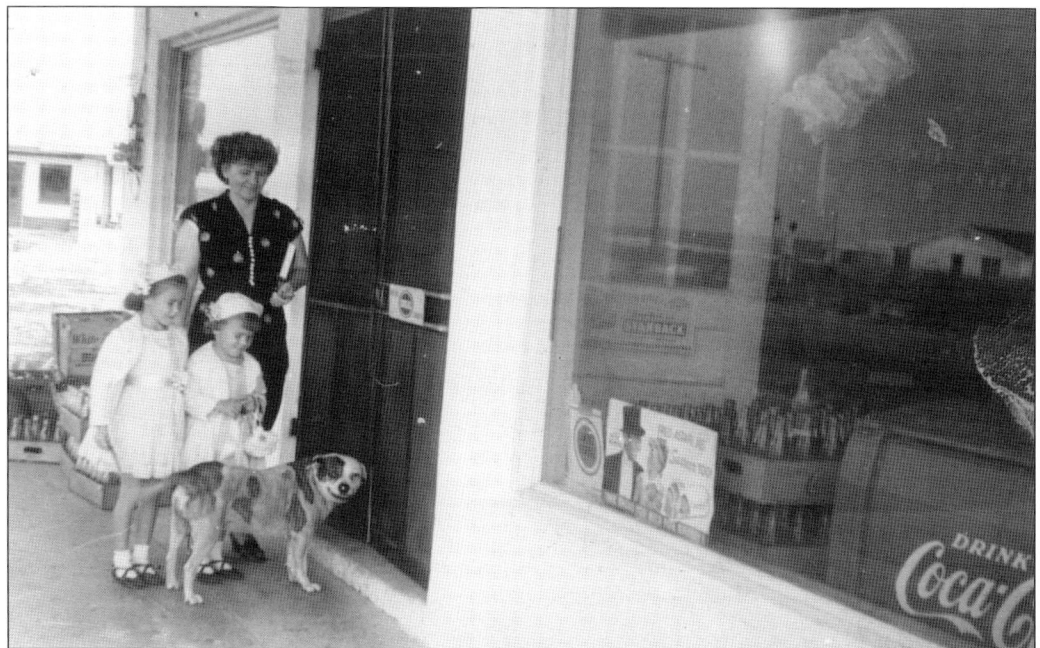

Estelle "Mom" Cathey enters her grocery store in the early 1950s with her granddaughters Cathey (left) and Sue Parker and her dog Trouble. The Mexico Beach Grocery was purchased by her son Bubba and his wife, Marion, and Estelle purchased the newly built adjoining sundries store, forming the Mexico Beach Shopping Center in the early 1950s. (Courtesy of the Parker family.)

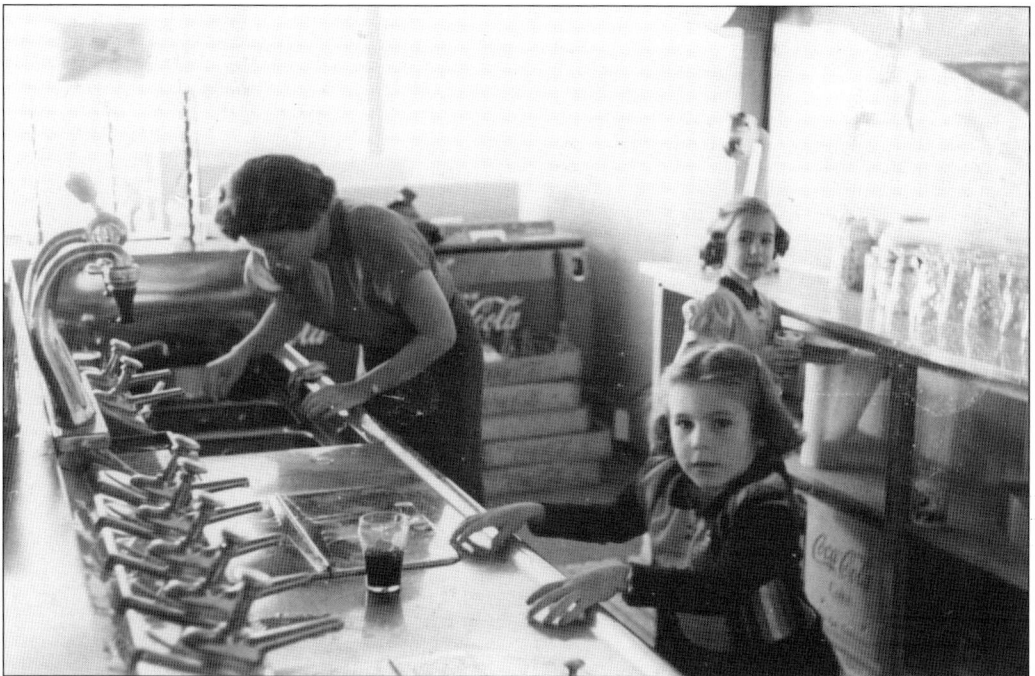

The Parker girls are at work at the soda fountain in the sundries store adjoining the Mexico Beach Grocery in 1952. Inky Parker and her daughter Sue are at the counter, and Cathey Parker is in the rear. (Courtesy of the Parker family.)

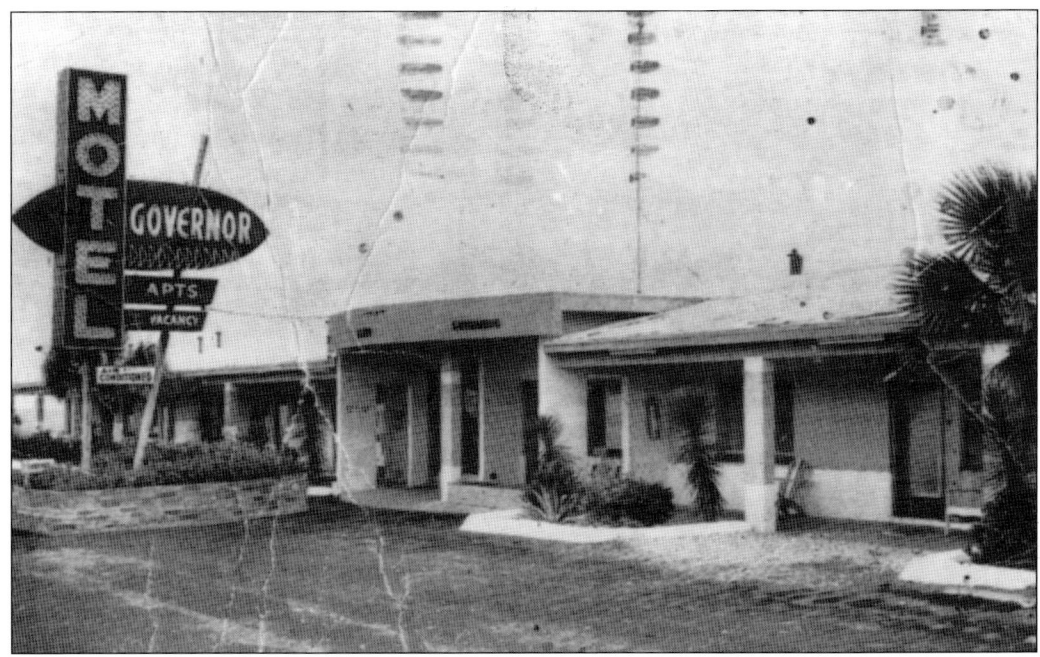

The Governor Motel, seen here in 1958, was owned and operated by Polly and Olen Hayes. In 1973, ownership of the property transferred to Demples Duncan, Ronnie Turner, Karen Ragen, and Debe Morgan. Don Baxter purchased the motel in 1976 and renamed it the El Governor. (Courtesy of Ronnie Turner.)

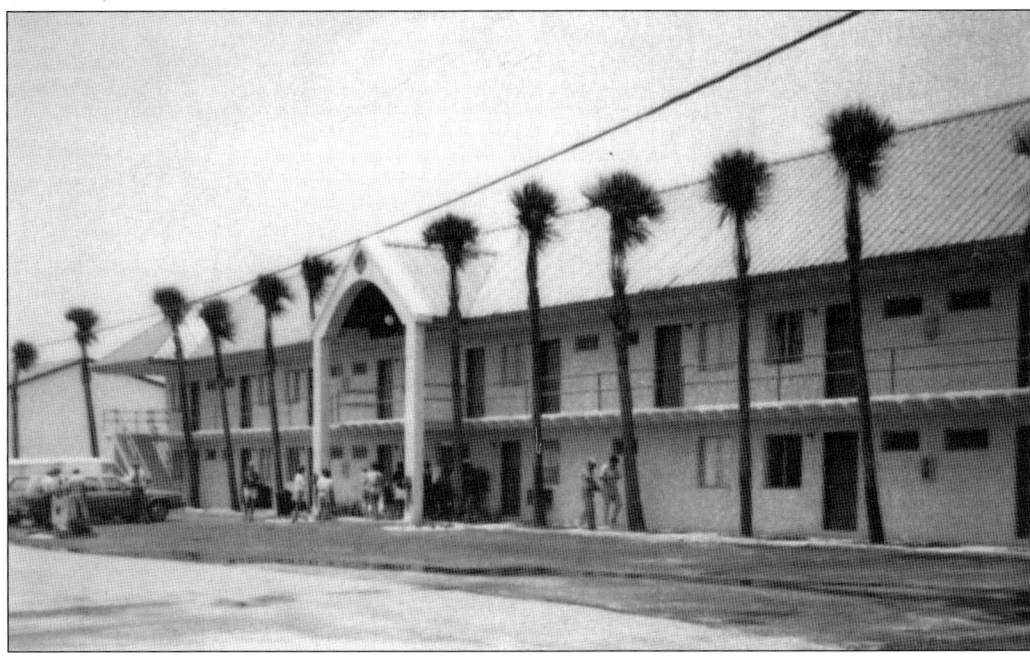

In 1989, the Hollanday Motel was renovated and reopened as the Big Game Club under the management of Joan Smithwick and the ownership of Randy Haney. In later years, the club became the Bluewater Inn and was managed by Leonard and Jeannette Giffin from 1995 until 2001, when it was sold to developer and contractor Jimmy Hambrick. (Courtesy of Joan Smithwick.)

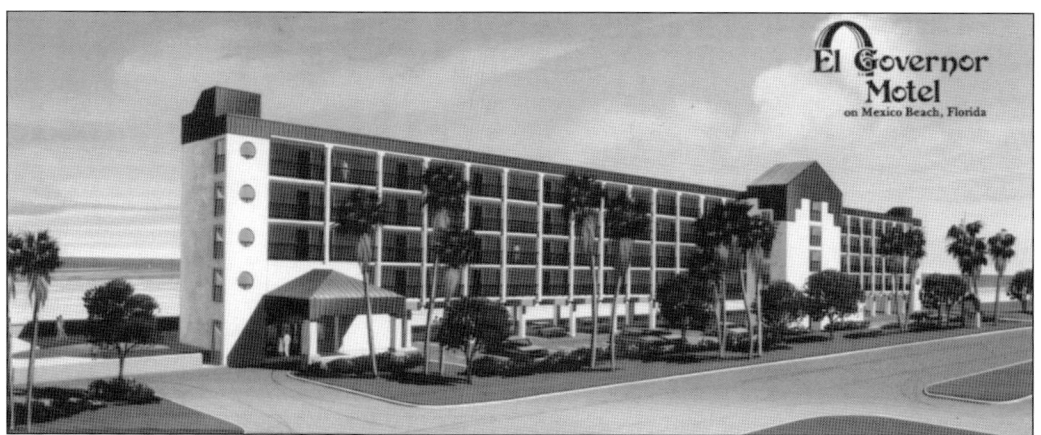

This artist's rendition of the proposed El Governor Motel was used for marketing and advertising purposes in the late 1980s. The 102-room motel was built in 1989. (Courtesy of Wylie Petty.)

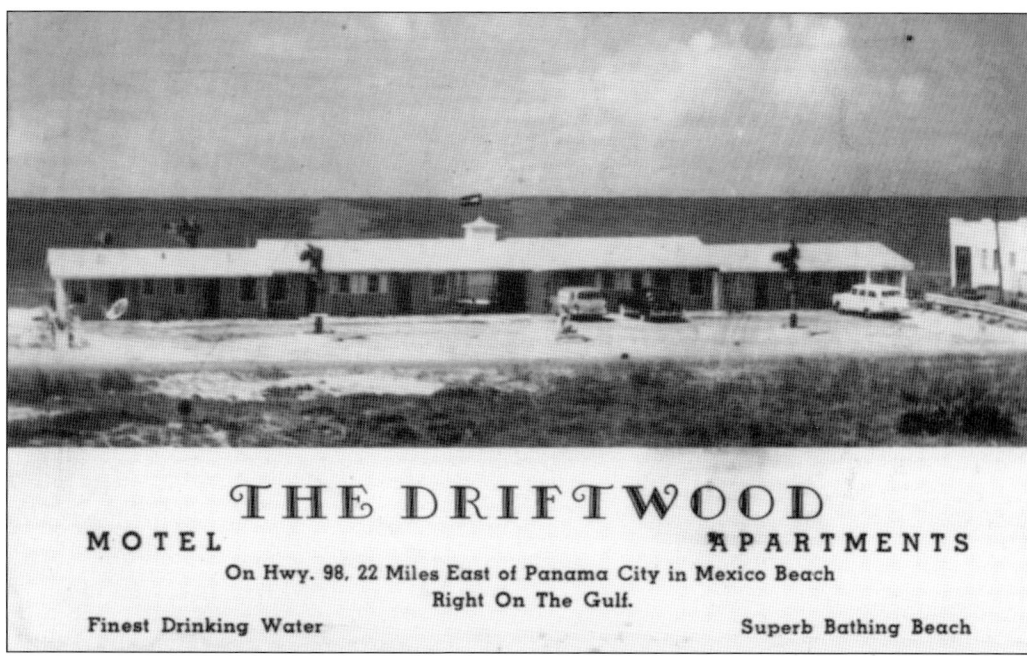

The Driftwood Motel and Apartments was built in 1950 and was made up of two buildings joined together by a breezeway in the center. Each building had four units. John Stokes, the owner, lived in the far right unit, leaving seven units for rent. Rooms rented for $12 a night. Highway 98 looked like a dirt road in this photograph. (Courtesy of Peggy Wood.)

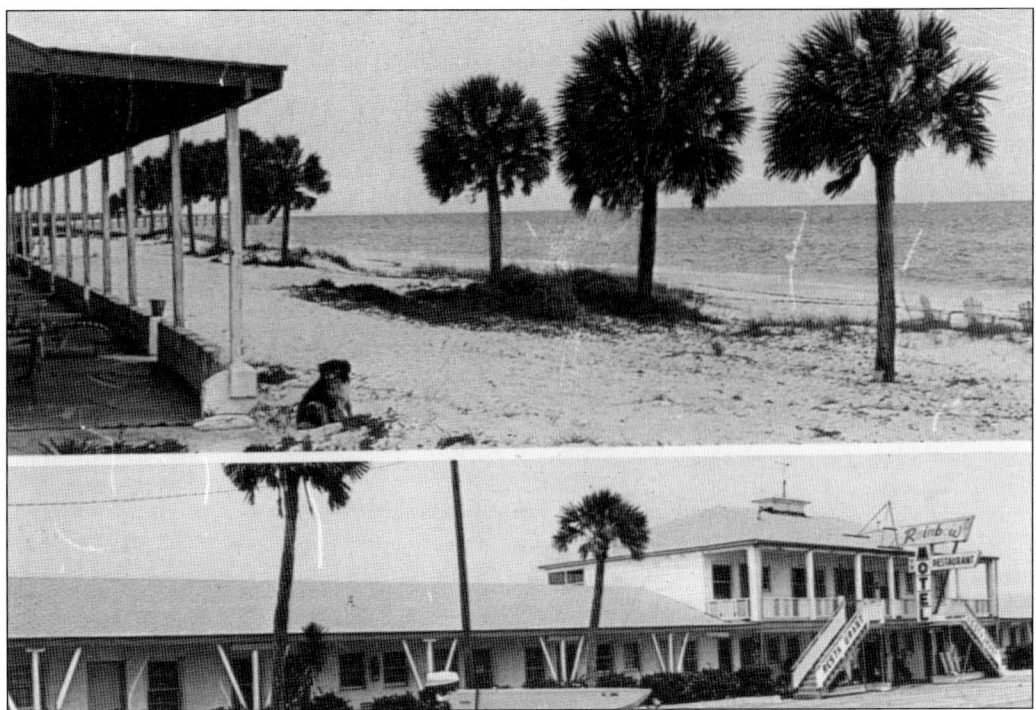

The Rainbow Motel was built by Edward Parker in the early 1950s. In its later years, the motel was owned and managed by local residents Bill and Millie Lyles. The top photograph shows the rear of the building, while the bottom shows the front. (Courtesy of the Parker family.)

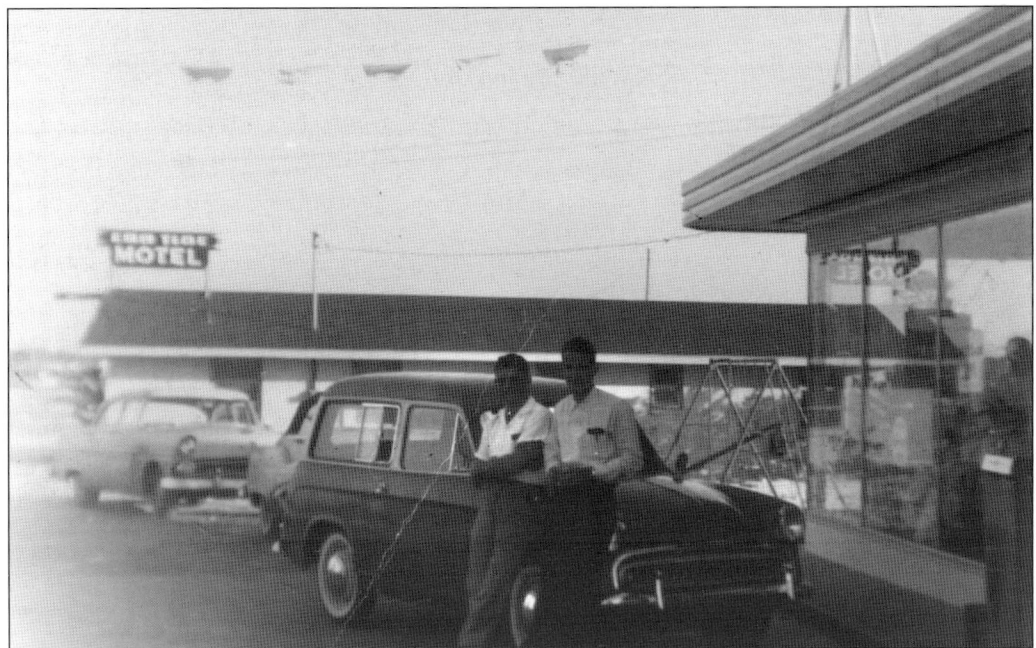

Barney Earley (left) and George Holland lean on a car at the Ebb Tide Motel and Pure Oil service station in the mid-1960s. The Ebb Tide was originally a two-unit motel, but Holland added five additional rooms in 1960. (Courtesy of George Holland.)

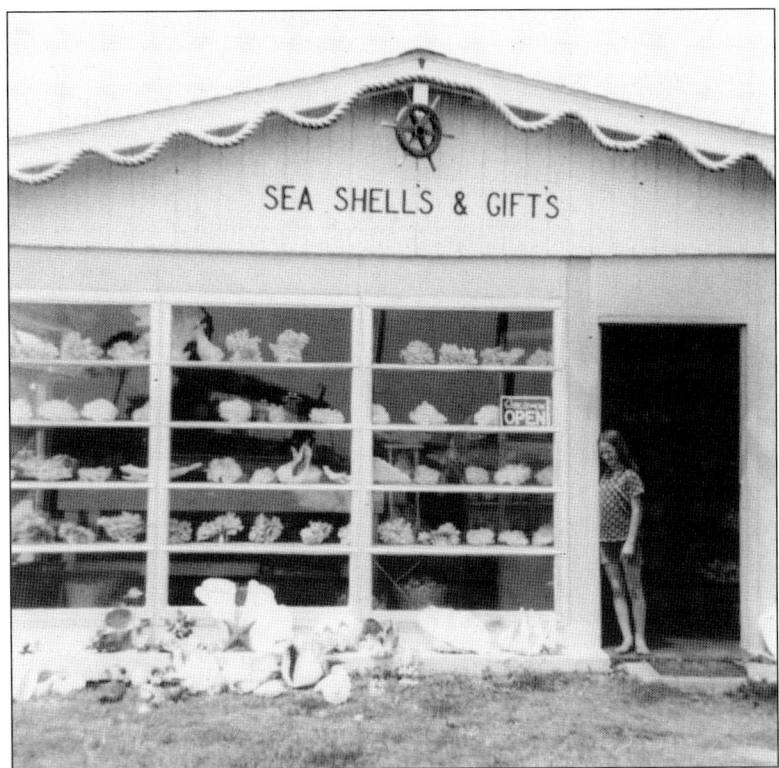

Elizabeth "Libby" Hunter, the daughter of Bennie and George Hunter, stands in front of the Shell Shack in the mid-1970s. Her brothers Fred, George III, and Harry still live in the area, and Elizabeth now lives in Indiana. Fred shrimps on his dad's boat, the *Miss Bennie*; "Little George" and his wife, Theresa, now own and manage the Shell Shack; and Harry and Bennie have both retired and live in Overstreet. George passed away in 2001. (Courtesy of Bennie Hunter.)

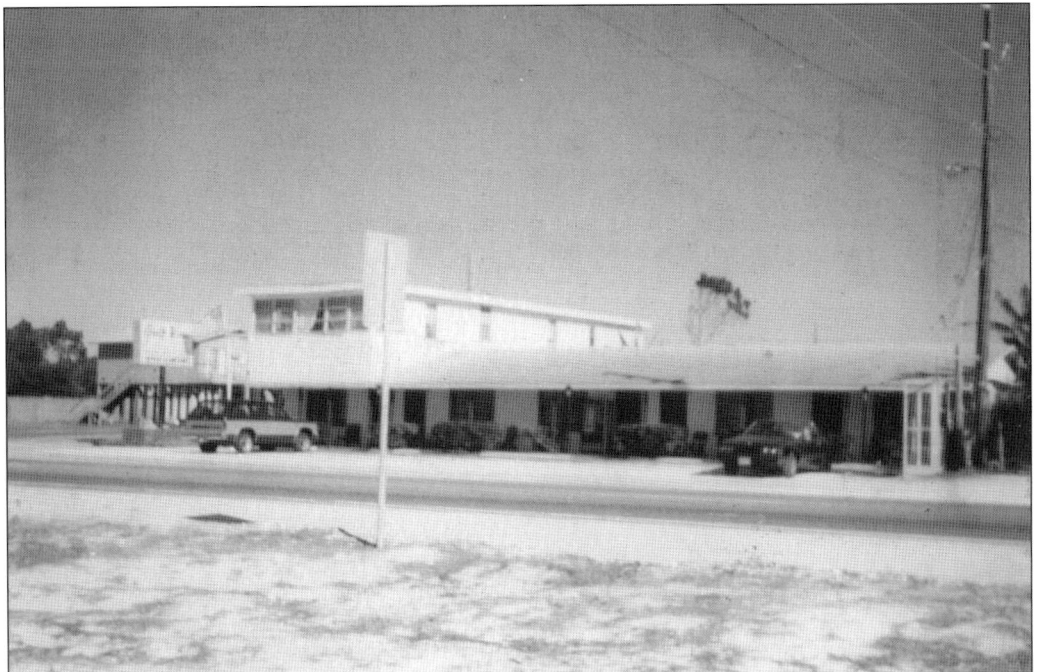

The Gulf View Motel, on the corner of Fourteenth Street and Highway 98, was built by Walter Buckalow in 1955. Current owners Charles "Brownie" and Elaine Smith purchased the motel in 1987 from Ed and Pansy Wysong. It is seen here in 1998. (Courtesy of Chuck Smith.)

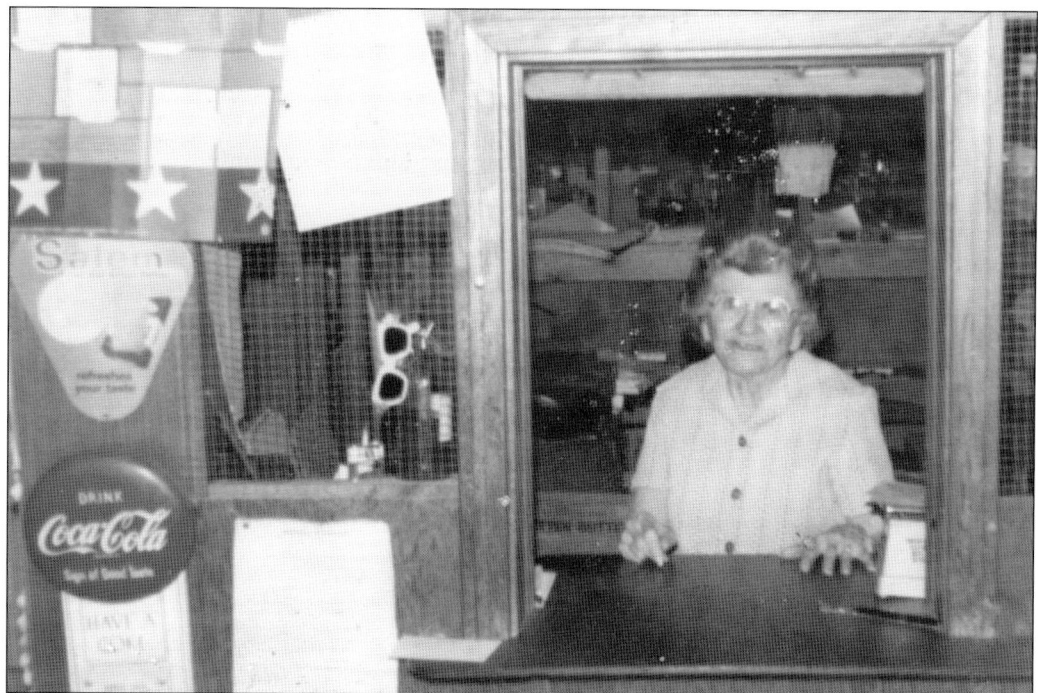

Estelle "Mom" Cathey was the postmistress in Mexico Beach for many years. The post office was located in the sundries store in the Mexico Beach Shopping Center. In the early days, the mail was delivered to the shopping center and kept in a cigar box. Estelle had daily "mail call" for local residents and military people who were stationed at Tyndall Field. (Courtesy of the Parker family.)

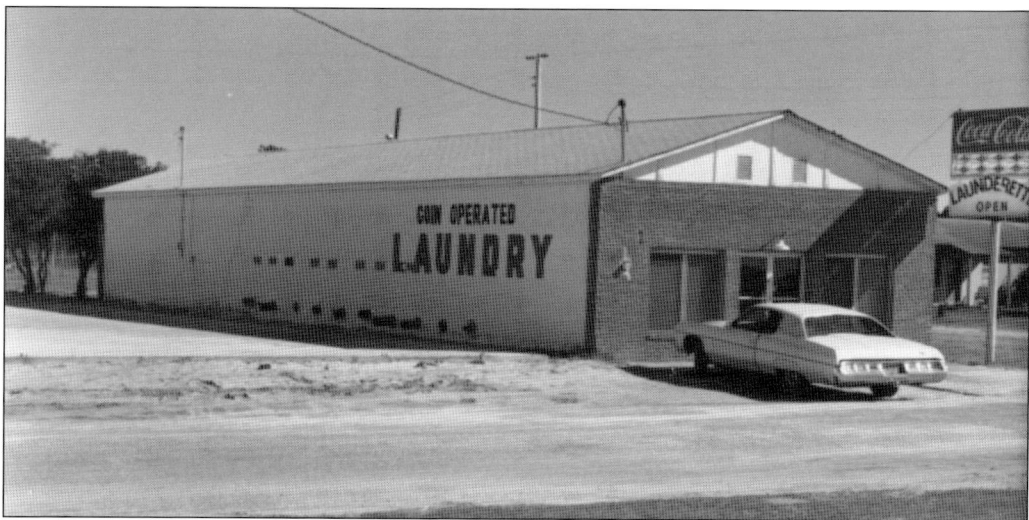

The Mexico Beach Laundromat, seen here in 1973, was originally a dry goods and hardware store owned by Leslie McCants and his wife, Ruth. The building was constructed in 1951. Church services were also held here until the Mexico Beach Methodist Church was built in the late 1950s. The building became a coin laundry in 1958, owned by Joe and Bea Hewett. Al and Helen St. Johns purchased the property in the early 1960s and sold it to Bubba and Marion Cathey in 1971. (Courtesy of Al Cathey.)

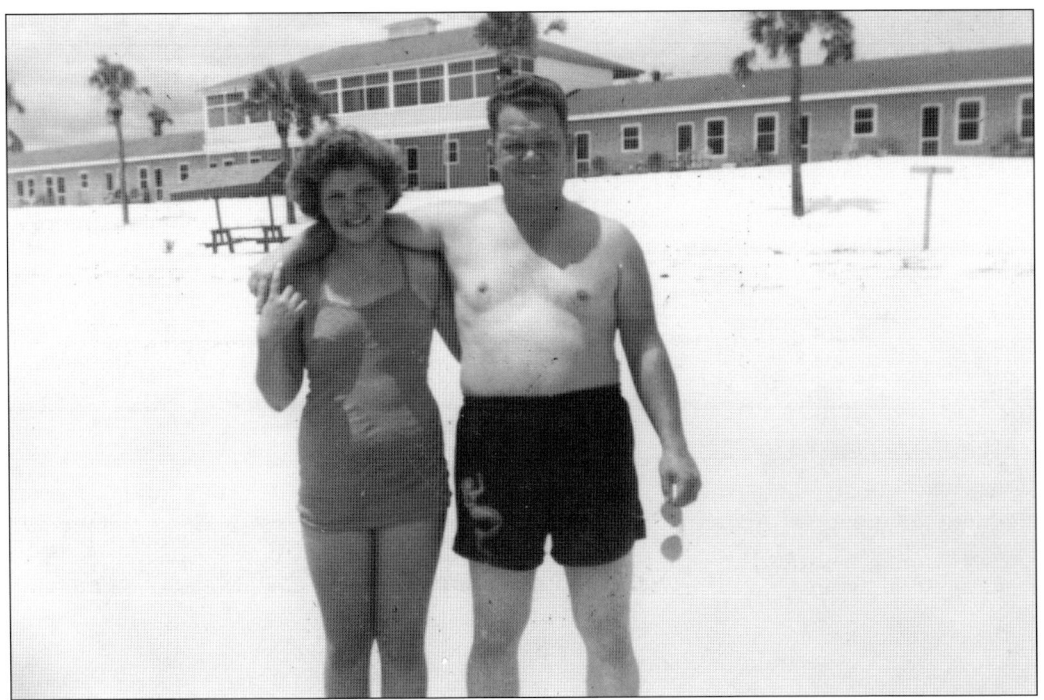

Nellie and Gordon Klope stand on the beach behind the Rainbow Motel in 1954. The Klopes made Mexico Beach their home in 1965. (Courtesy of Nellie Klope.)

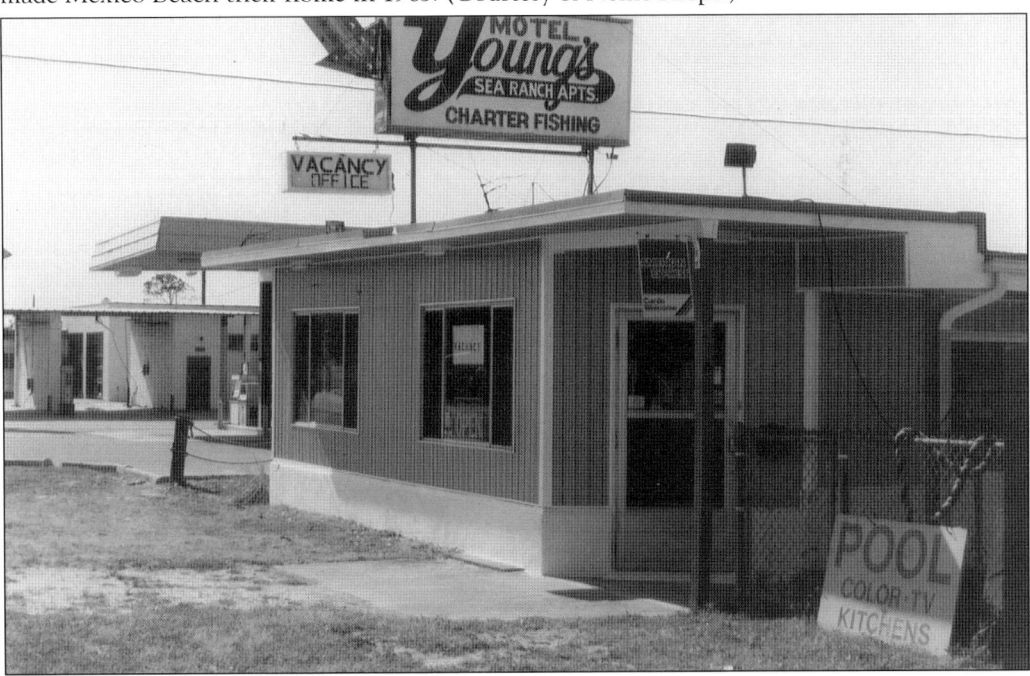

Sonny and Virginia Young purchased the Gulf Cabanas Motel in 1982 from Helen and Al St. John. Young's Sea Ranch Apartments was remodeled into five efficiency apartments. The Youngs sold the property to B.J. Barwick in 1997, and the name was changed to Ocean Breeze. (Courtesy of Virginia Young.)

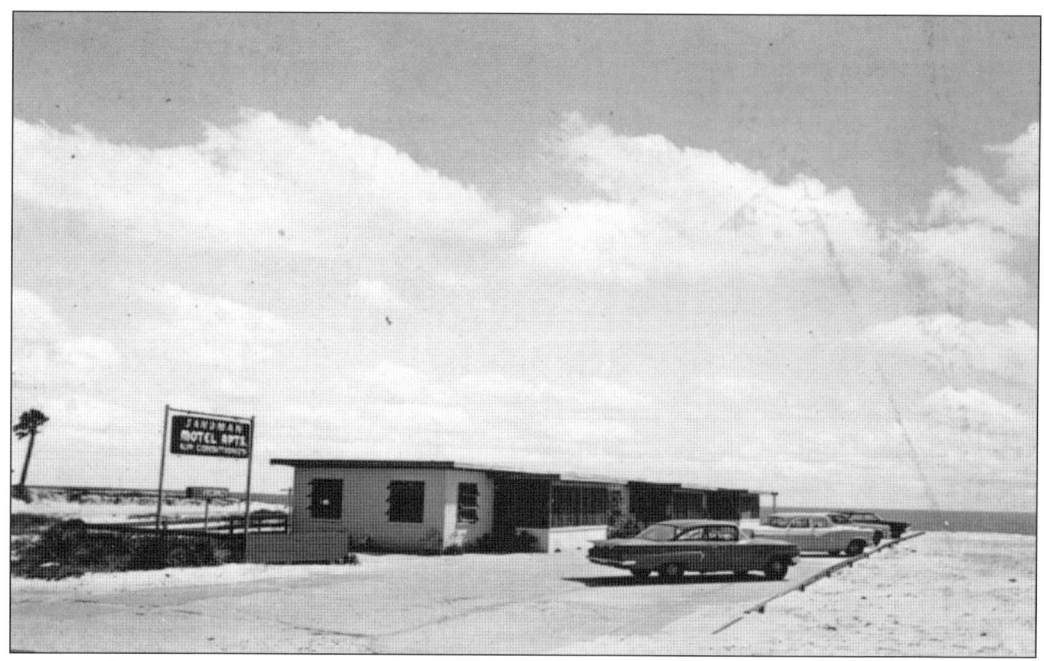

The Sandman Motel and Apartments was located at 2303 Highway 98, the current location of The Vue Condos. The motel was built by Harlem and Clyde Allen in the mid-1950s and managed by Jessie Stafford through the mid-1960s. (Courtesy of Cathey Parker Hobbs.)

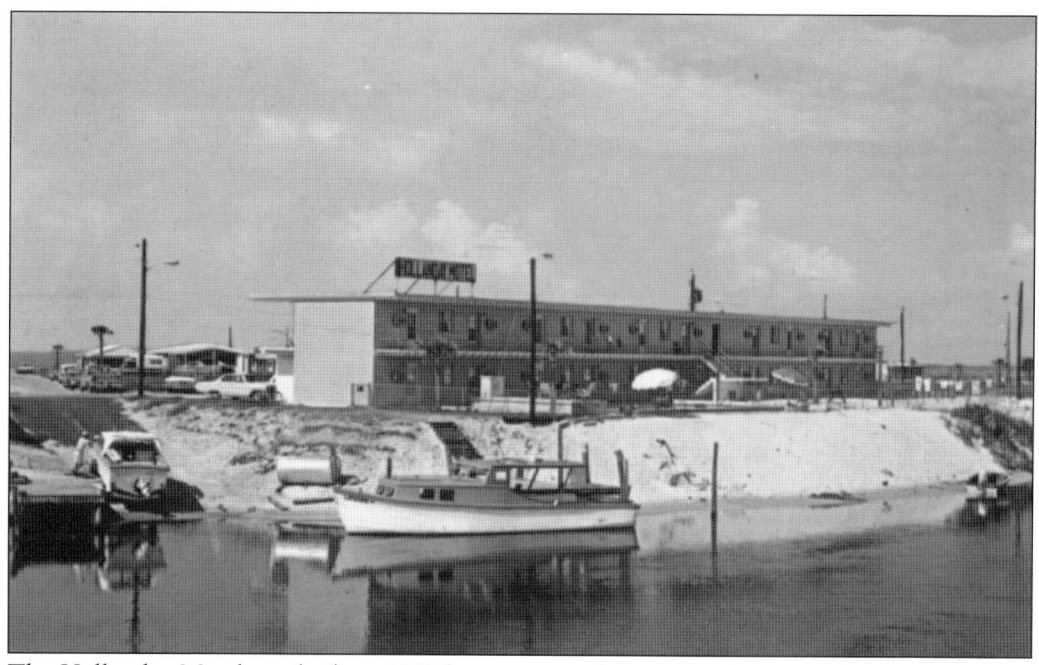

The Hollanday Motel was built in 1962 by owners and operators George and Louise Holland. Located on the canal, it was ideal for tourists and fishermen. (Courtesy of Louise Holland.)

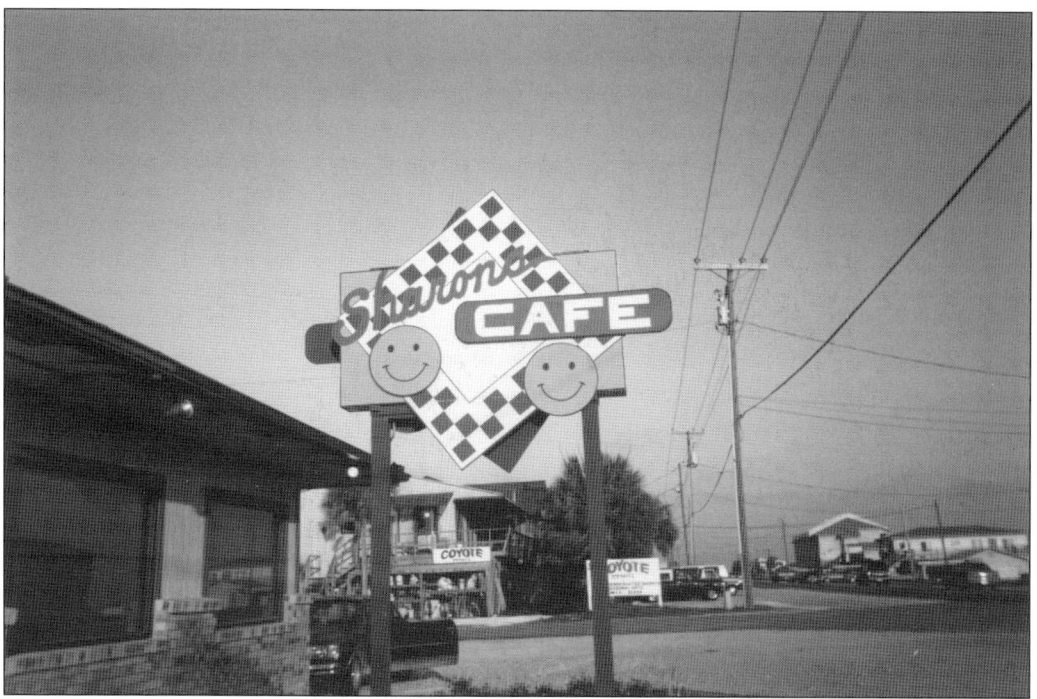

Sharon's Café was built in 1988 by J.T. Barineau. Eight months later, he sold it to Sharon Call, and it remains a popular breakfast and lunch restaurant today. (Courtesy of Cathey Parker Hobbs.)

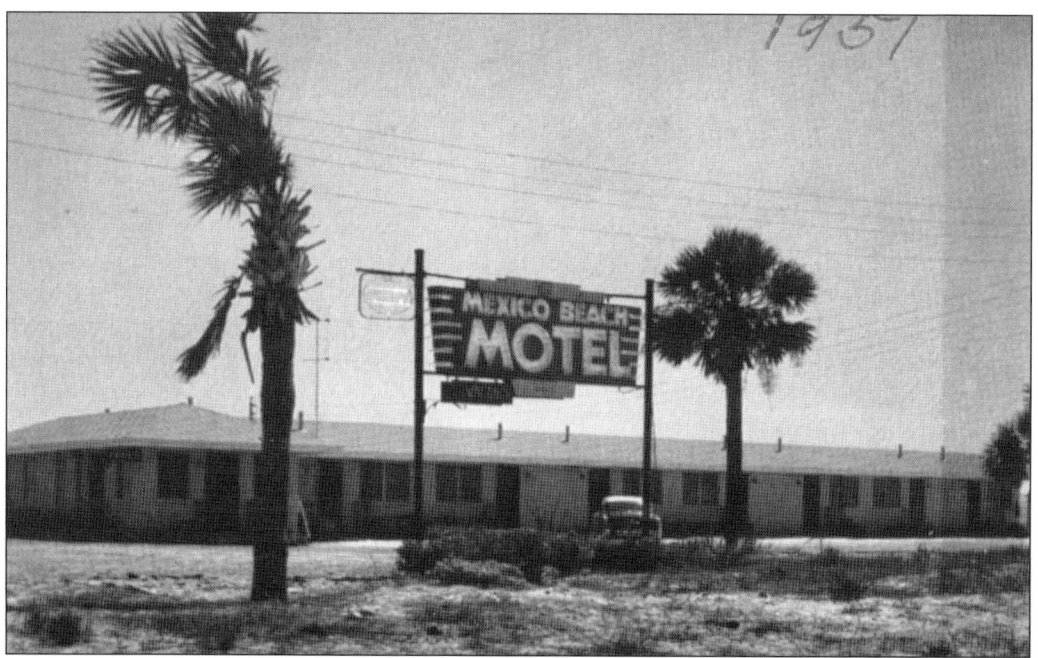

The Mexico Beach Motel was built in the early 1950s by Teet Newcomb. The property was later purchased and seasonally operated by new owners Ed and Betty Corry and their family. (Courtesy of Jim Corry.)

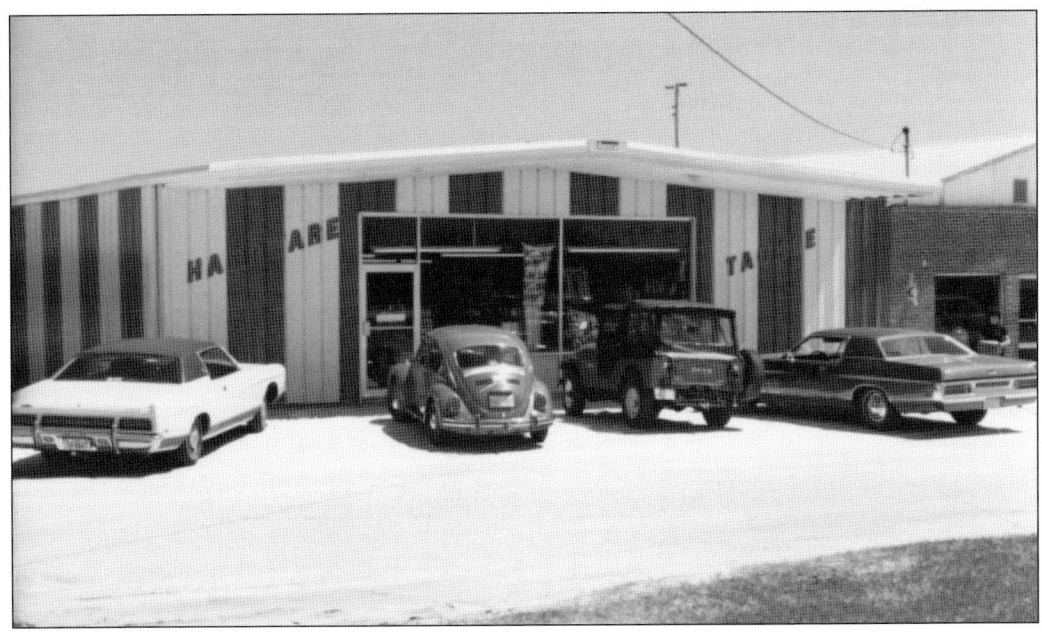

Cathey's Hardware and Tackle opened for business in April 1974. Bubba and Marion Cathey operated both the grocery and hardware stores until the grocery was sold to Joe and Sylvia Whaley in 1976. After Bubba's untimely death in 1979, Marion, along with her son Al and dedicated 20-year employee and friend Dana Angerer Boyer, managed and operated the hardware store. Marion retired in 1991. (Courtesy of Al Cathey.)

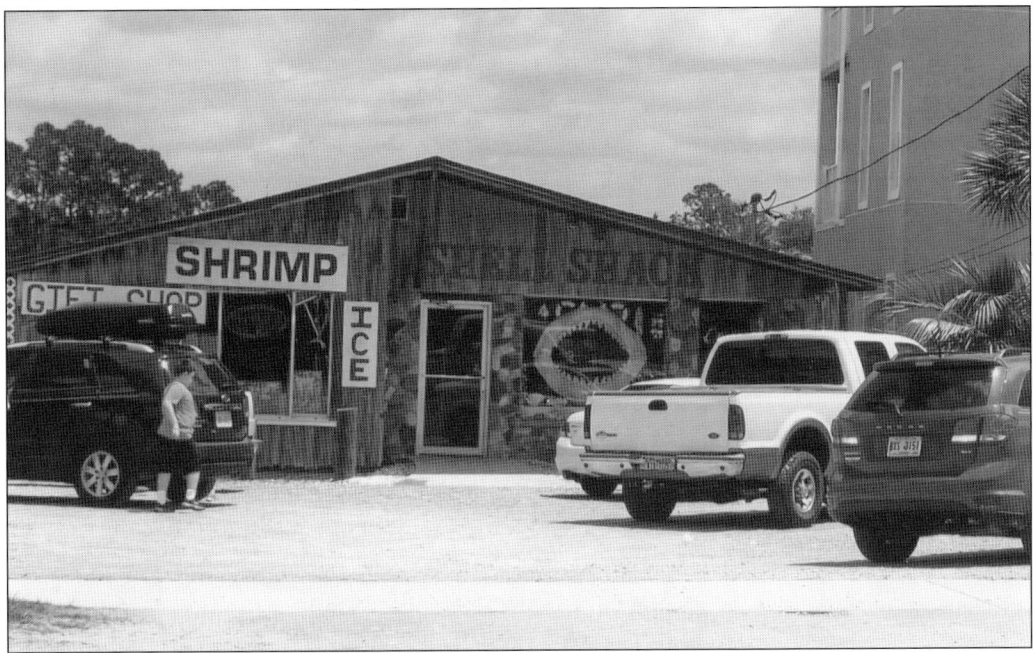

The Shell Shack, a family-owned and -operated business, has been part of Mexico Beach for over 40 years. George and Bennie Hunter originally opened it in 1971 as Bennie's Bait and Tackle, and the name was changed a few years later. The business still operates today as a third-generation mom-and-pop fish market and retail shop. (Courtesy of Bennie Hunter.)

Five

PIONEER FAMILIES

Charlie and Inky Parker moved from Blountstown to Mexico Beach in 1949 with their two daughters, Cathey (left) and Sue (right). Their daughter Nan was born in 1958. Inky's mother, Estelle "Mom" Cathey, and her 13-year-old son also made the move with them, as her husband had recently passed away. Charlie took over the development of the new land in Mexico Beach with Inky at his side, and Estelle Cathey ran the first grocery store. (Courtesy of the Parker family.)

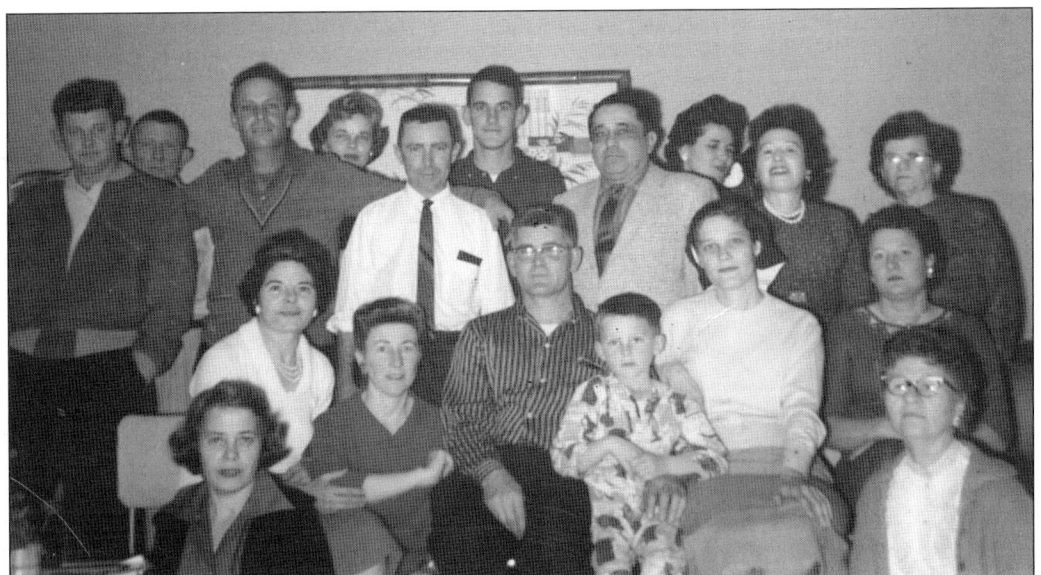

These pioneers got together at the Earley family home for a housewarming party in the mid-1950s. From left to right are (first row) a Mrs. Sheppard, Annie Chewning, Inky Parker, Barney Earley, Chris Earley, Mary Earley, Bea Hewitt, and Jessie Stafford; (second row) Bubba Cathey, Joe Hewitt, Charlie Parker, Morris and Betty Missler, and Estelle "Mom" Cathey; (third row) Jimmy Chewning, Louise Holland, George Holland, and Marion Cathey. (Courtesy of Chris Earley.)

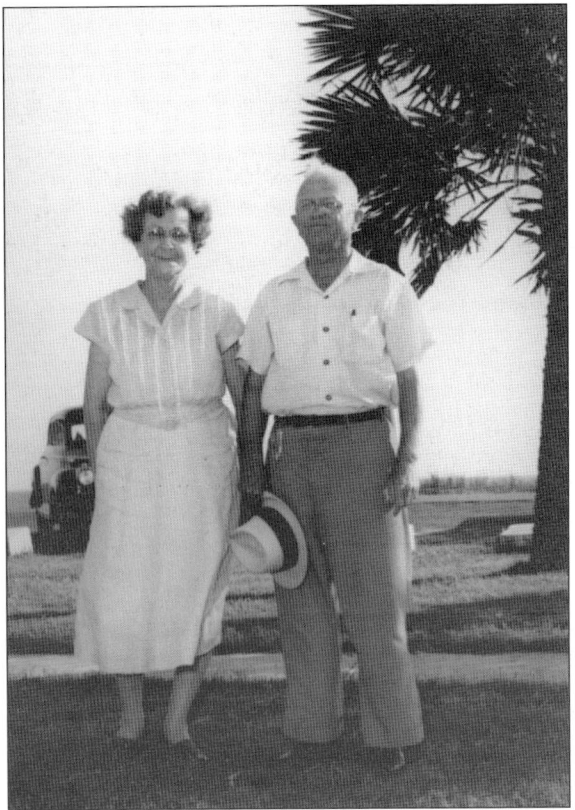

Gordon "G.U." Parker and his wife, Maude, are seen here at Wayside Park in the early 1950s. Parker moved his family from Alabama to Blountstown in 1918 to go into the lumber and land-purchasing business. He had a reputation of being a land man with vision, wisdom, and integrity. In 1946, Parker, his cousin W.T. McGowin, and J.M. Wainwright purchased the 3.5-mile stretch of land that would become Mexico Beach. (Courtesy of the Parker family.)

The Cathey family is seen here in 1964. Bubba and Marion Cathey and their son Al moved from Memphis, Tennessee, to Mexico Beach in 1953. That same year, baby Janie Cathey became the family's first Mexico Beach native. Bubba and Marion owned and operated the Mexico Beach Grocery for 23 years. From left to right are Marion, Janie, Bubba, and Al. (Courtesy of Al Cathey.)

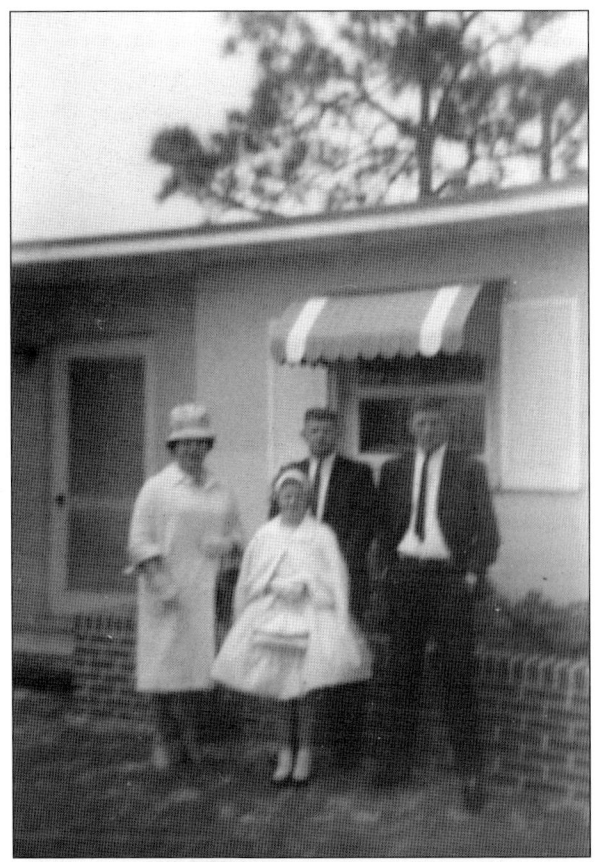

In 1971, city attorney Fred Witten (far right) conducts the oath of office to the newly elected city council members and the second mayor of Mexico Beach. They are, from left to right, Pollye Hayes, Elizabeth Thompson, Tollie Mullins, and Mayor William F. Lyles. (Courtesy of Ronnie Turner.)

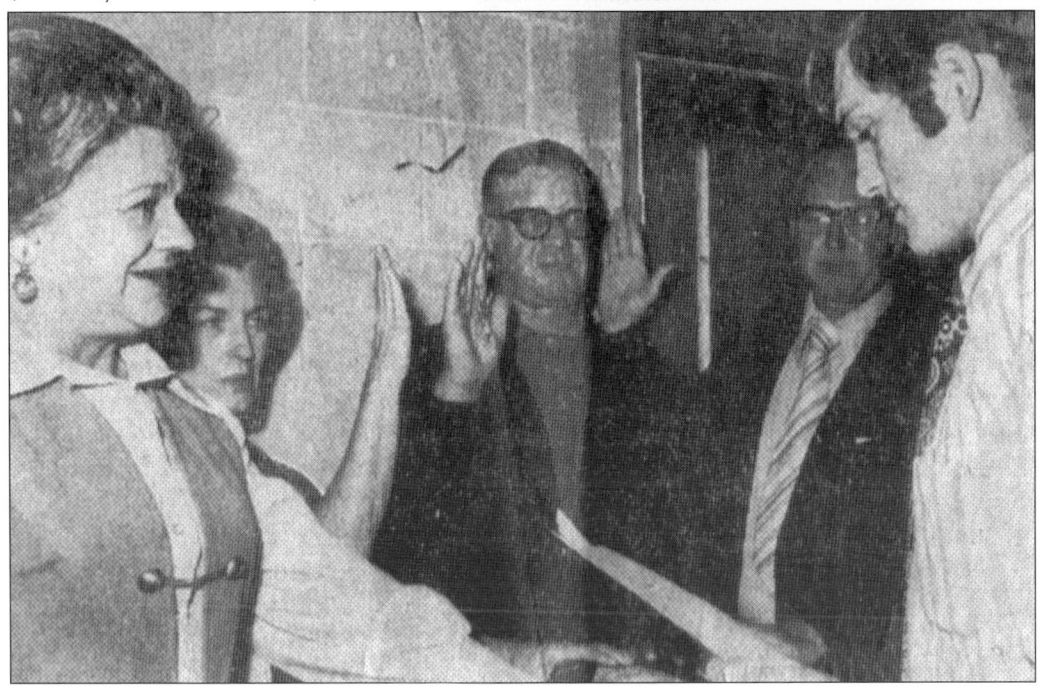

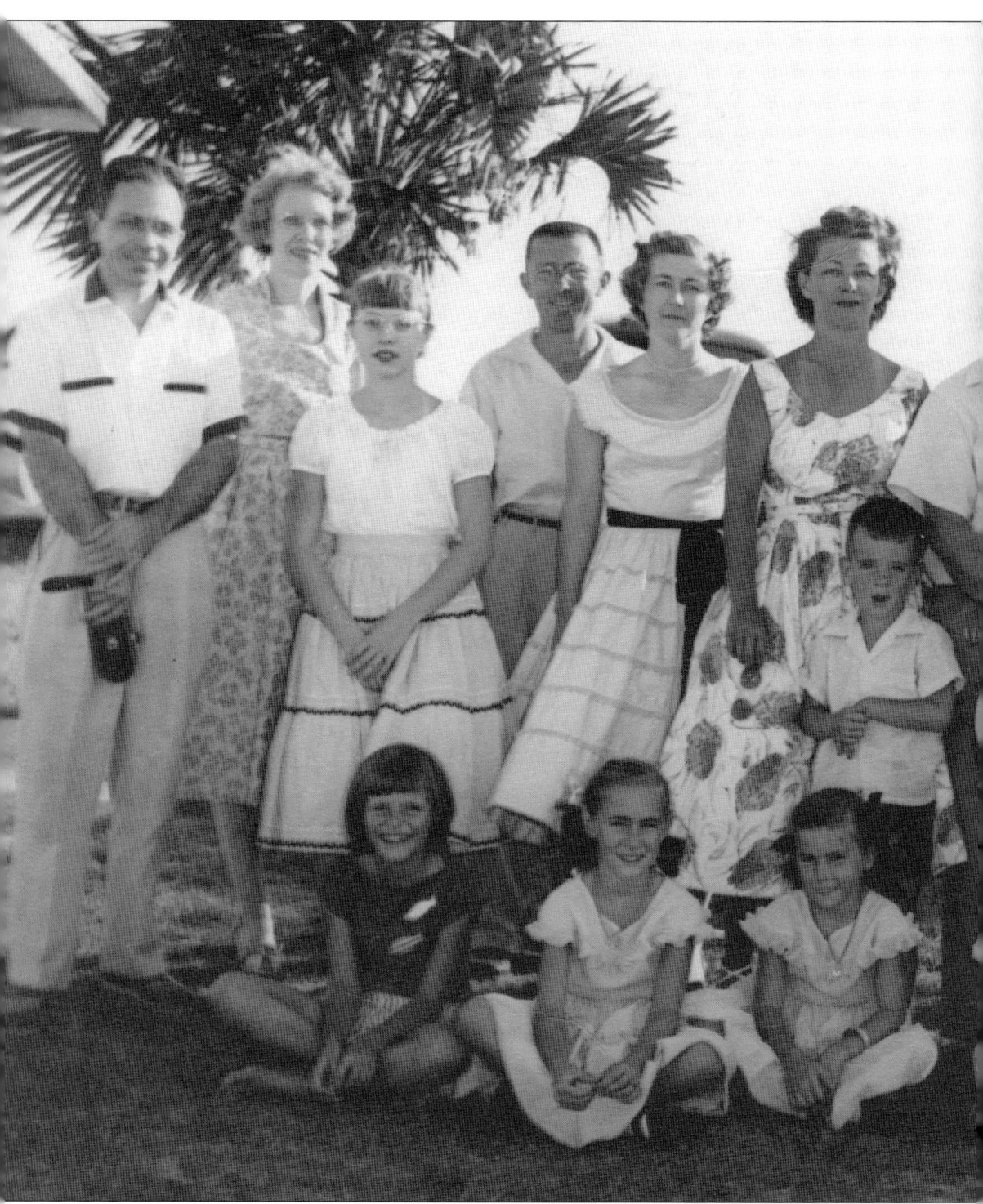

Seen here at a Parker family reunion at Wayside Park in the mid-1950s are, from left to right (sitting) Linda Barrett, Cathey Parker, Sue Parker, and Gordon Parker; (standing) John Gordon Parker, Emily Parker, Terry Parker, Charlie Parker, Inky Parker, Virginia Parker Troutman with

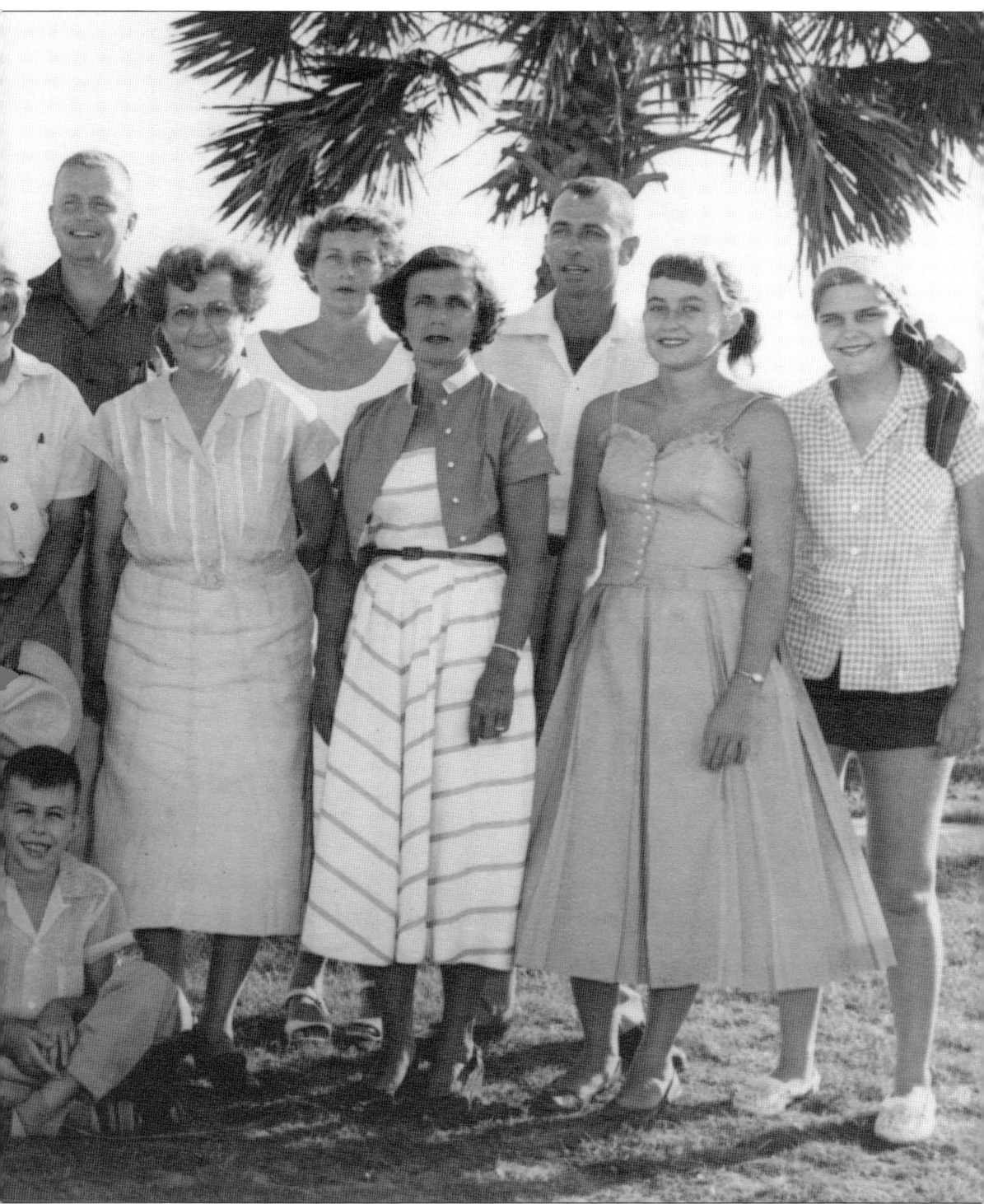
Brent Troutman in front of her, G.U. Parker, Edward Parker, Maude Parker, Jessie Parker, Helen Parker Rainey, James Parker, Joan Parker, and family friend Julie Leonard. (Courtesy of the Parker family.)

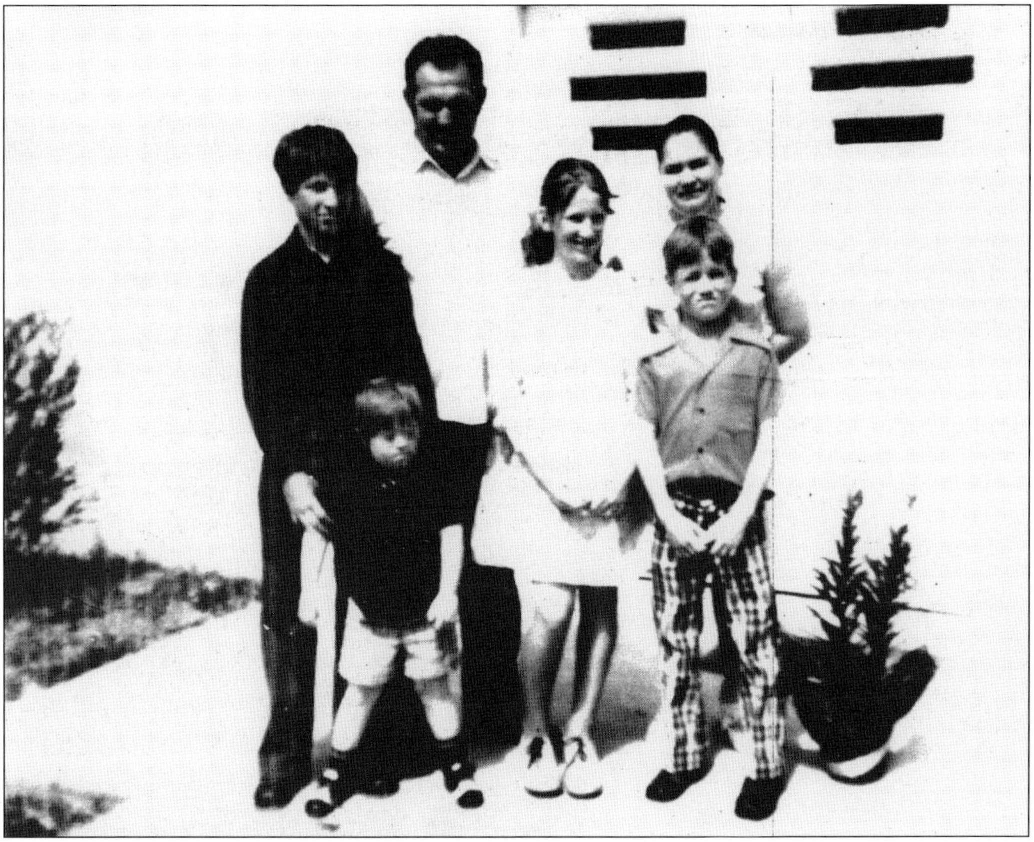

In the late 1960s, George and Bennie Hunter built a structure that would house their business and residence. George Tapper financed the first dry-storage marina on Mexico Beach, which the Hunters opened as Bennie's Bait & Tackle Box. In the mid-1970s, the family turned to seashells and the business was renamed the Shell Shack. From left to right are Harry, Fred, George, Libby, Bennie, and George III. (Courtesy of Bennie Hunter.)

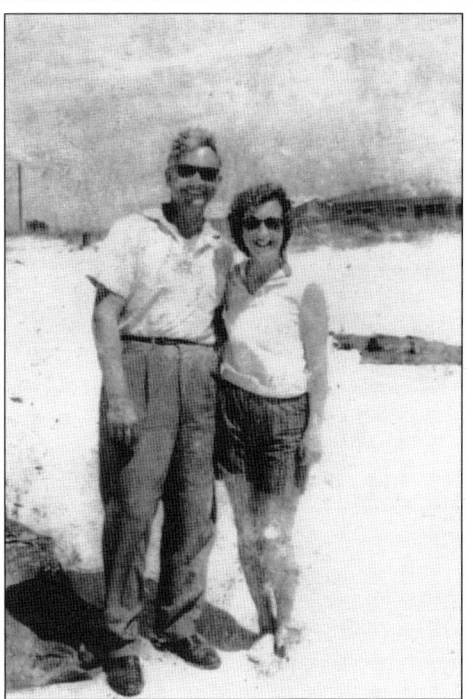

Ed and Betty Corry enjoy time together on the beach in the late 1950s. The Corry family lived in Quincy and made Mexico Beach their second home. They owned the Mexico Beach Motel, along with multiple rental properties. (Courtesy of Jim Corry.)

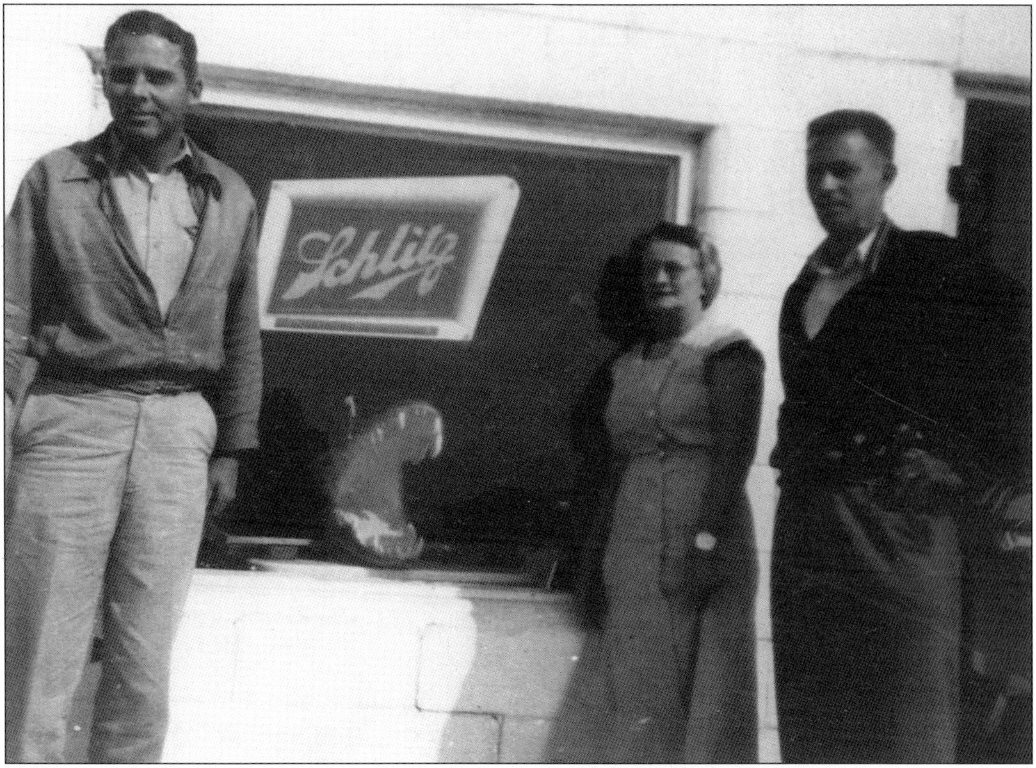

There were two places in Mexico Beach where one could find out all the local news: the post office and Roy's Club. Roy Conoley (left) is seen here showing off his prized stuffed alligator with his friends Dorothy and Harold Scott. Scott was in the Canadian Air Force and came to Tyndall Field for training. The Scotts stayed in Mexico Beach and became friends with Conoley. (Courtesy of Roy Conoley Jr.)

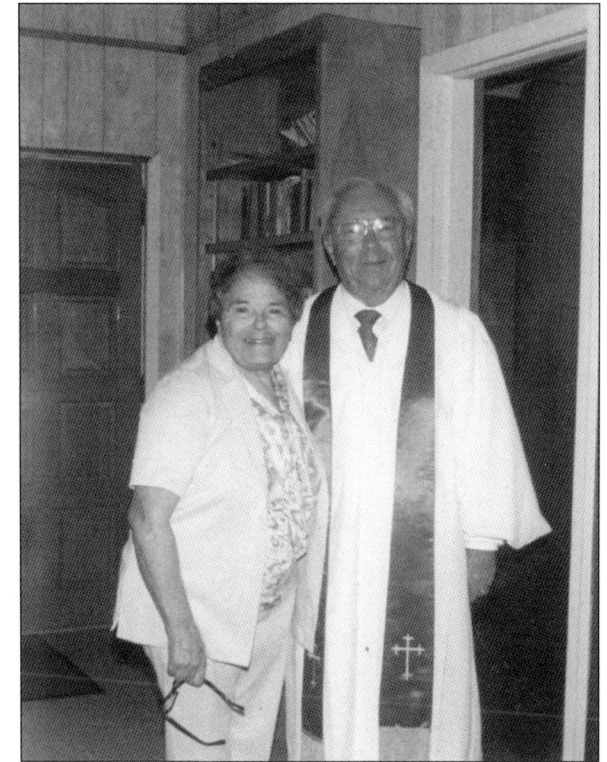

Annie Chewning was a charter member of Mexico Beach Methodist Church and the church organist for many years. Her husband, Jimmy, was instrumental in the building of the sanctuary and the educational building. Annie is seen here with Charlie Parker. (Courtesy of the Parker family.)

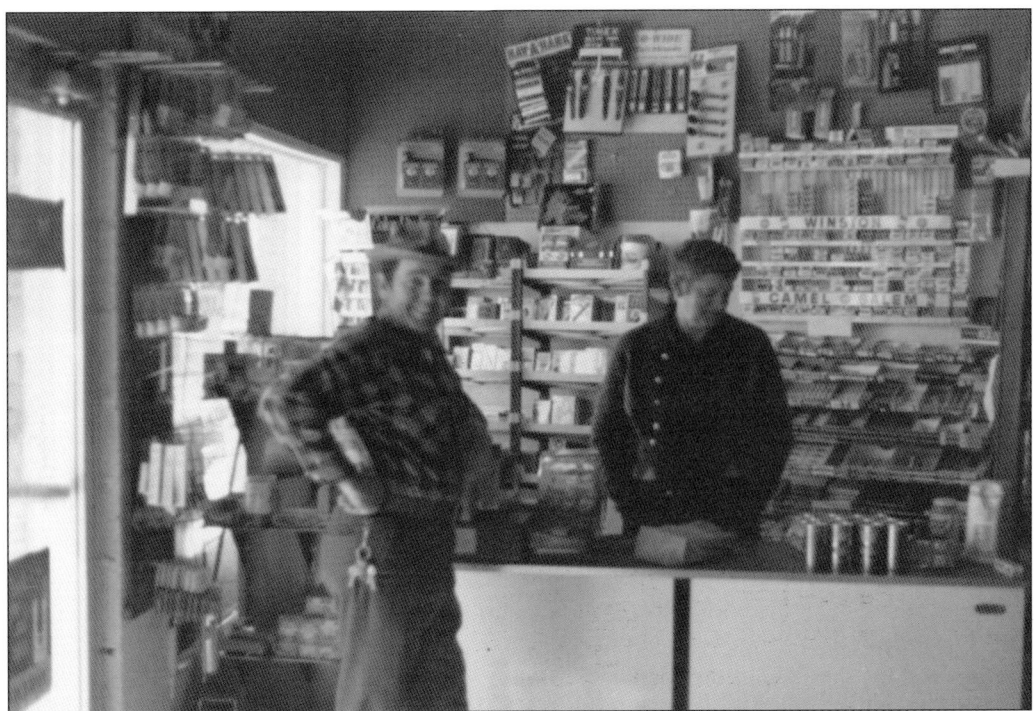
Johnny "The Mailman" Bulger (left) and Bubba Cathey (right) are seen here at the counter in the Mexico Beach Grocery in the early 1970s. (Courtesy of Al Cathey.)

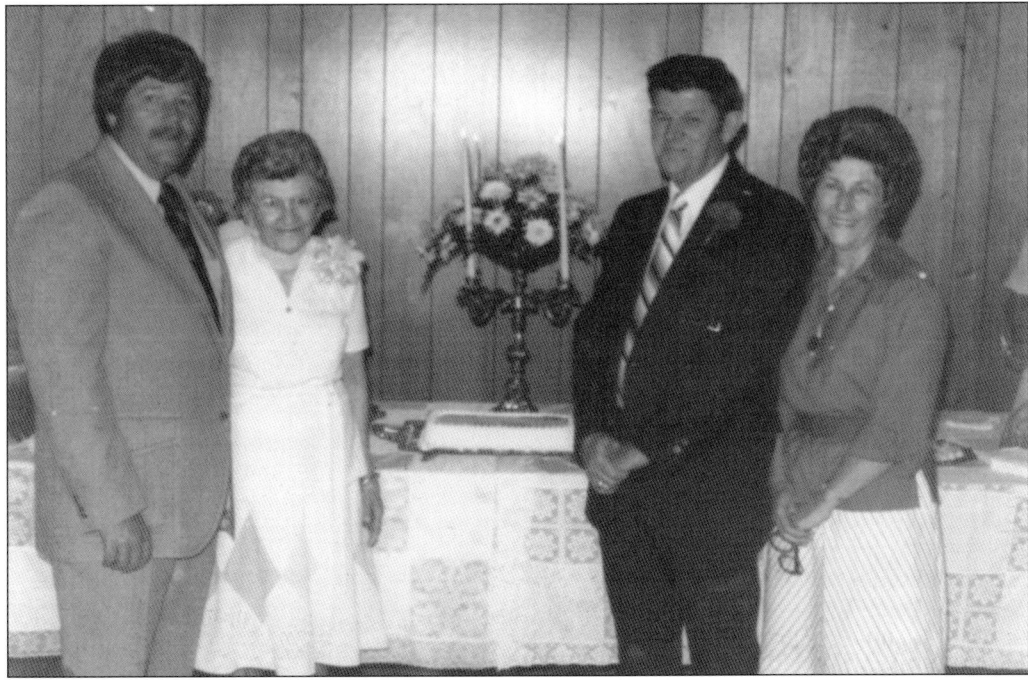
A celebration was held for Estelle "Mom" Cathey's retirement from the postal service in 1976. Flanking her are her son Val Cathey (left), her son Bubba Cathey (third from left), and her daughter Inky Parker (far right). (Courtesy of the Parker family.)

School was a wonderful time for the children growing up in Mexico Beach. They loved their bus driver, Roland Hardy, who was from the Overstreet area. He was known to every student in the county as Sam. This photograph was taken during a class trip in May 1968. (Courtesy of Cathey Parker Hobbs.)

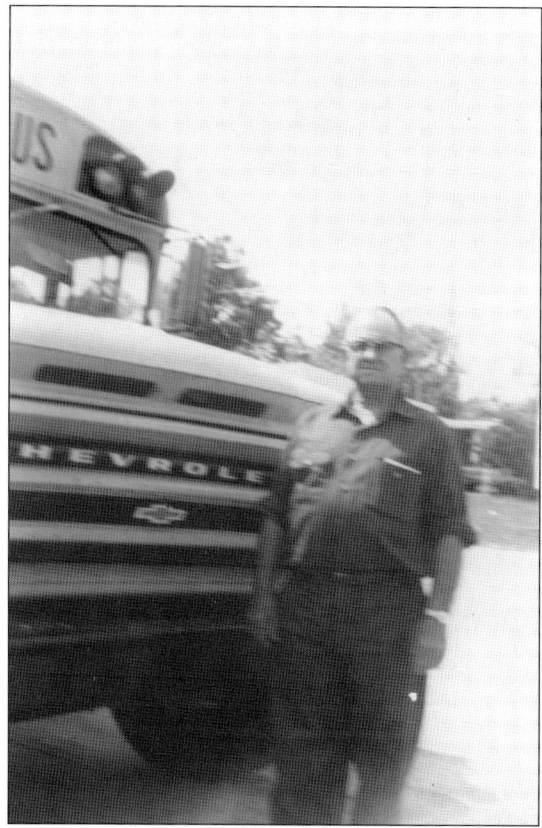

Henry Hogue worked with Parker Realty and the Mexico Beach Corporation for many years, helping with development, reading water meters, laying pipe, and maintaining the water plant. He is seen here at work in 1981. (Courtesy of Cathey Parker Hobbs.)

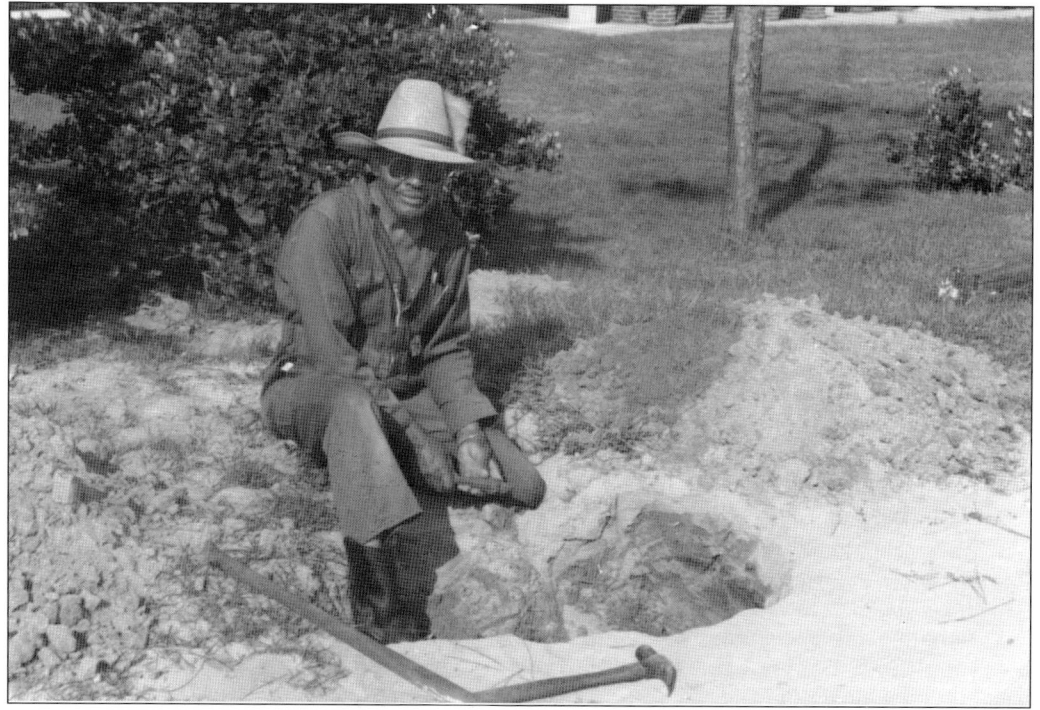

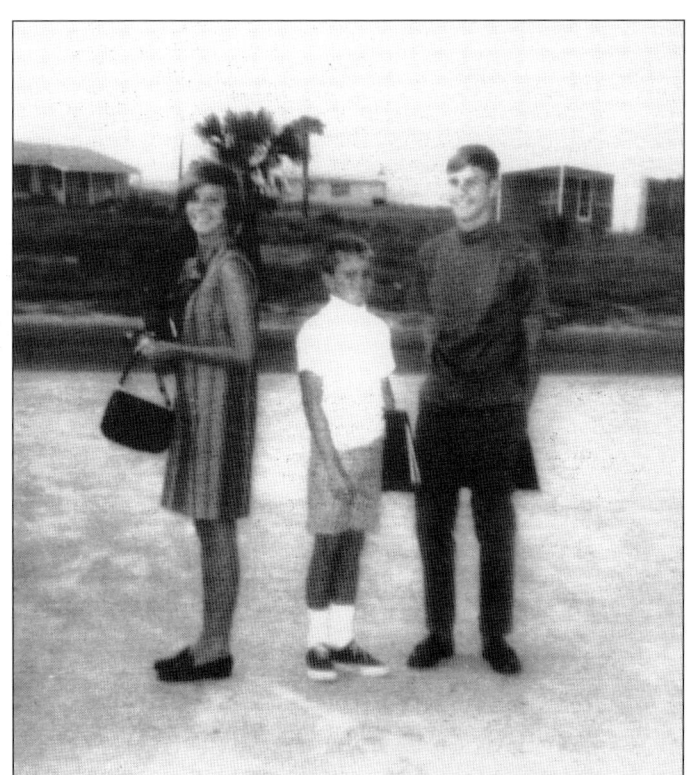

From left to right, the Holland children, Julie, Mark, and Eddie, stand in front of the Hollanday Motel awaiting the school bus in the early 1960s. (Courtesy of Louise Holland.)

A Guilford family reunion was held on Thanksgiving, 1973. Seen here from left to right are (first row) sons Jimmy, Bobby, and Chuck; (second row) daughter Alice, Gertrude and James ("Mom" and "Pop"), and daughter Maxine. Their son Carl (not pictured) was on active duty in the Air Force. (Courtesy of Jim Guilford.)

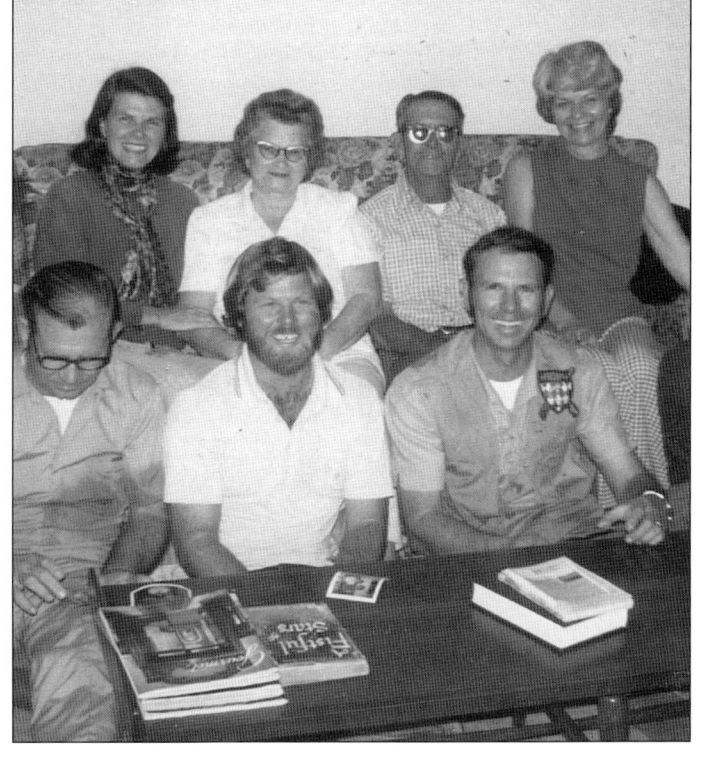

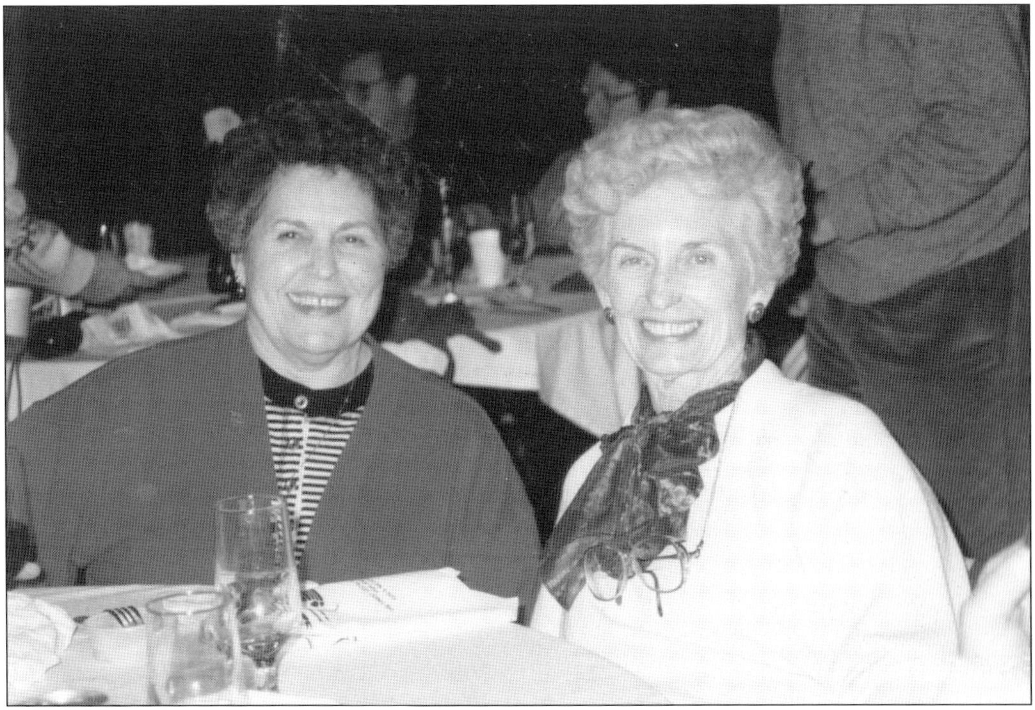

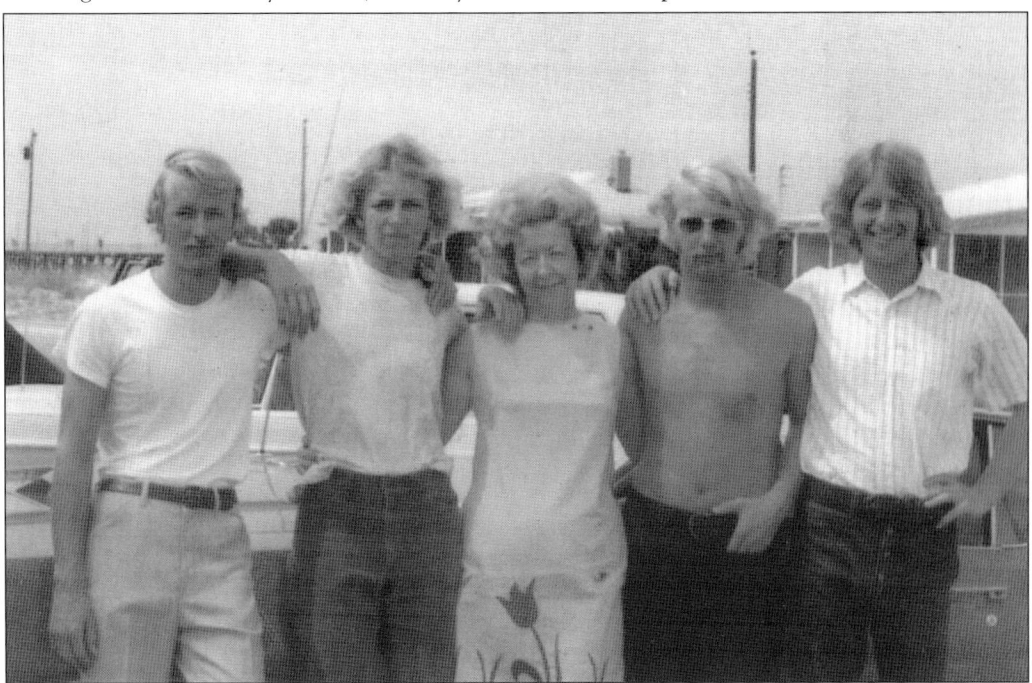

Longtime friends and early pioneers Marion Cathey (left) and Elizabeth Thompson (right) enjoy time together in the early 1990s. (Courtesy of Richard Thompson.)

Betty Corry and her sons (from left to right) Jim, Steve, Jack, and Bill enjoy a summer day in the 1960s. The Corry boys were frequently helping with the repairs and maintenance on the family's motel and rental cottages. (Courtesy of Jim Corry.)

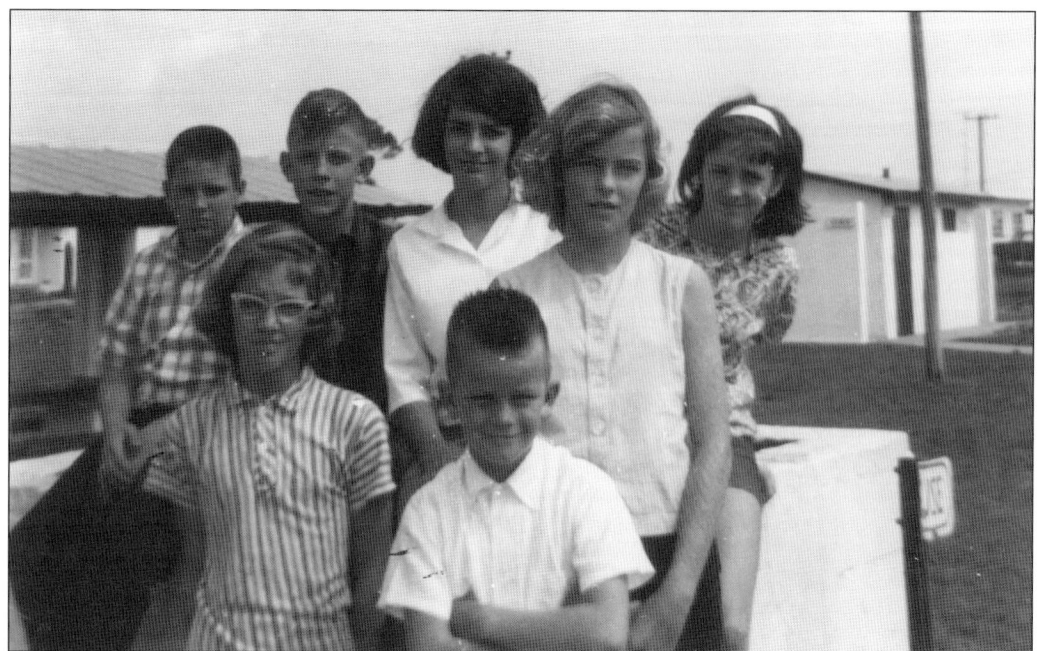

A Holland family reunion was held at Wayside Park in 1965. Seen here are, from left to right, (first row) Jo and Mark Holland; (second row) John Wright and Eddie, Kay, Julie, and Pam Holland. Wayside Park was located at Highway 98 between Seventh and Eighth Streets. (Courtesy of Louise Holland.)

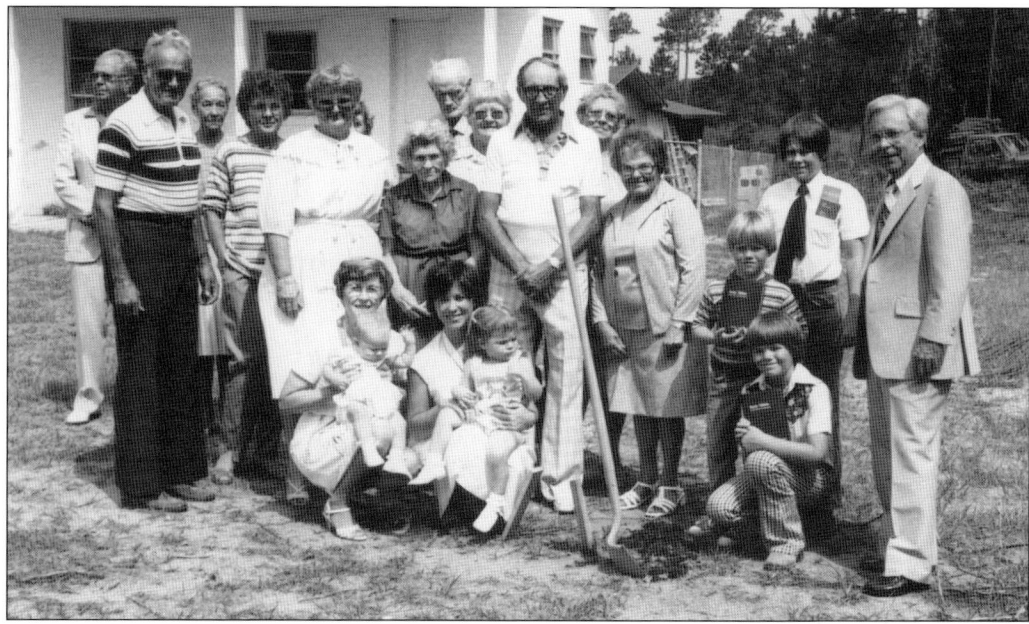

This photograph shows the ground-breaking ceremony for the Mexico Beach Methodist Church Fellowship Hall in 1982. Kneeling in front are Inky Parker, holding her granddaughter Brooke Adkison, and Nan Parker Adkison, holding her daughter Frances Adkison. Among those standing are, in no particular order, Ernie Donahue, Arch Gardner, Estelle "Mom" Cathey, Frank Golson, Annie Chewning, and pastor Charlie Parker. (Courtesy of the Parker family.)

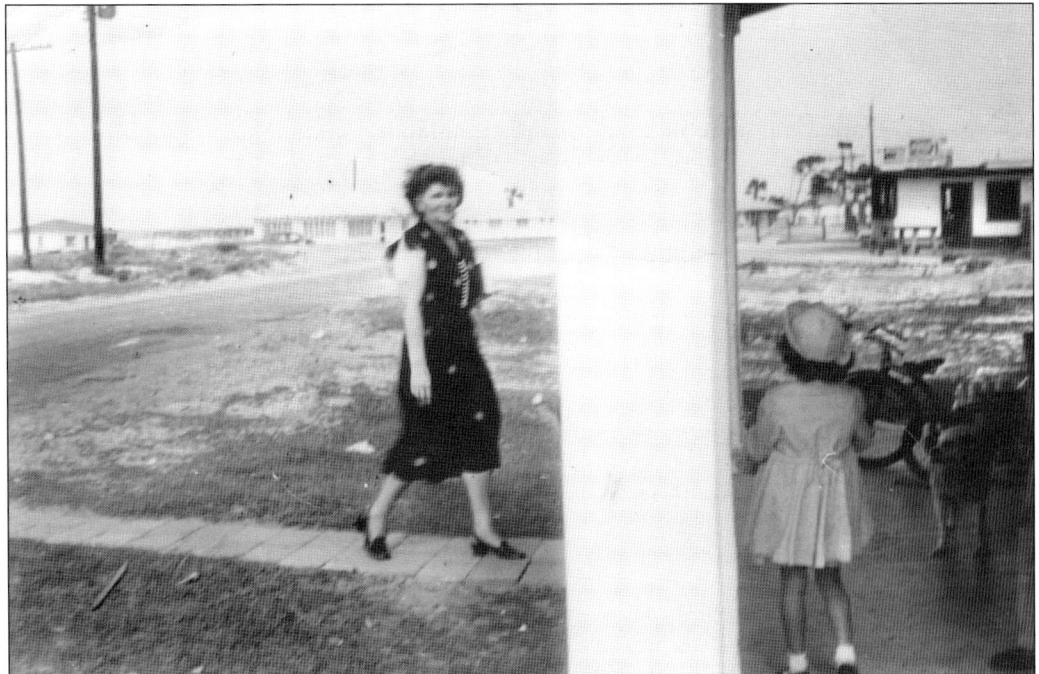

Estelle "Mom" Cathey walks to her Mexico Beach Grocery in the early 1950s as her granddaughter Cathey Parker and her dog Trouble await her arrival. In the background is the drive-in and patio owned by Pete Comforter. (Courtesy of the Parker family.)

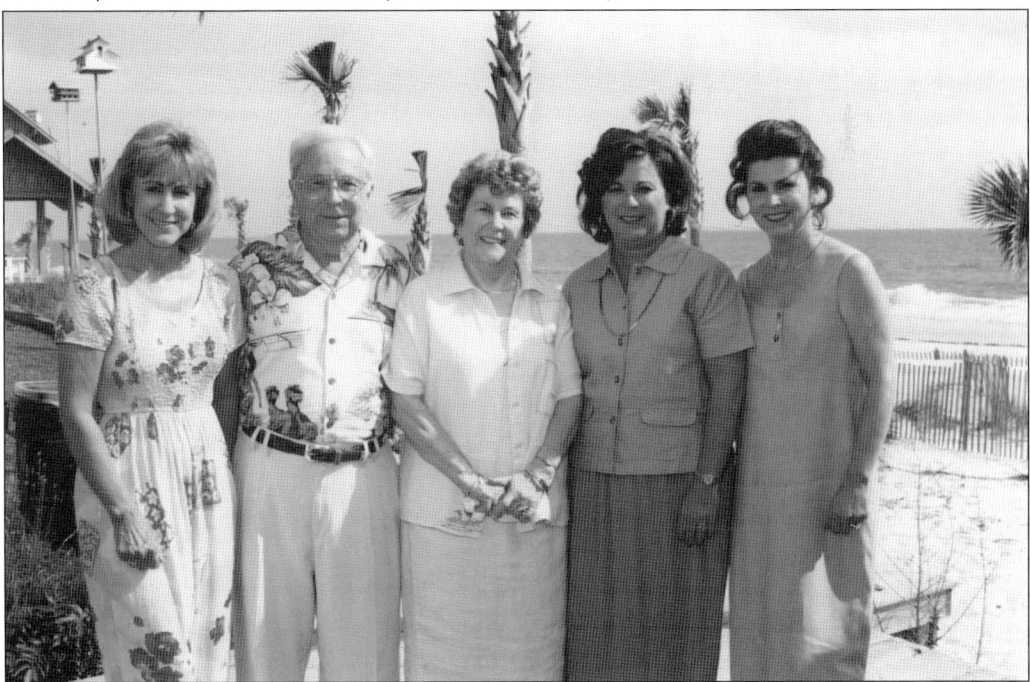

The Parker family went to the Driftwood Inn to celebrate Charlie and Inky Parker's 55th wedding anniversary in 1994. From left to right are Cathey Parker (Hobbs), Charlie and Inky Parker, Nan Parker (Adkison), and Sue Parker (Thomas). (Courtesy of the Parker family.)

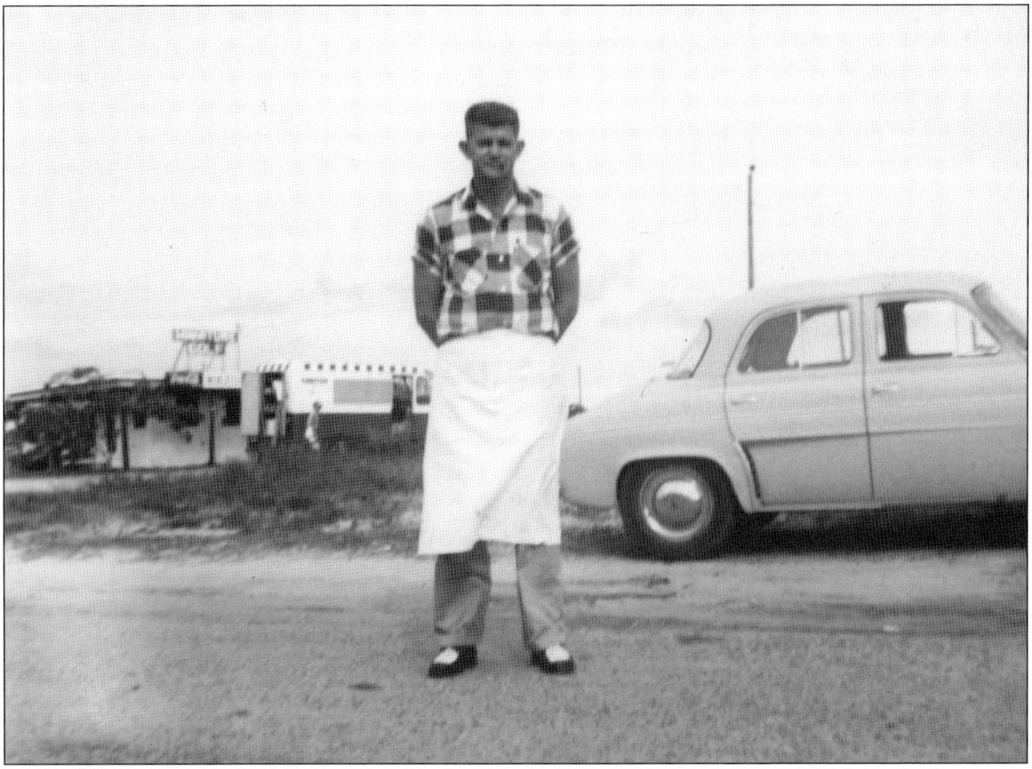

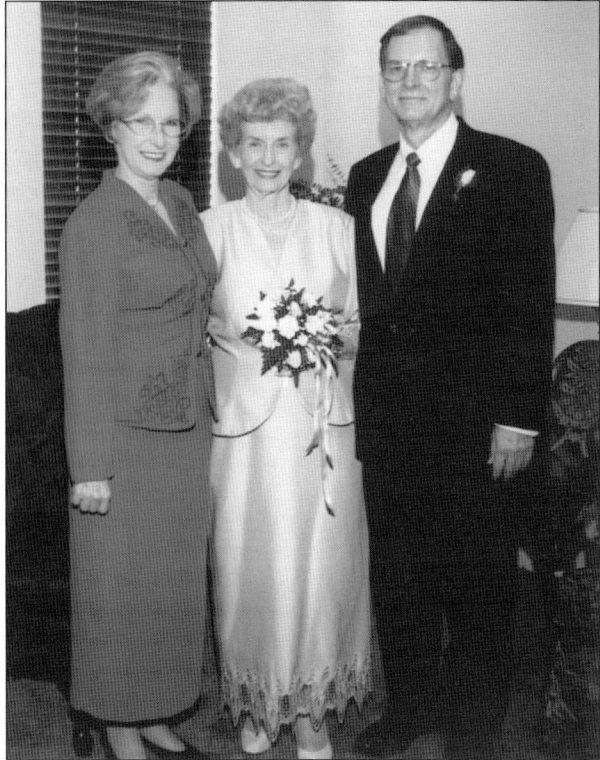

Bubba Cathey fashions his butcher apron outside the Mexico Beach Grocery in the early 1960s. (Courtesy of Al Cathey.)

Elizabeth W. Thompson and her family moved to Beacon Hill in 1951. She became a realtor in the late 1950s, one of the first women to become a licensed real estate agent in the Mexico Beach–Gulf County area. In 1961, her combined residence and Thompson Realty office was at the corner of Nineteenth Street and Highway 98. Affectionately known as "Miss Liz," she passed away in 2007. Elizabeth (center) is seen here with her daughter Carol Thompson Rish (left) and son Richard E. Thompson. (Courtesy of Richard Thompson.)

Six
MAKING MEMORIES

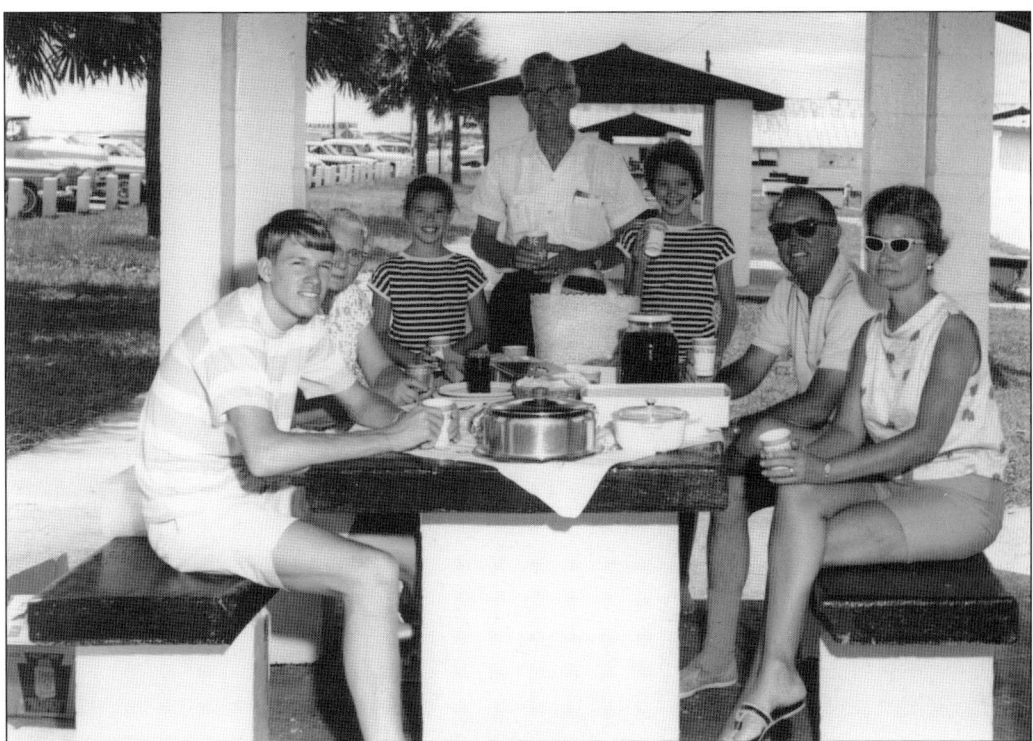

A group gathers at Wayside Park for family fun and recreation in 1965. Wayside Park was located on Highway 98 and Eighth Street and was used frequently by residents, travelers, and tourists. The park had covered tables with benches, bathrooms, and shower facilities. In the early 1980s, the state abandoned the park and the property was sold. The skating rink is seen in the background of this photograph. (Courtesy of Florida State Archives.)

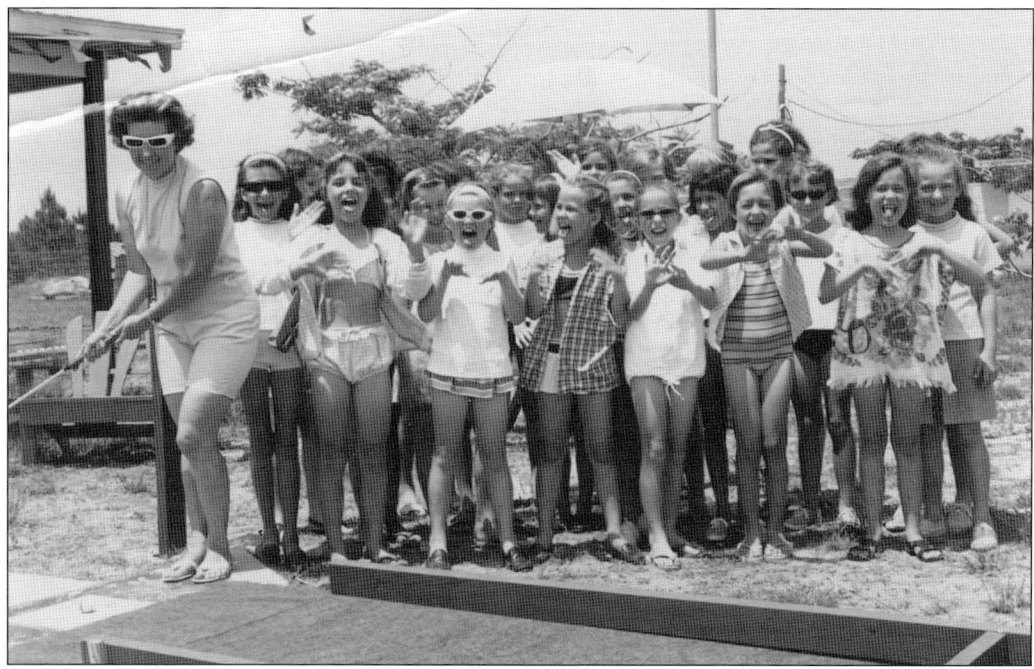

Scout leader Inky Parker and her Girl Scouts play putt-putt golf in Mexico Beach in the late 1960s. The Scout troop members are, from left to right, (first row) Inky Parker, Linda Griner, Cindy Freeman, Gail Kirkland, Janis Schweikert, Nan Parker, Joni Shores, and Priscilla Ash; (second row) Melody Smith, Terry Gay, Cheryl Parker, Jolyn Parrott, Marcia Biggins, Sandra Tootle, and Vicky Boyd. (Courtesy of the Parker family.)

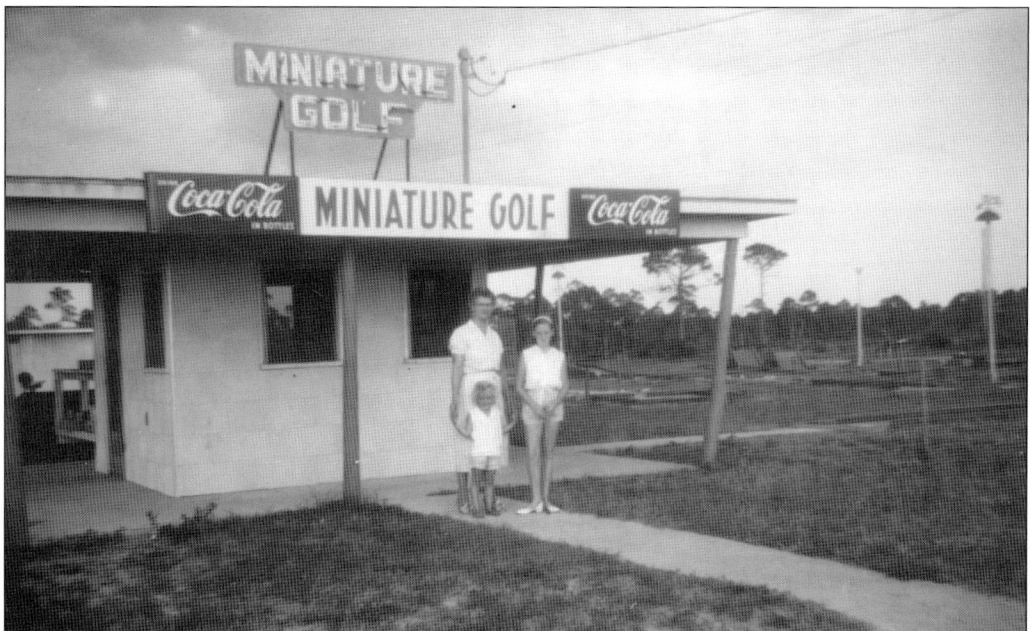

Manager Jessie Stafford stands in front of the snack stand and check-in counter at the 18-hole, lighted miniature golf course in 1956. Stafford's helpers are her niece Janie Cathey (front left) and Janie's cousin Diana Barger (right) from Memphis. (Courtesy of Al Cathey.)

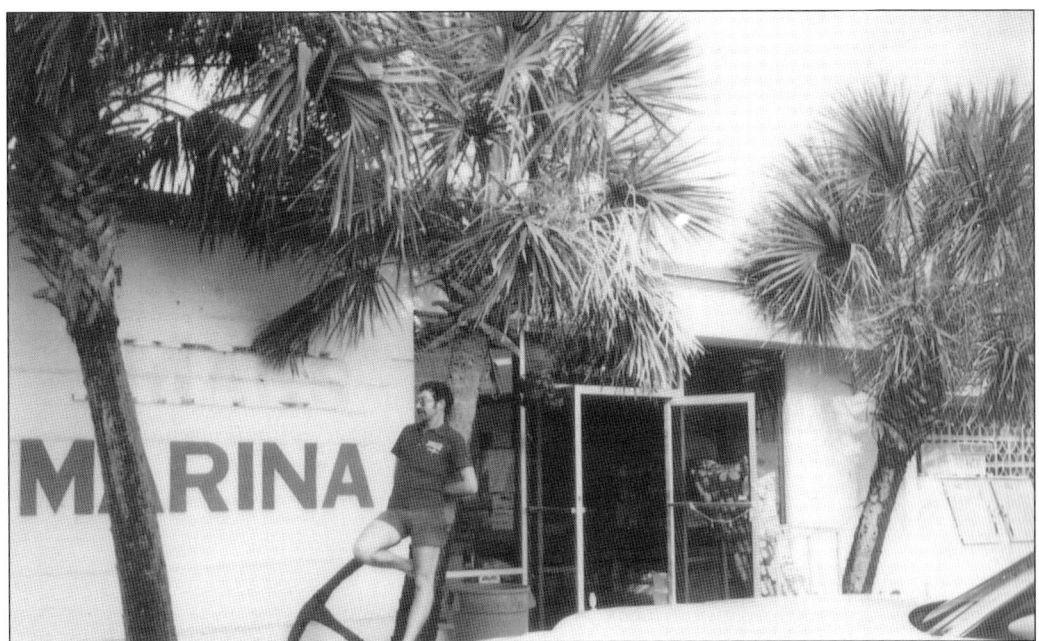

The original marina building was constructed by George Tapper in the late 1950s, and the business was named for his beloved Saint Bernard dog Hennessey. Tom and Linda Marquardt purchased the property from Tapper in 1977. Over the next 35 years, the Marquardt family, with their daughters Chrystina and Amanda, expanded and grew the business into a full-service marina serving Mexico Beach and the surrounding area. Tom Marquardt is seen here in 1978. (Courtesy of Tom Marquardt.)

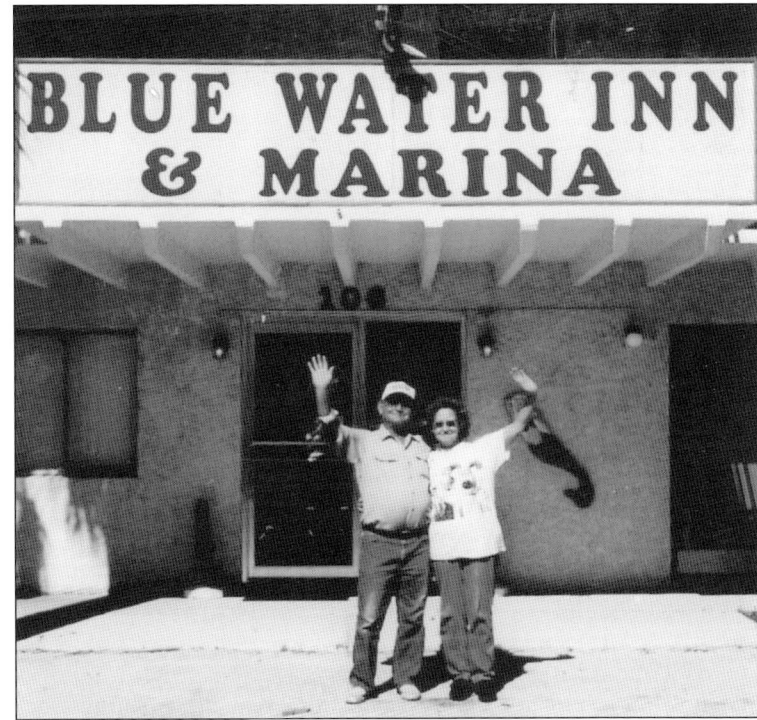

Standing in front of the Blue Water Inn and Marina in 1999 are managers Leonard and Jeannette Giffin. The building was sold in 2001 to Jimmy Hambrick, who remodeled the motel into a condominium complex in 2002. (Courtesy of Jeannette Giffin.)

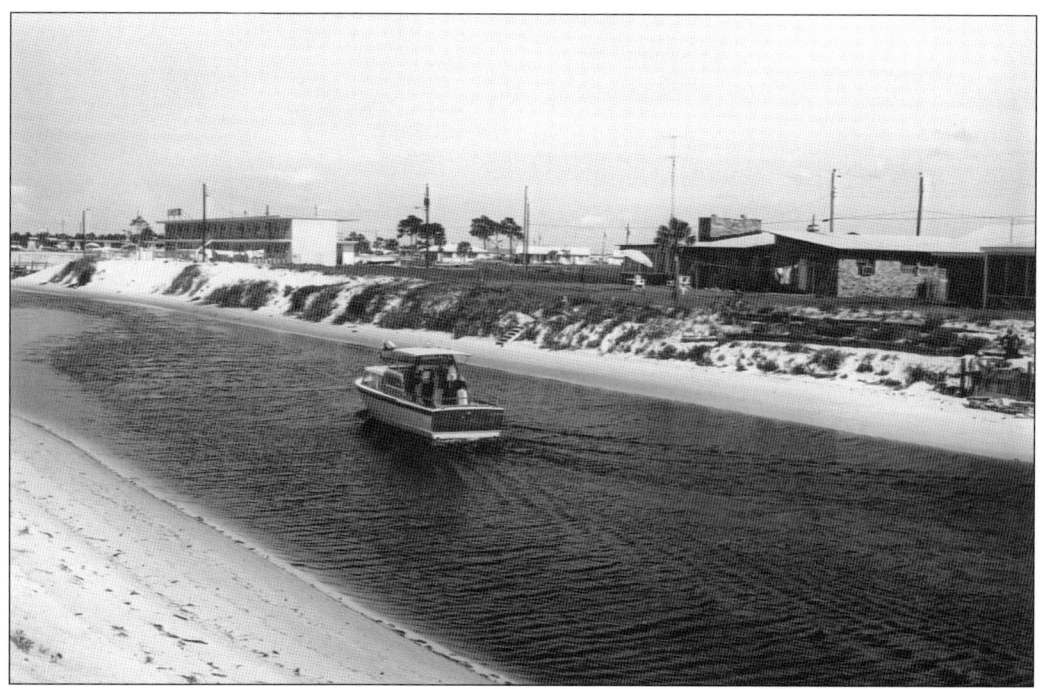

A lone boat travels up the Mexico Beach Canal in 1964. Serving as an area recreational facility, the canal is the only safe haven for small craft between Port St. Joe and Panama City. (Courtesy of the Parker family.)

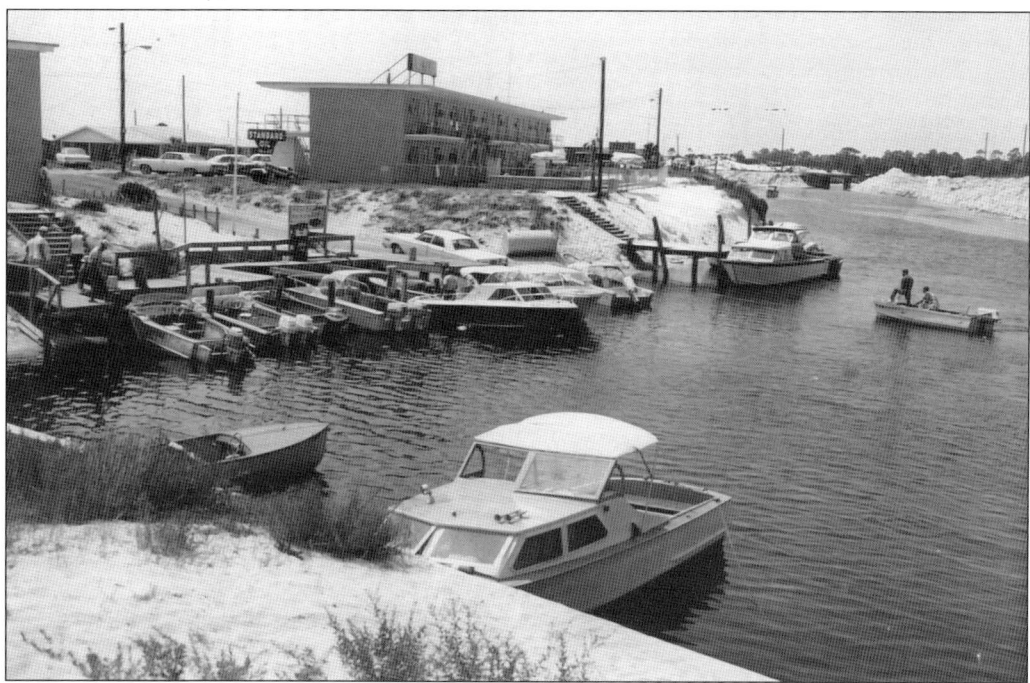

The Mexico Beach Canal was a hub of activity in this mid-1960s photograph. Fishermen and boaters congregated at the Mexico Beach Marina, the county boat ramp, and the Hollanday Motel to start and end their day on the Gulf. (Courtesy of George Holland.)

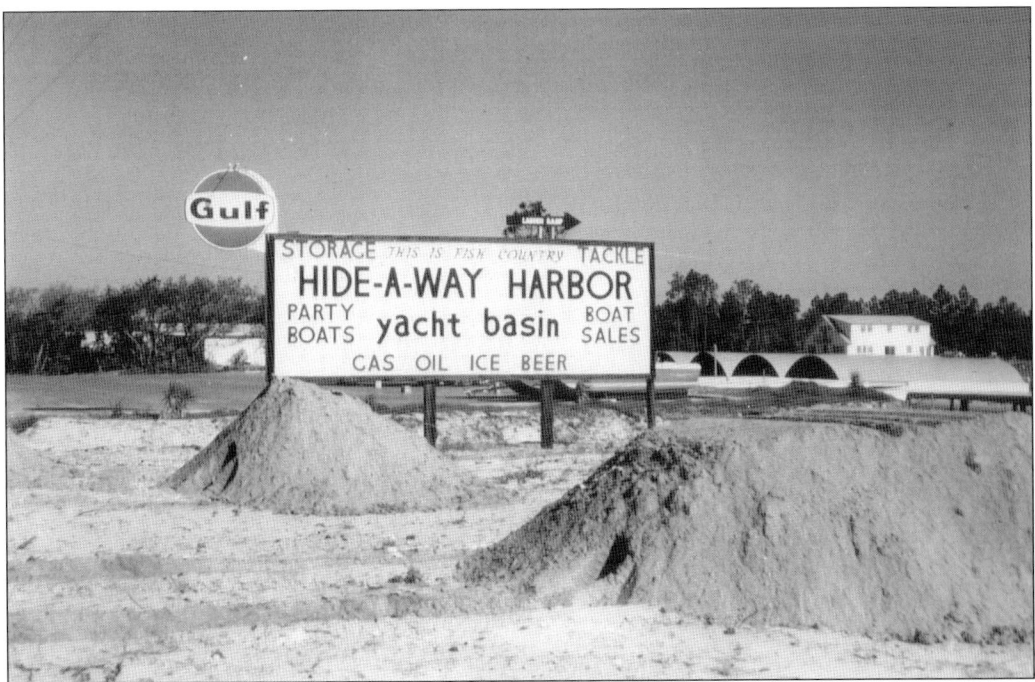

The Hide-A-Way Harbor Marina was built in 1967 by owners Bill Hughes and Don Waddell. In 1973, it was expanded to include covered boat slips and then expanded again in 1976. The business, on the north side of Highway 98 at the end of the pier road (Thirty-seventh Street), was sold in 1994 to Jim and Kay McCullough. (Courtesy of Bill Hughes.)

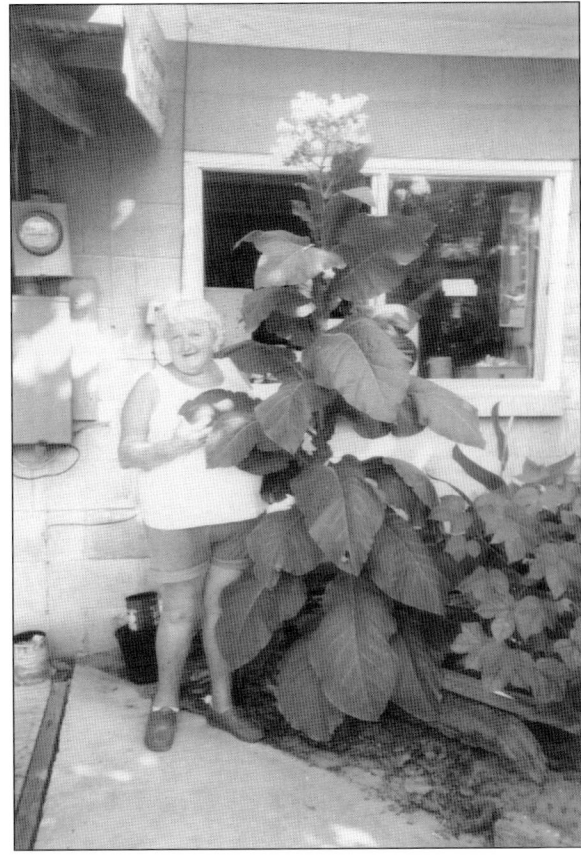

Wilberta J. Hamilton, known as "Mrs. Birdie," worked for owner Bill Hughes in the management and day-to-day operations of Hide-A-Way Harbor Marina from 1973 to 1993. A devoted and dedicated employee, she was instrumental in the success of Hughes's business. Mrs. Birdie was a special member of the Mexico Beach community and was loved and adored by many. (Courtesy of Bill Hughes.)

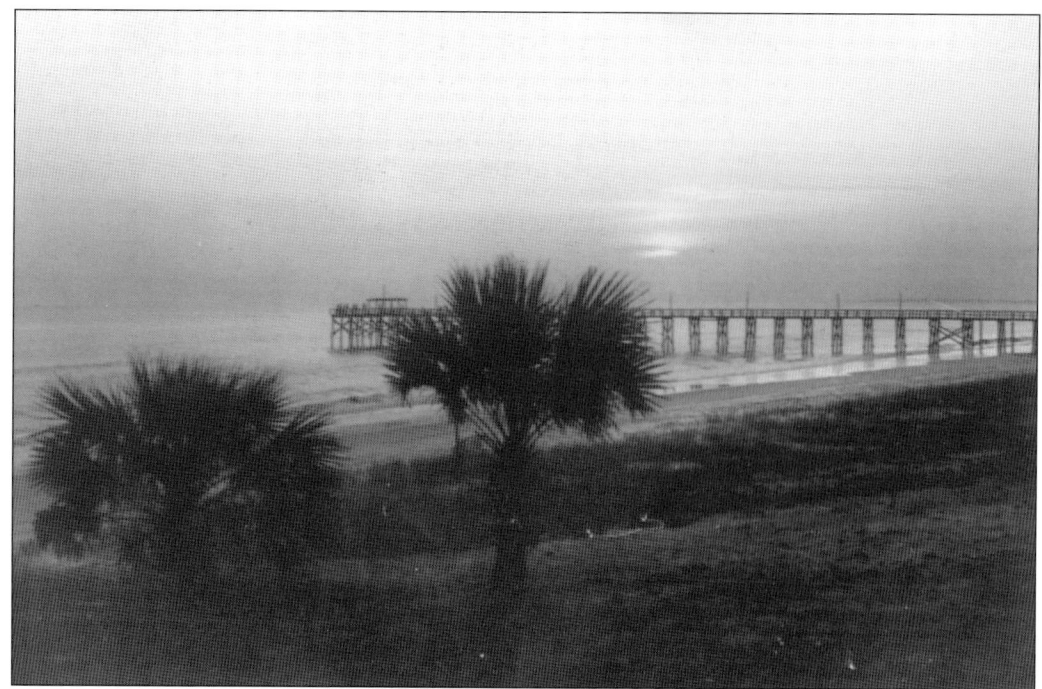

The Surf Pier was located at 816 Highway 98, across from what is now Killer Seafood. The pier was constructed behind the Surf Restaurant in 1961 by Charles M. Parker. It was destroyed during Hurricane Eloise in 1975. (Courtesy of the Parker family.)

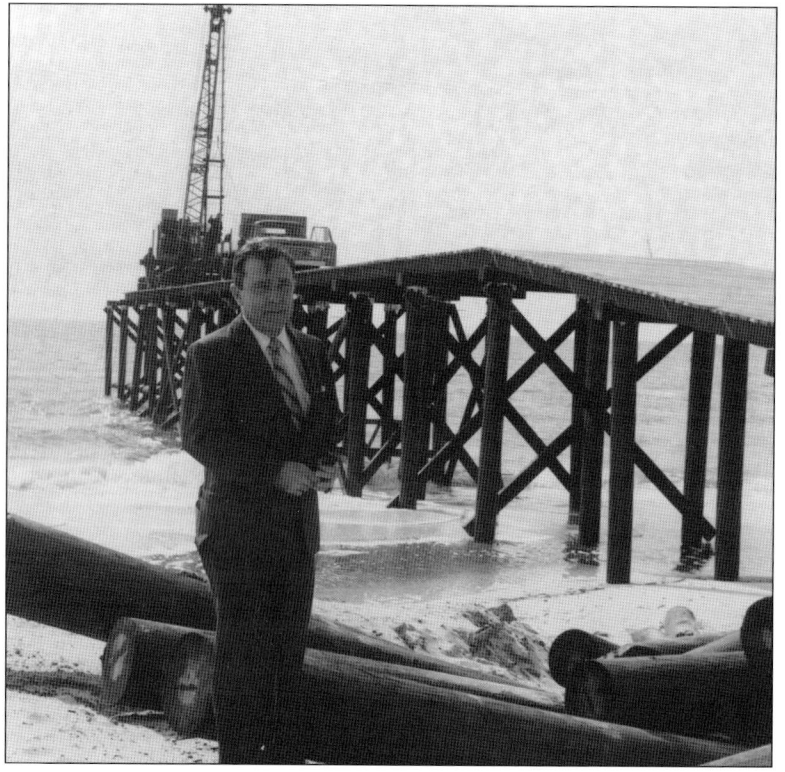

Charlie Parker is seen here overseeing the construction of the Surf Pier in 1961. (Courtesy of the Parker family.)

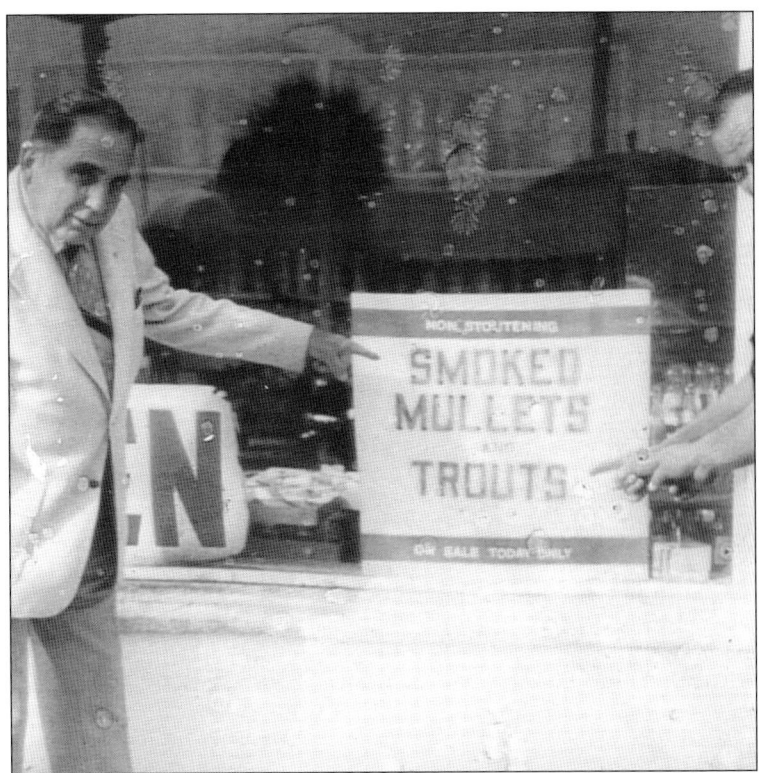

Roy Conoley (left) and Leroy Sherman show off Conoley's world-famous "Smoked Mullets and Trout" sign. Shortly after Conoley passed away, Roy Conoley Jr. gave the sign to good friend and patron Gen. Ken Stromquist. Today, with the general's permission, this sign proudly hangs in Cathey's Ace Hardware. (Courtesy of Roy Conoley Jr.)

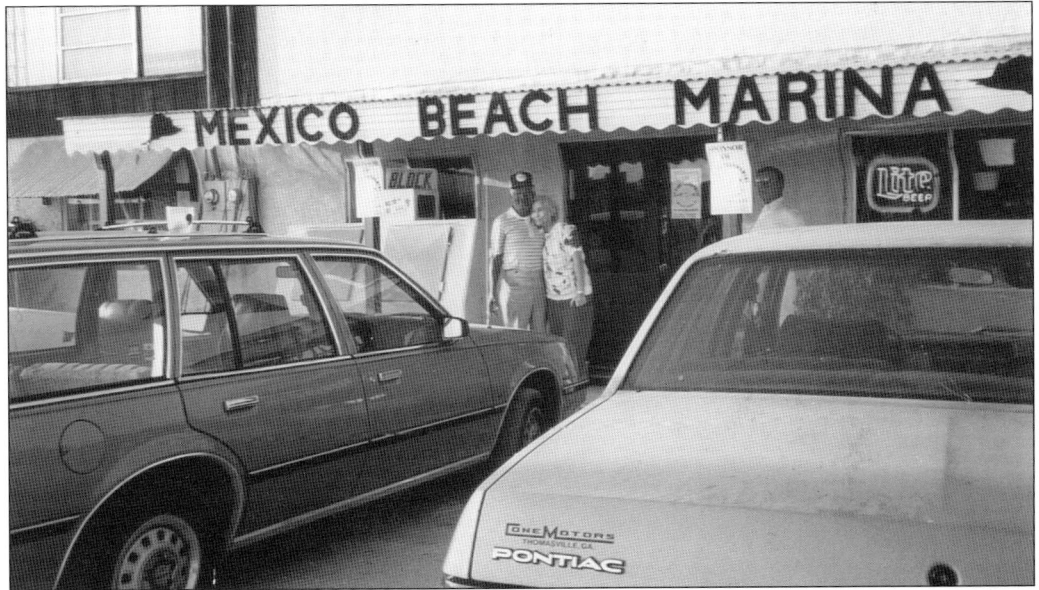

The Mexico Beach Marina was reconstructed in the early 1960s by Red Dove of Dothan, Alabama. The marina was operated for 20 years by the Hooks, followed by Tom and Susie Hudson, who operated the marina from 1985 until it sold in 2001. This late-1980s photograph shows the Hudsons standing in front of the marina. Tom was the mayor of Mexico Beach from 1988 through 1994. With her vibrant personality, Susie was active in many community events. (Courtesy of Cathey Parker Hobbs.)

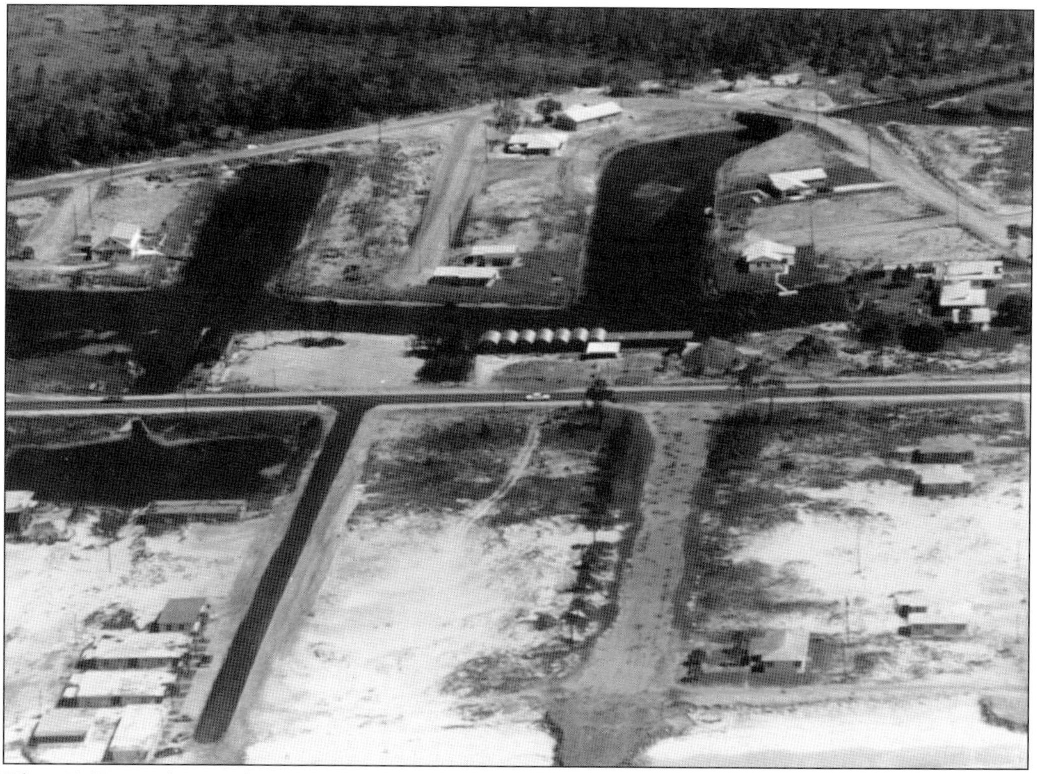

This 1967 aerial view shows the covered boat slips of the newly constructed Hide-A-Way Harbor Marina and a few scattered homes on the north side of Highway 98. At the end of South Thirty-Seventh Street is the beach cottage of George and Amy Tapper. Behind the Tapper cottage, facing South Thirty-sixth Street, is the Driggers-Hatcher cottage. Up the road toward the highway are the two Owens family cottages. (Courtesy of Bill Hughes.)

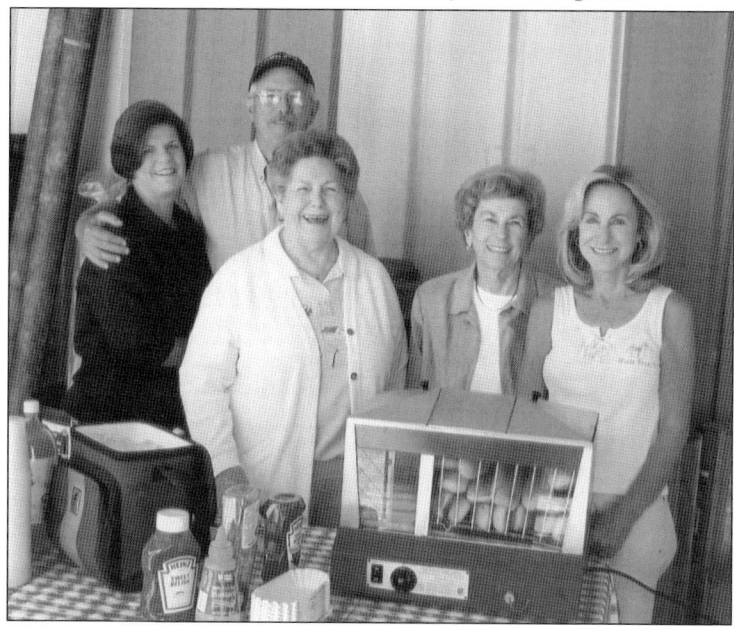

Friday Franks was a popular lunch event for several years at Cathey's Ace Hardware. Hot dogs were served using the old hot dog cooker from the putt-putt golf snack shop. The community was invited, and fun was had by all. Seen here from left to right are Carol and Al Cathey, Marion Cathey, Inky Parker, and Cathey Parker Hobbs. (Courtesy of Al Cathey.)

Seven
EARLY BEACH COTTAGES

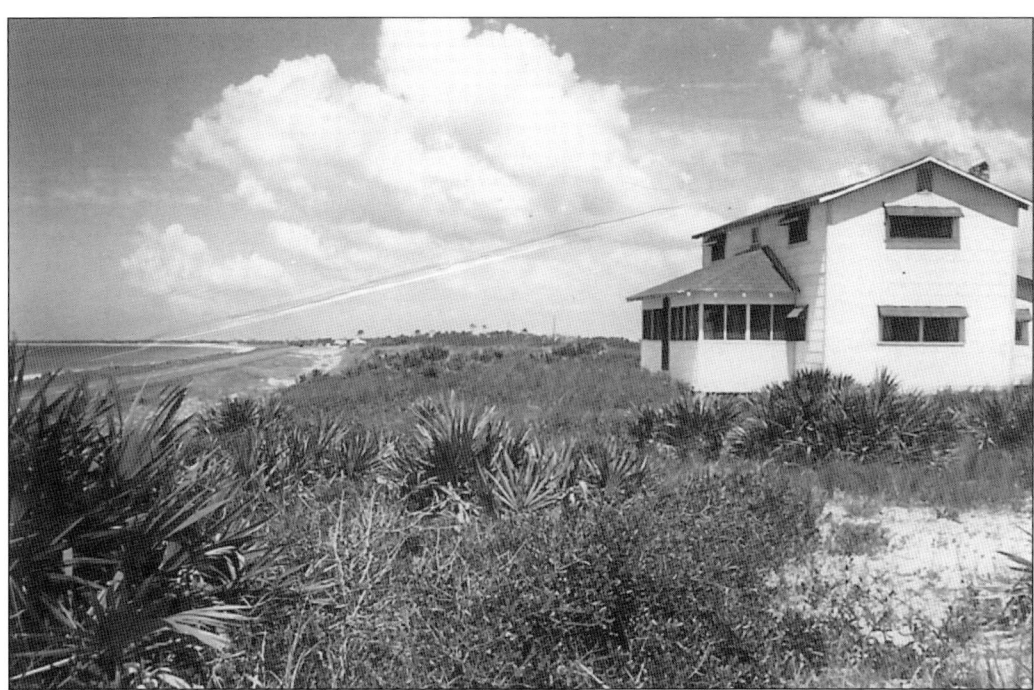

The strip of Gulf view land running parallel to Highway 98 from Route 386 west to Sea Street was negotiated for purchase by Marianna native Floie Packard, the wife of John C. Packard, in 1946. Due to the size of the property, Packard found buyers from her hometown, thus the name Marianna Hill. Seen here in 1947 is the lonely Finlayson house on the bluff. (Courtesy of Cathey Parker Hobbs.)

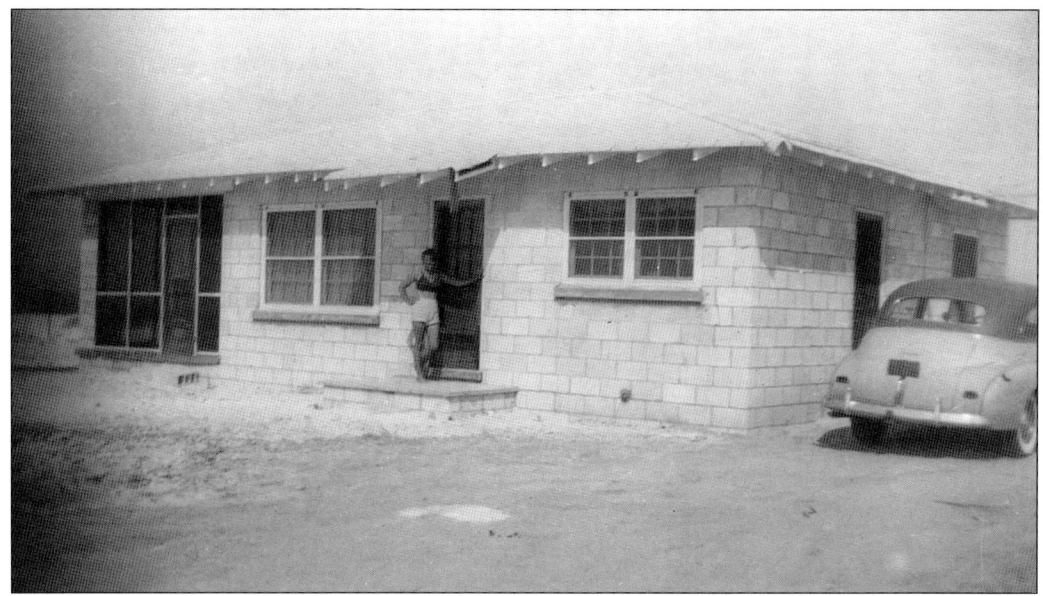

LuLu Varnador stands in the doorway of her beach house in the early 1950s. The house, known as Sandpiper, is located on South Twenty-fifth Street and remains in the family today. (Courtesy of Sue Tatum.)

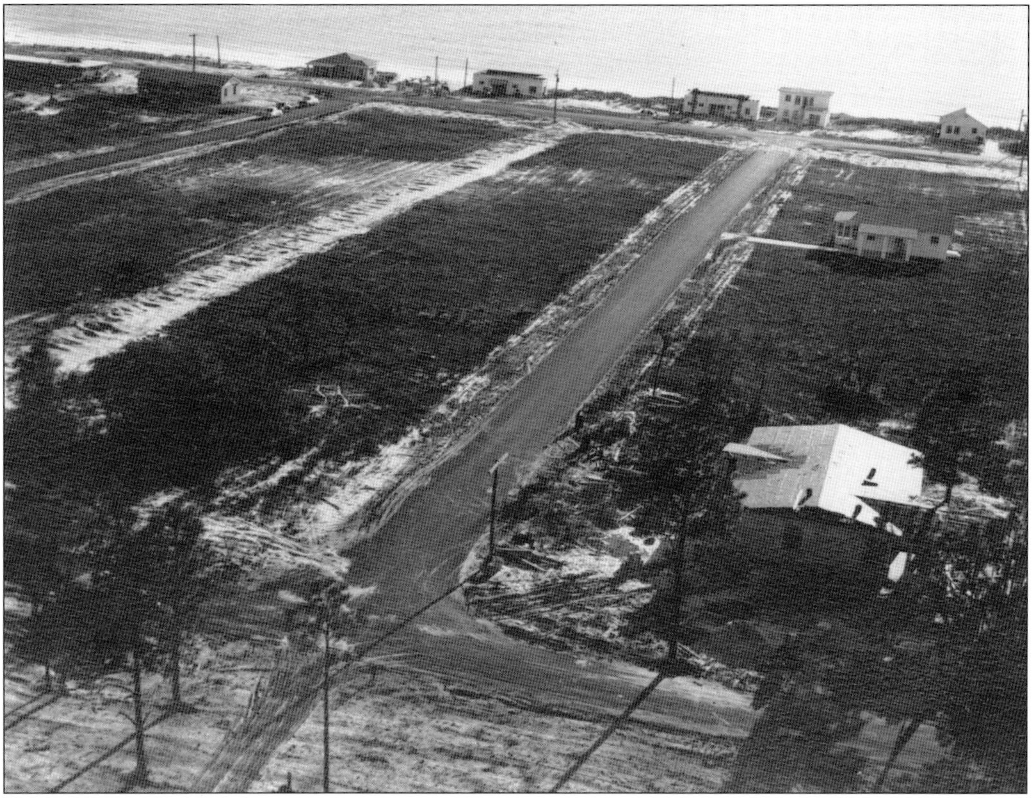

This view down Twentieth Street was taken from the Mexico Beach water tower in 1954. (Courtesy of Al Cathey.)

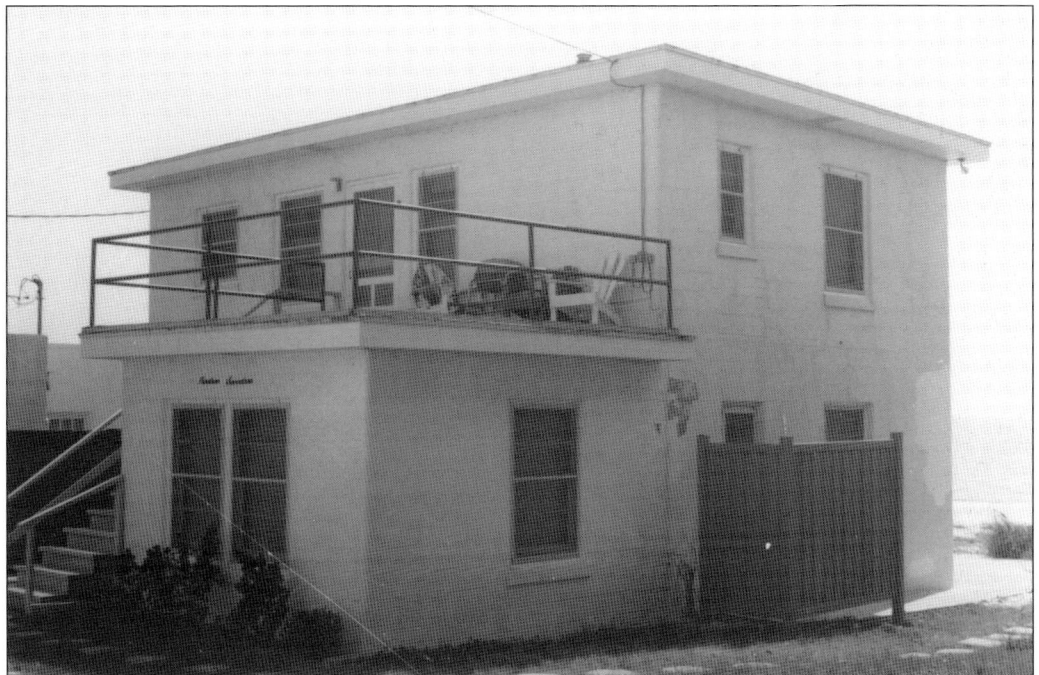

This duplex at the end of Twentieth Street and Highway 98 is seen here in 1952. The house was built by Ruth Costin Soule, the sister of Naomi Brock. The property was purchased in 1971 by Sue and Dick Coyner of Tallahassee. The house was a casualty of Hurricane Opal in 1995. (Courtesy of Sue Coyner.)

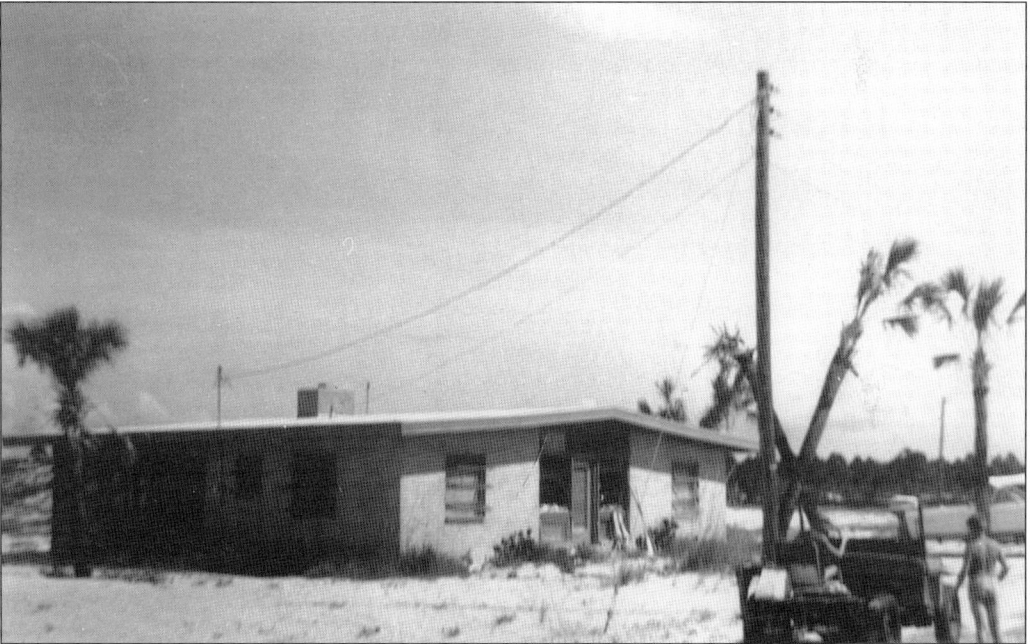

The beach house of Dr. Joe and Marion Hendrix is seen here in 1957. Although it looks different today, the house remains at the end of Canal Parkway and is still used by the Hendrix children, Joe, Bill and Mitzi, and their families. (Courtesy of Joe Hendrix Jr.)

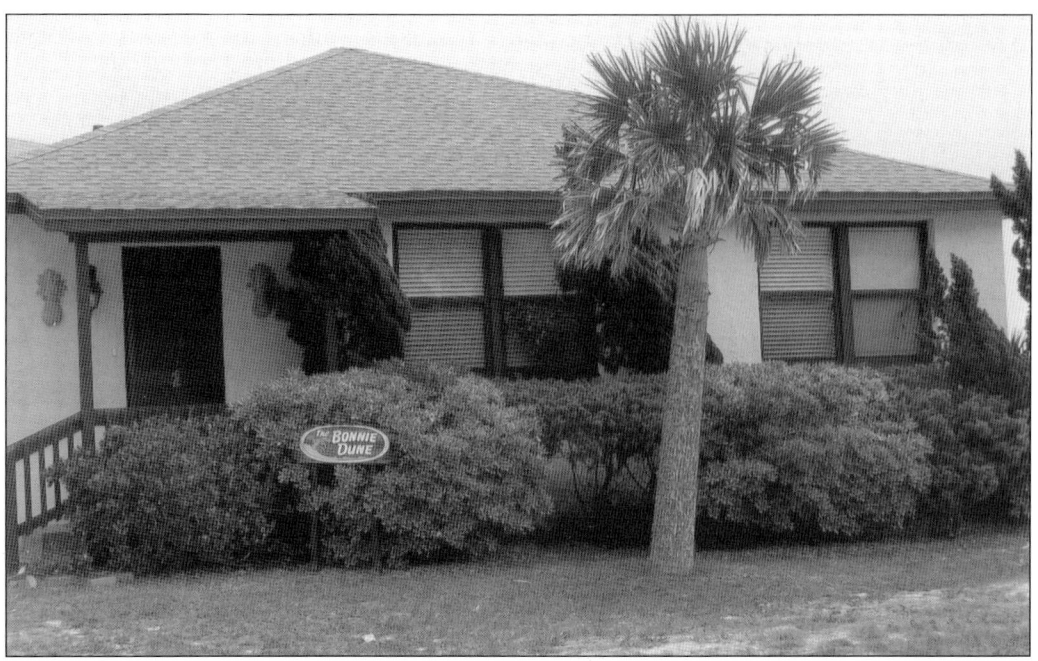

In 1950, Paul and Betty Fensom built this Gulf-front beach home at the end of Twenty-first Street and Highway 98. The beach house was used extensively by the Fensoms and their children Chesley, Jim, and Judy throughout the 1950s, 1960s, and 1970s. In her later years, Betty sold her home in Port St. Joe and moved to the beach. (Courtesy of Cathey Parker Hobbs.)

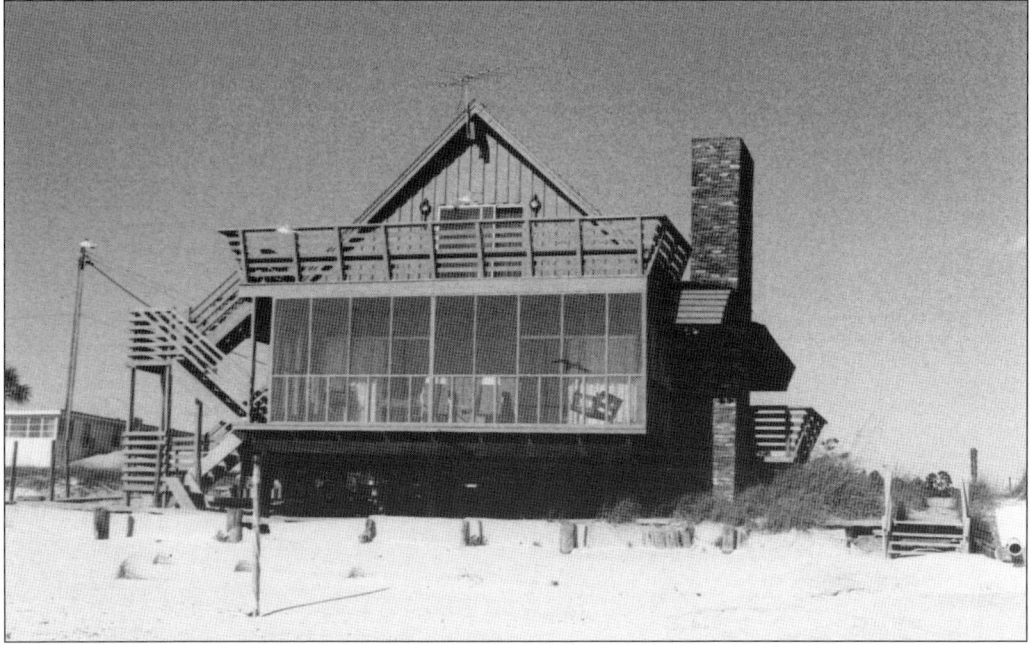

The Parker beach cottage, at 1401 Highway 98, was built by Charlie Parker in 1975 with lumber he had cut at the sawmill in Wewahitchka. He told Inky, his wife, that it would be a waste not to use it. Since then, the beach cottage has made many great family memories for the Parker family and all the families that have rented it over the years. (Courtesy of the Parker family.)

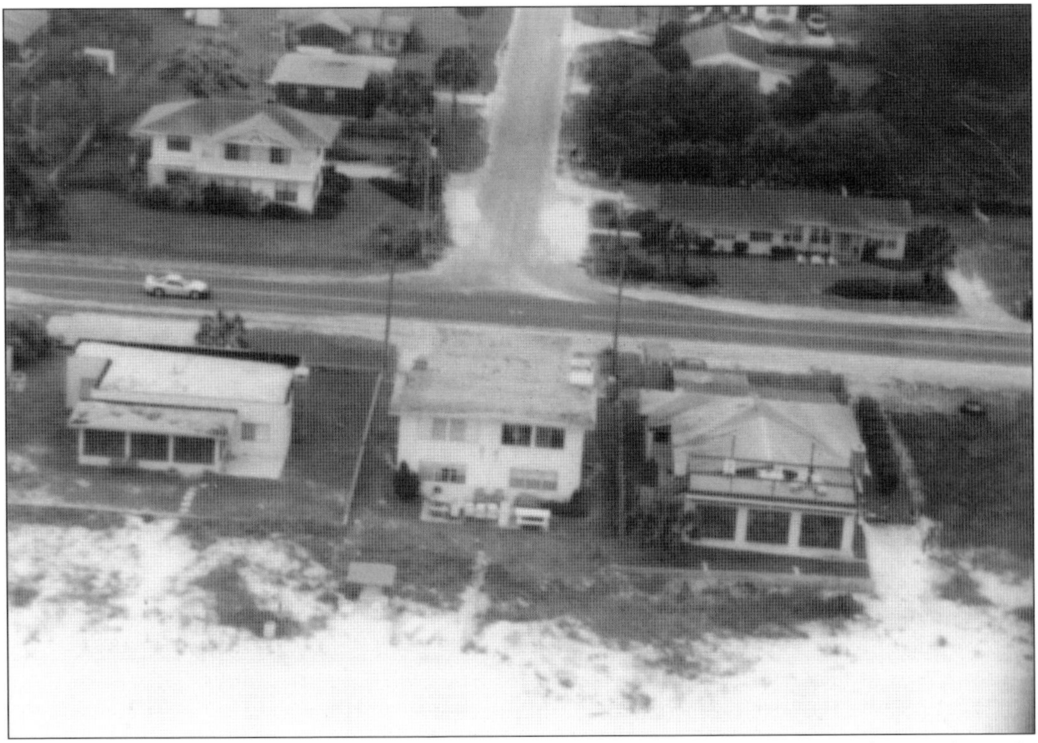

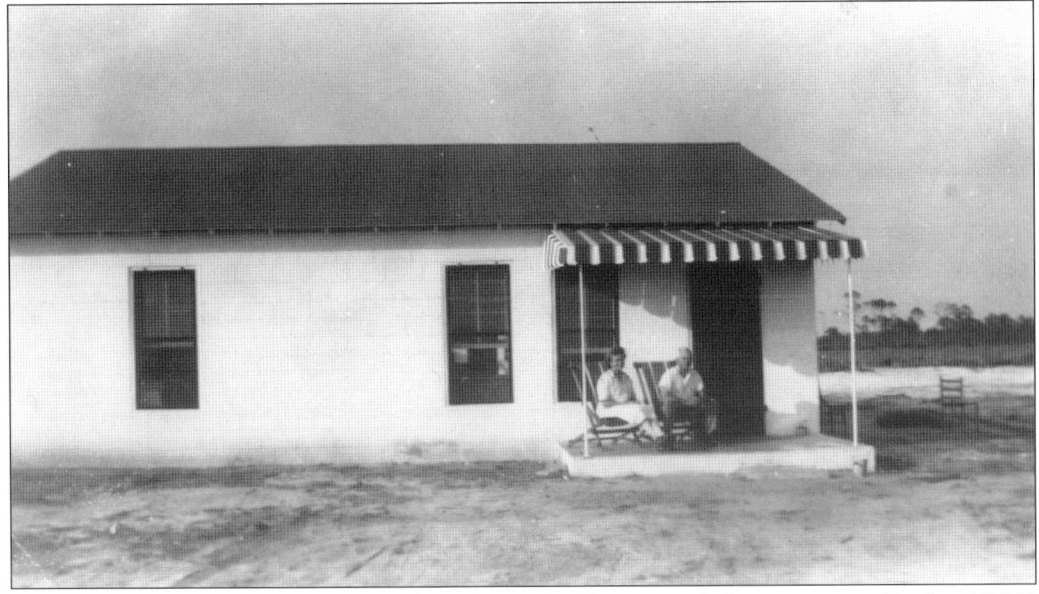

This aerial view of the intersection of Nineteenth Street and Highway 98 was taken in the early 1990s. The three Gulf-front buildings are, from left to right, the Joe Cliffton house; the Gulfwind Apartments, owned by Mr. and Mrs. Bob Frye of Tallahassee; and Bob Davis's house. Across the highway on the left is the 1986 home of Elizabeth Thompson, and across Nineteenth Street from her home is her long-standing Thompson Real Estate office. (Courtesy of Bob Frye.)

At their beach cottage built in the early 1950s at 104 Twenty-sixth Street, owners Gordon "G.U." and Maude Parker are seen sitting on their porch. (Courtesy of the Parker family.)

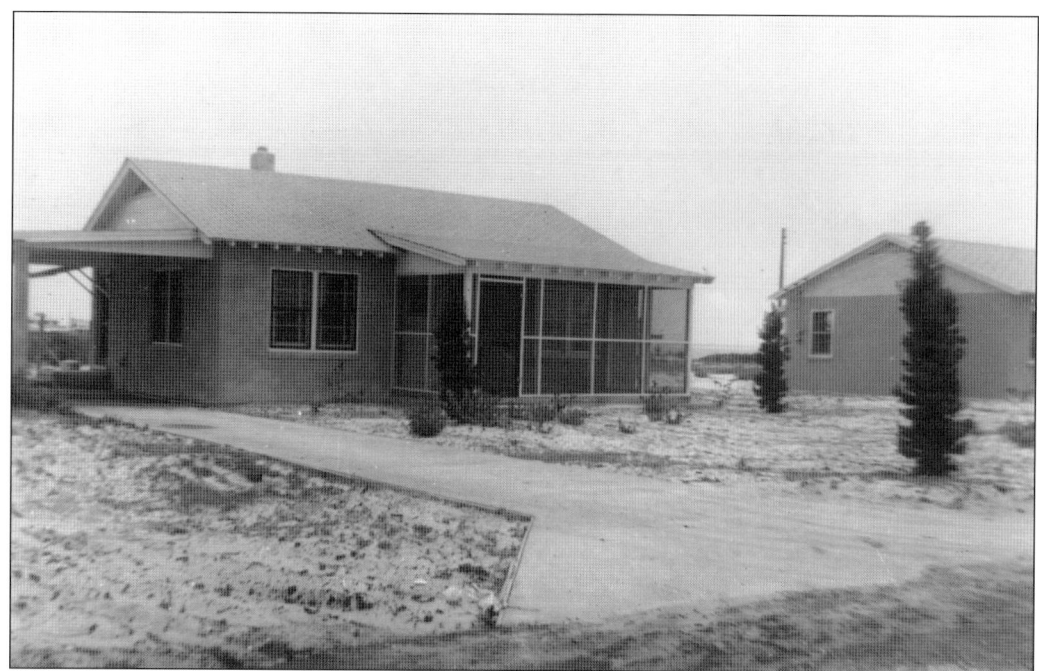

Located on North Twenty-seventh Street was the home of Estelle "Mom" Cathey, the owner of the sundries store from the mid-1950s until her death in the early 1980s. (Courtesy of Cathey Parker Hobbs.)

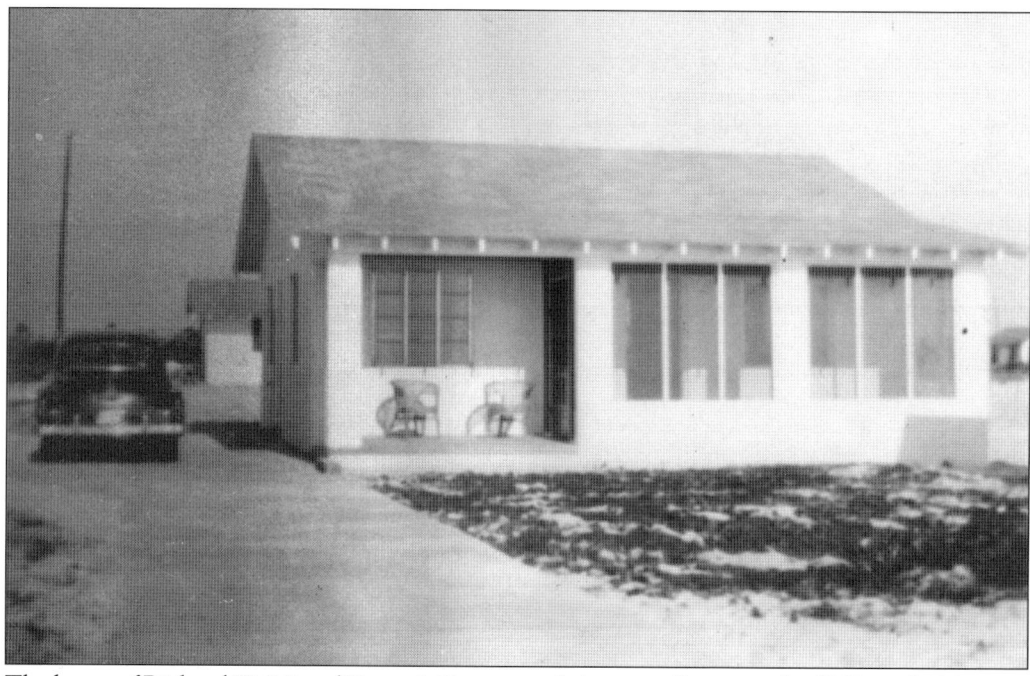

The home of Richard "R.L." and Tommie Fortner and their son Sonny in the 1950s and 1960s was located on Highway 98 overlooking the dedicated beach. In those days, Sonny Fortner, Herman Collier, and Tommy Williams were impressive skaters at the skating rink owned by Lee Williams, Tommy's dad. (Courtesy of Sonny Fortner.)

Eight
Past and Present

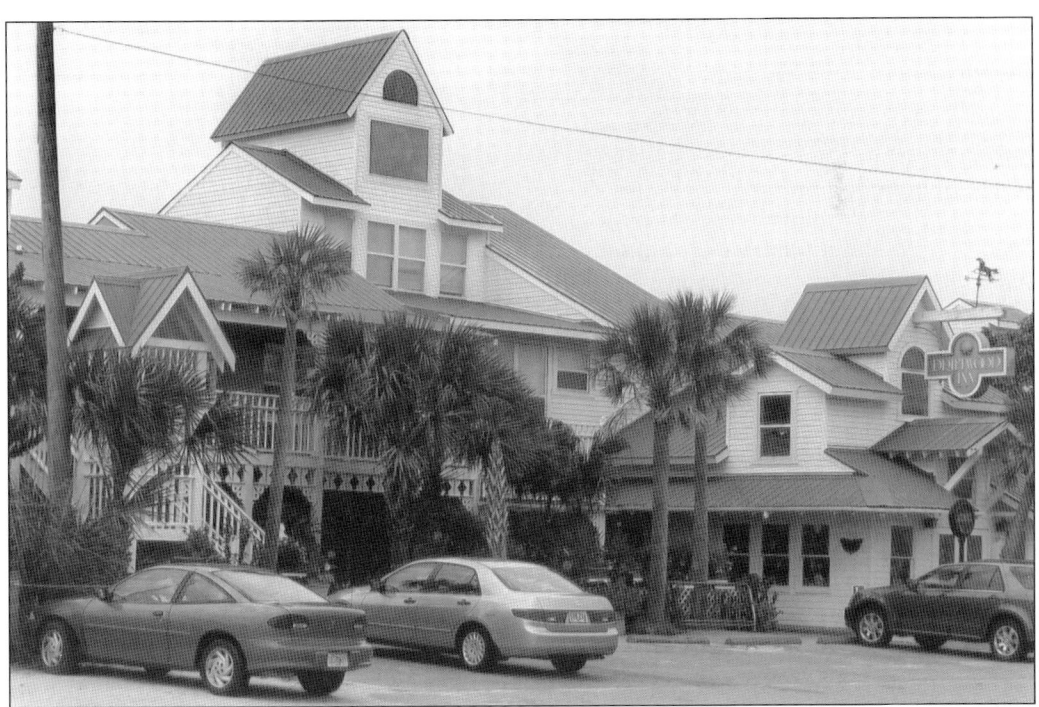

The Driftwood Motel has been in operation in Mexico Beach since the early 1950s. Present owners Tom and Peggy Wood purchased the property in August 1975. On June 6, 1994, fire destroyed the building; it was then rebuilt and reopened in May 1995. Over the years, the Wood family—Tom and Peggy and their children Shawna, Bart, and Brandy—has continually upgraded and improved the lodging facility. (Courtesy of Peggy Wood.)

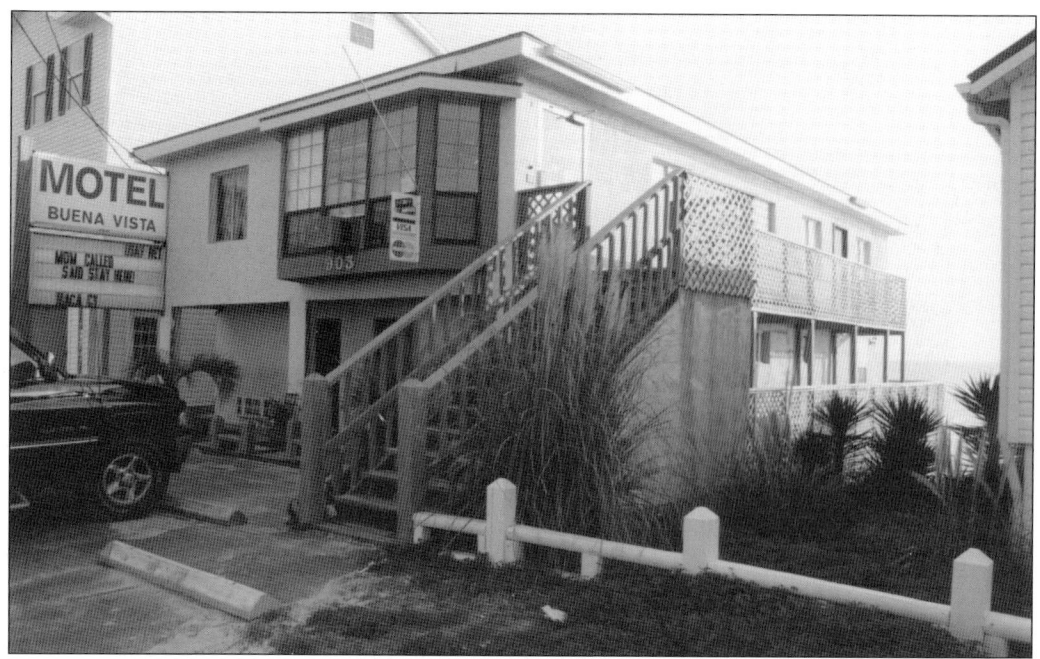

Currently a six-room motel owned and operated by Michael Kent, the Buena Vista Motel was built in 1974 by James Gaddis. Charles and Patricia Kent purchased the motel in 1991 and remodeled the building after Hurricane Opal. The motel sits across the street from Gulf Foods. (Courtesy of Mike Kent.)

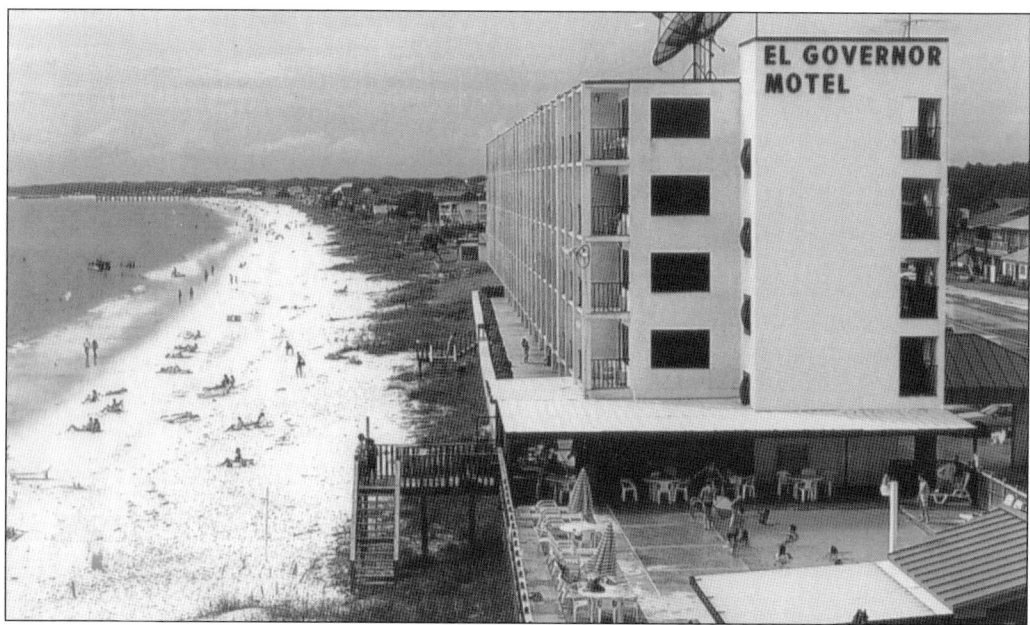

The El Governor Motel is a perfect place to spend a Mexico Beach vacation. Attractively decorated rooms face the gorgeous white sand beach, just a few steps from the Gulf of Mexico. Complete with a gift shop, wine and spirits, a heated swimming pool, and an outdoor picnic area, the four-story motel also has Jet Ski and parasailing rentals on site. Managed by Wylie Petty, the El Governor Motel is owned by Dorothy Baxter and family. (Courtesy of Wylie Petty.)

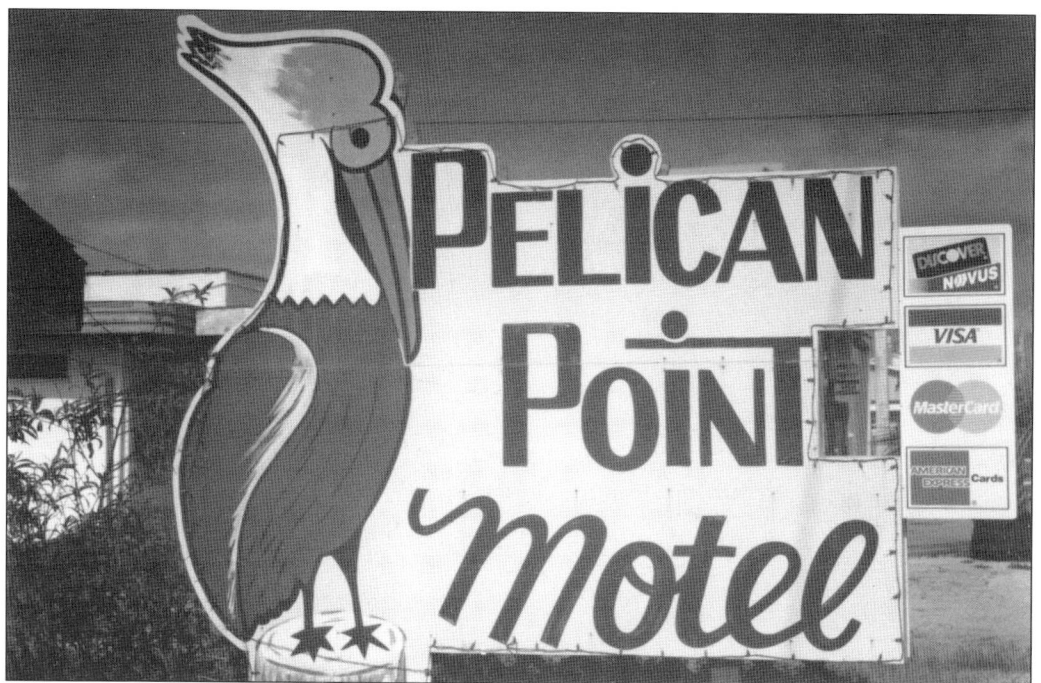

In 1991, the Ebb Tide Motel became the Pelican Point Motel and was operated and managed by Wylie Petty and Mark Grier. Teresa Crowe purchased the property in 1993 and sold it in early 2000 to developer Bill Beatty, who constructed the Treasure Palms townhomes. (Courtesy of Cathey Parker Hobbs.)

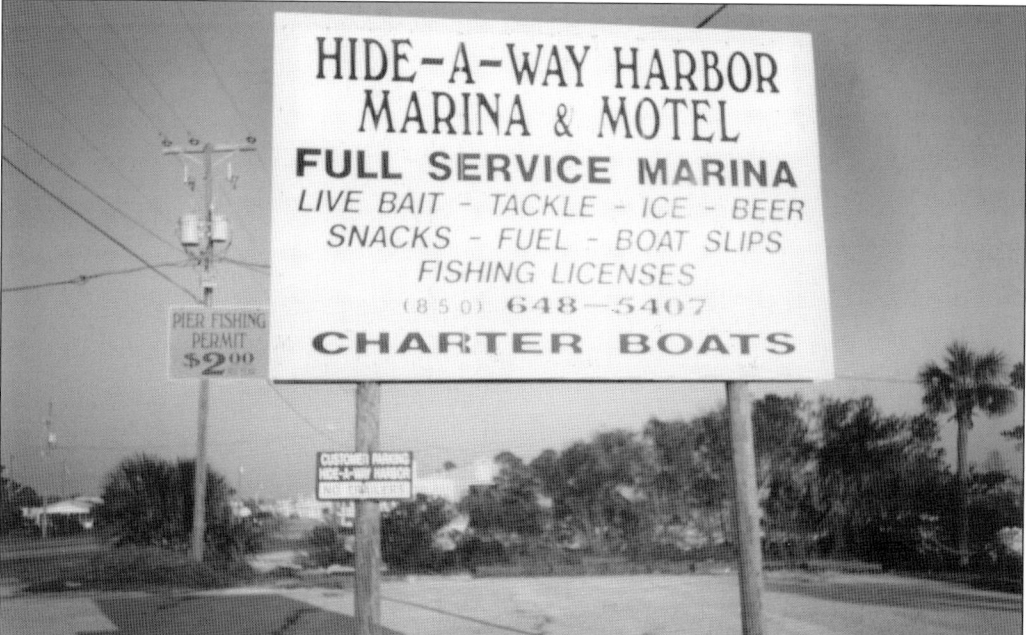

The Hide-A-Way Harbor Marina & Motel was located across from Tommy T's on Highway 98. The only remaining trace of the marina is the infamous, now closed city boat ramp situated at North Thirty-seventh Street. (Courtesy of Bill Hughes.)

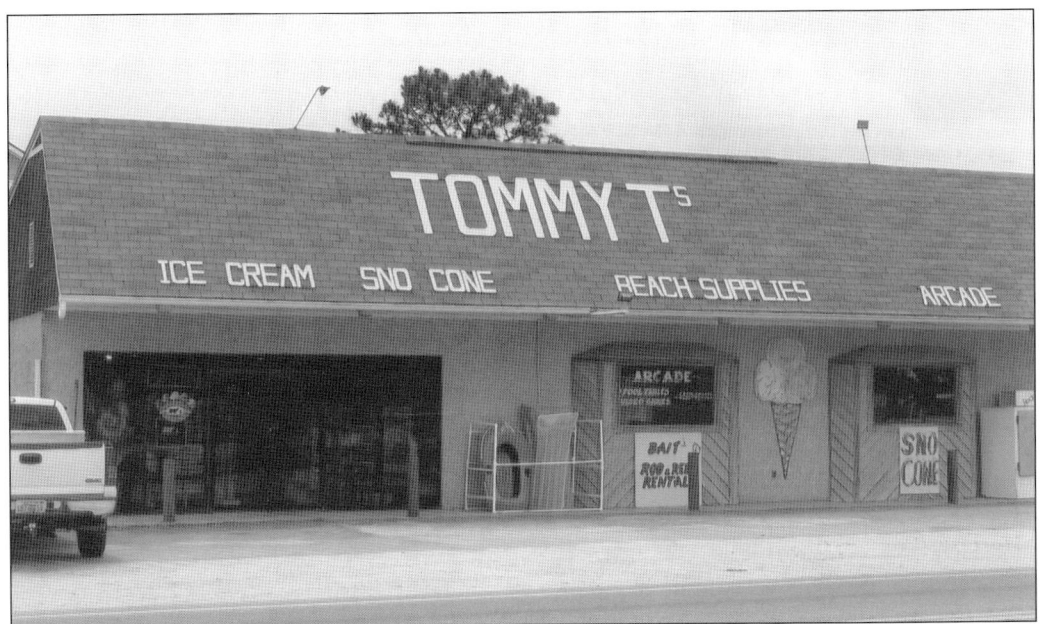

Tommy T's has served as the main Mexico Beach hangout for young people for 30 years. Built in 1983, the business opened as Nichol's Alley and was operated by Dennie and Joan Nichols. In 1985, Tommy Pitts assumed management of the popular game room, ice cream shop, and beach supply store. The building remains under the ownership of Earl Nichols. (Courtesy of Cathey Parker Hobbs.)

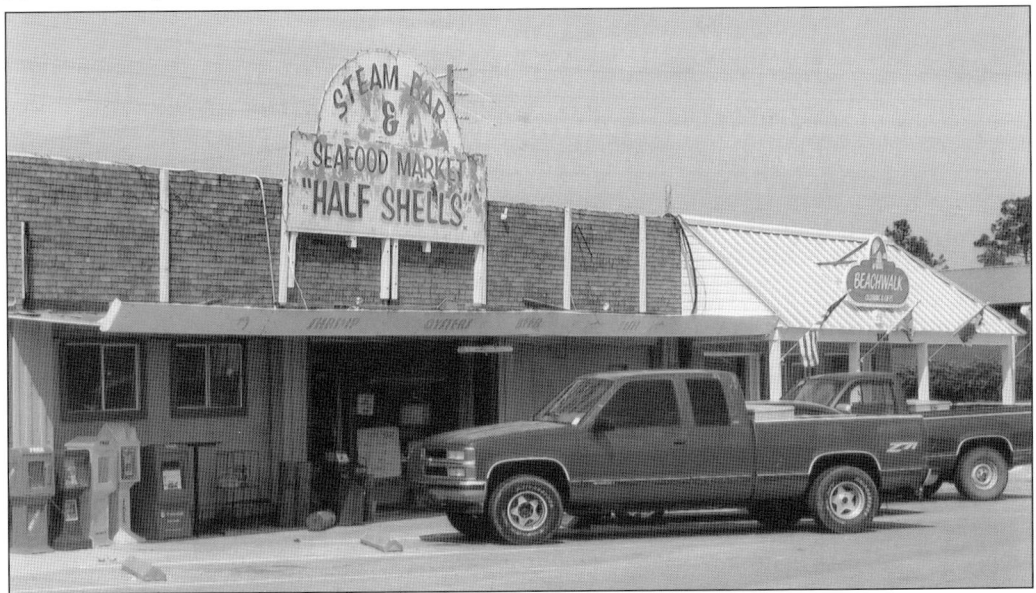

In 1976, Jack and Lynn Kerigan purchased the sundries store at left from Estelle "Mom" Cathey. Through the years, the building has been home to Kerigan's Cargo, Sarah Anne's Surf Shop, Fat Jack's, Jam's, the Sand Bar, Half Shells (opened by Kevin Bradley in 1999), and Mango Marley's. In 1976, the Mexico Beach Grocery, located at right, was purchased by Joe and Sylvia Whaley. In 2001, they had the building remodeled to accommodate the relocation of Beachwalk. (Courtesy of Lynn Kerigan.)

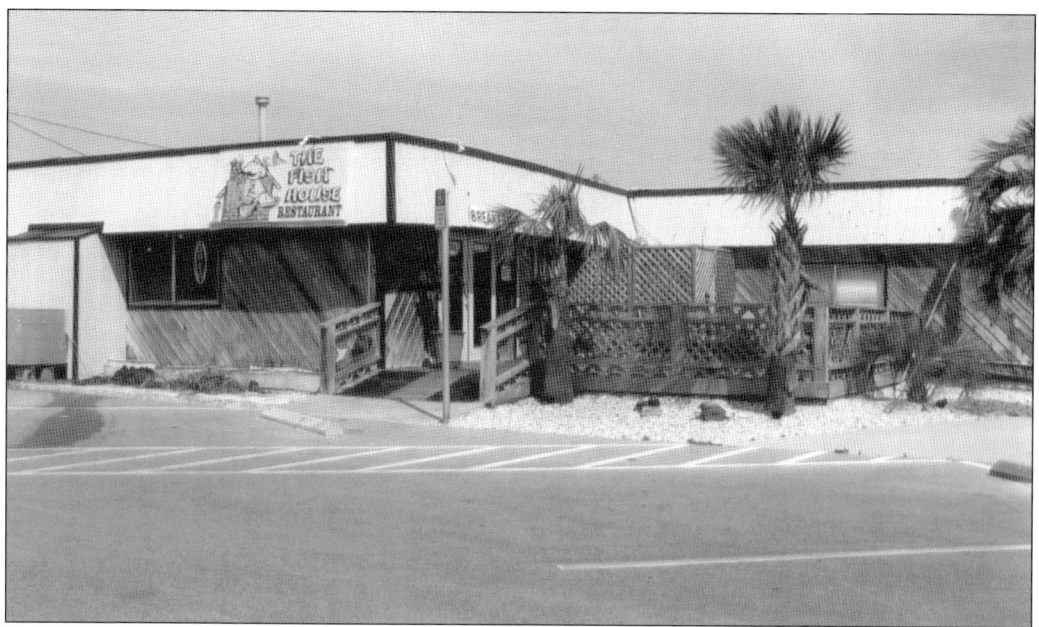

The location of this local restaurant was originally a small building with an open porch that operated as a sandwich shop called Daisy Queen. In 1979, Chris King purchased the property from Gary Carlston. The King family renovated and expanded the building and opened the Fish House Restaurant. Current owner Carol Dow purchased the restaurant in 1994. Today, the Fish House remains a local favorite. (Courtesy of Cathey Parker Hobbs.)

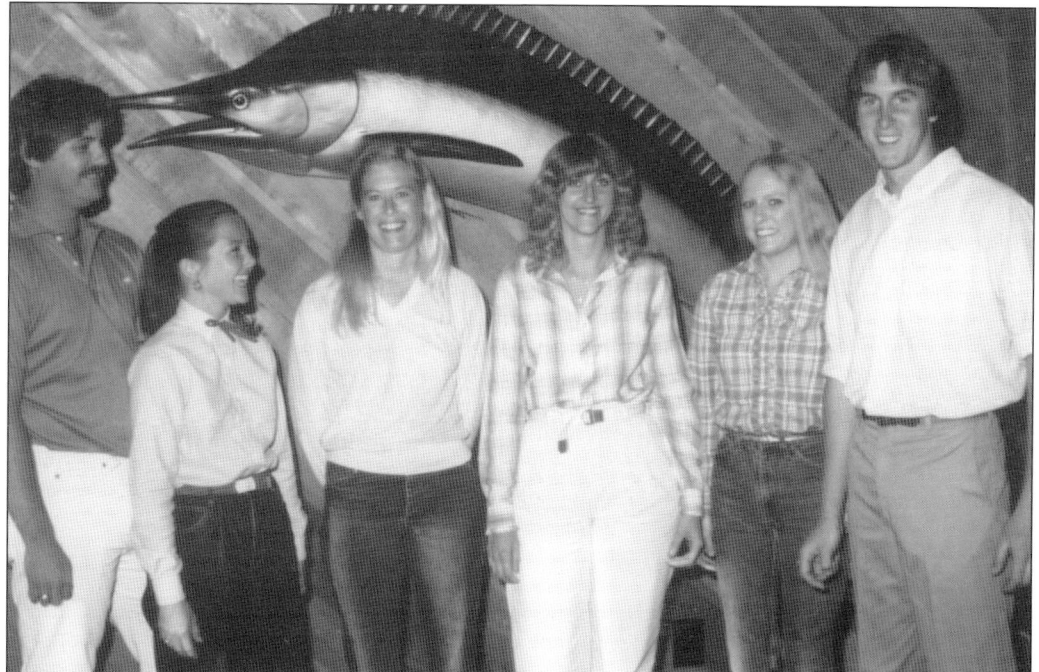

The staff of the Fish House Restaurant's Back Room are seen here in 1981. They are, from left to right, Chris King, Gay Best, Leslie Bell, Rhonda Vise, Ruby Schell, and Pat Kerigan. (Courtesy of Lynn Kerigan.)

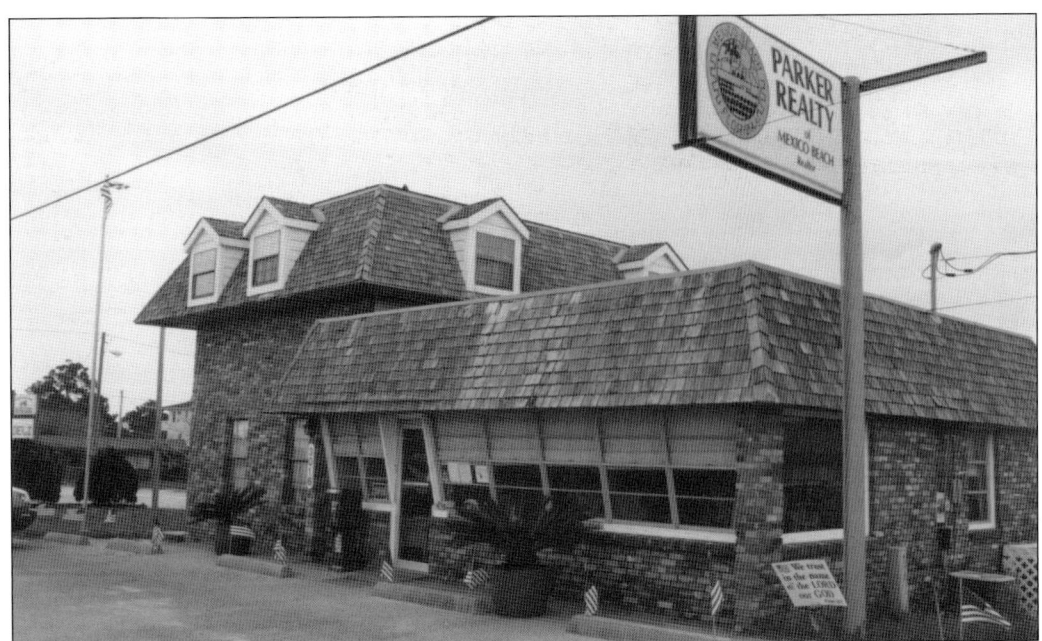

In the late 1950s, Charlie and Inky Parker moved their Parker Realty office from the rear of the Mexico Beach Grocery to its current location on Highway 98. The second story was added in 1981, and the building was renovated into its current state in 2002. After Charlie Parker's death in 2003, their oldest daughter, Cathey Parker Hobbs, became the owner and active broker of the family business. (Courtesy of Cathey Parker Hobbs.)

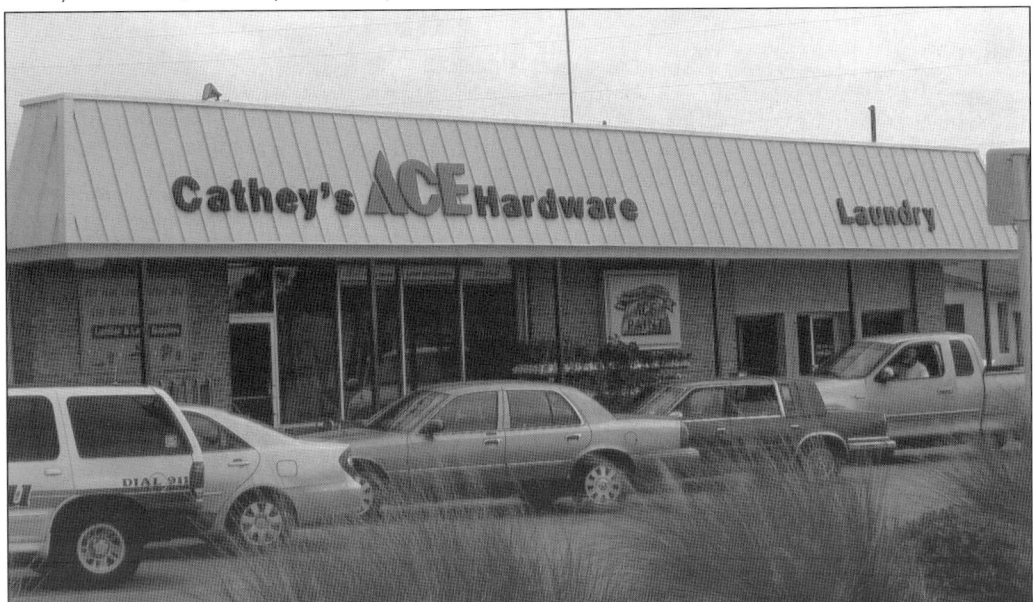

In 1979, Cathey's Hardware and Tackle was renamed Cathey's Ace Hardware. The third-generation family-owned business continues today. Al and Carol Cathey, with their youngest son, Lee, maintain and operate the hardware store. Their oldest son, Brian, owns and manages Cathey Construction and Development. The Cathey family has owned and operated a retail business in Mexico Beach for 60 years. (Courtesy of Al Cathey.)

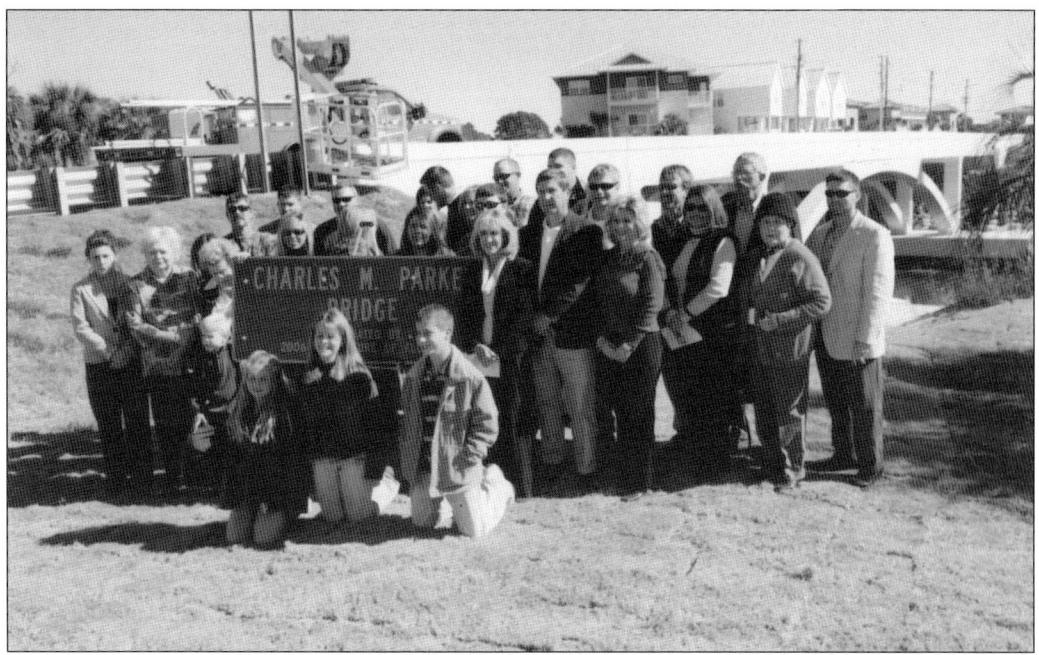

The Charles M. Parker Bridge dedication ceremony was held on December 5, 2006. Parker devoted his life to making Mexico Beach what it is today—"our paradise." The bridge was named in his honor to recognize his accomplishments. Seen here enjoying the occasion is his wife, Inky, along with many family members and friends. (Courtesy of the Parker family.)

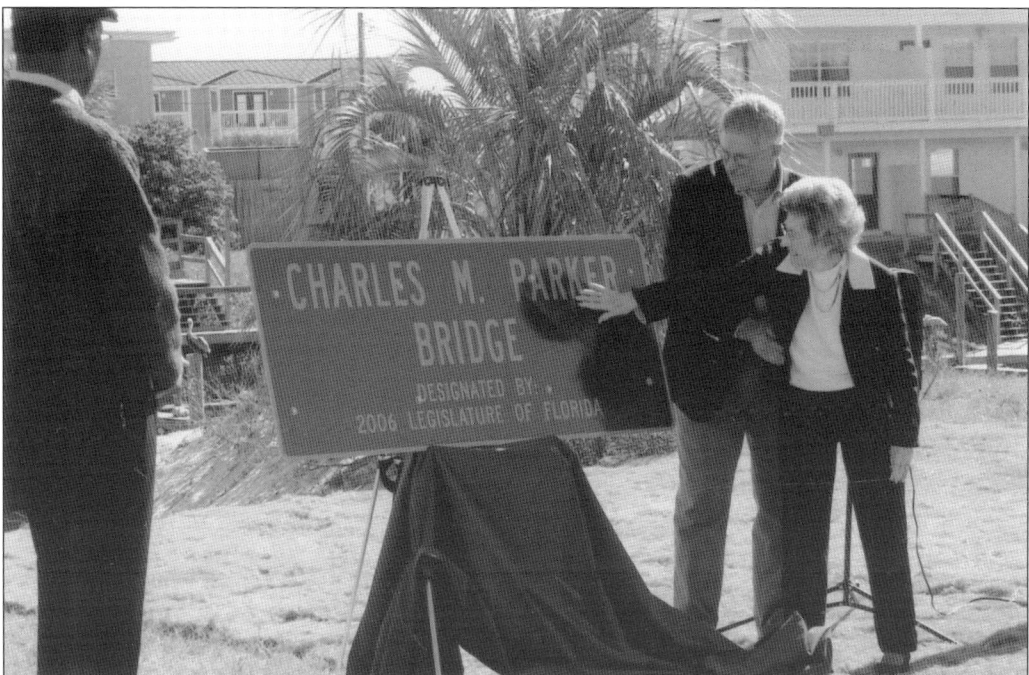

Inky Parker shares a special moment with her nephew, Mayor Al Cathey, at the dedication ceremony of the Charles M. Parker Bridge in 2006. The bridge is located at the west entrance to Mexico Beach. (Courtesy of the Parker family.)

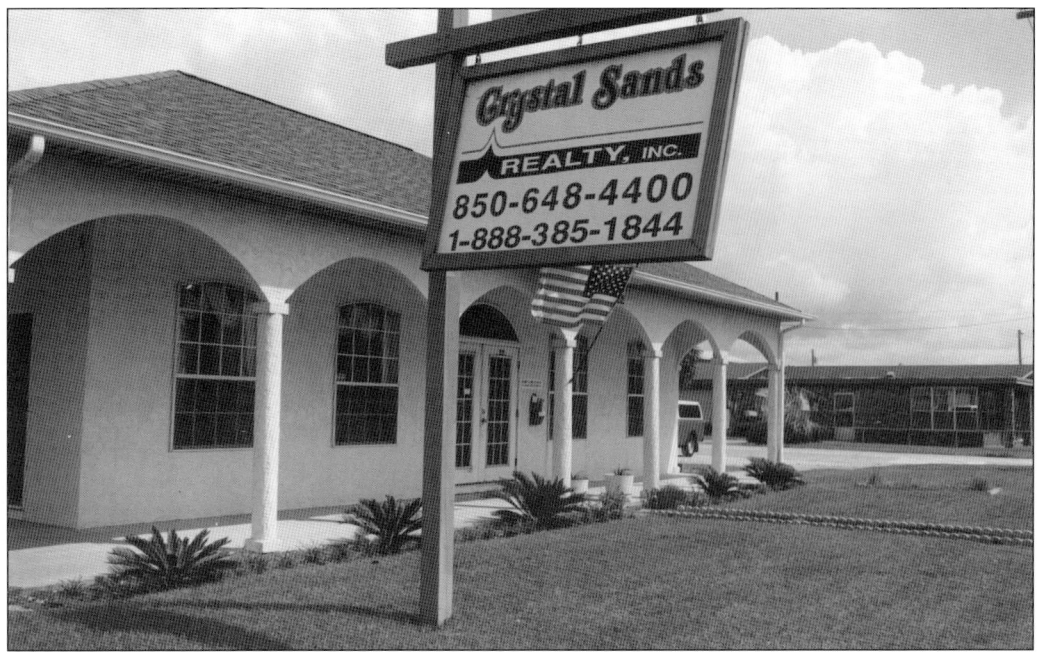

In 1998, Crystal Sands Realty began operations at 900 Highway 98 under broker Janice Brownell. In 2005, owner George Duren opened Blue Water Realty. The property is now the home of Living Water Lutheran Church. (Courtesy of Cathey Parker Hobbs.)

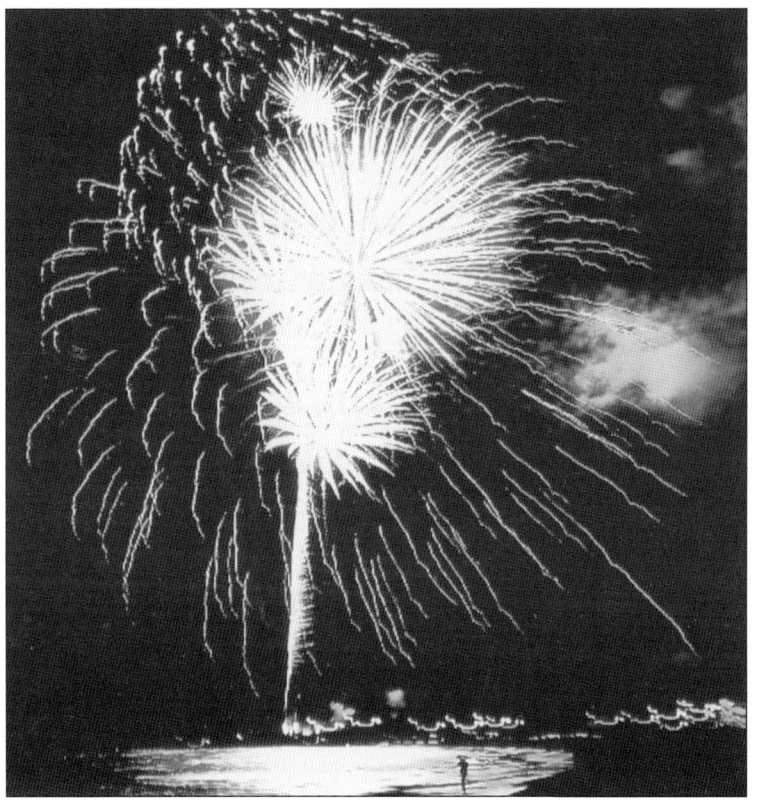

The Fourth of July "Best Blast on the Beach" fireworks display has been a much-anticipated annual celebration in Mexico Beach since 1998. The first Special Events Committee was organized by Dana Angerer Boyer and included members Bill Bloesma, Peggy Wood, Carol Dow, Mora Rich, Wylie Petty, Carrie Stomp, and Jennifer Poole. (Courtesy of Hilary Patterson.)

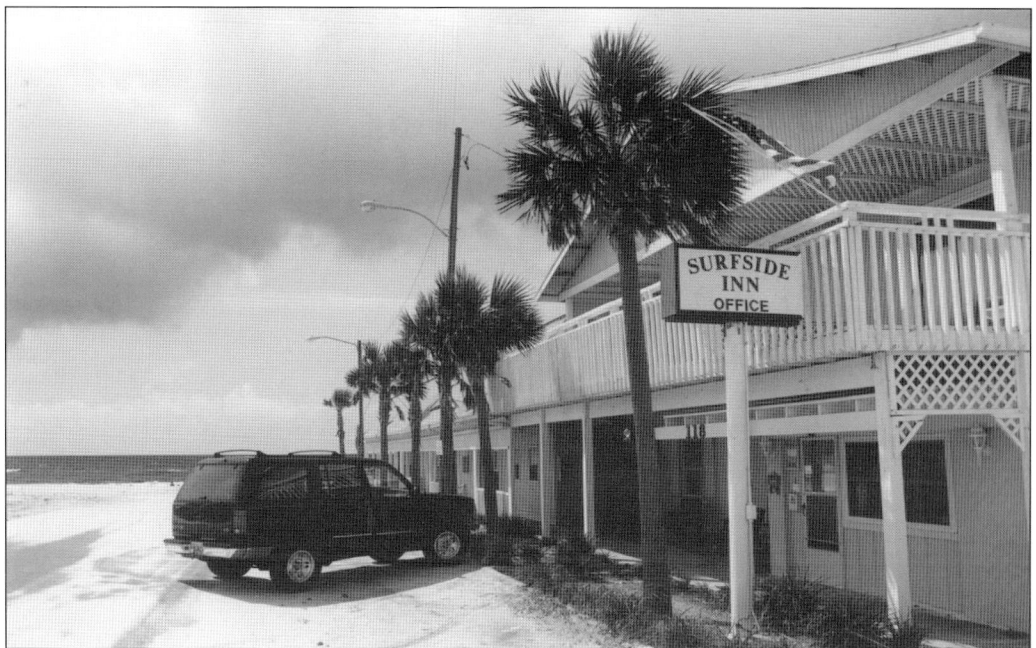

Built in the late 1950s, the Surfside Inn was located at the end of South Thirty-eighth Street. In 1959, Ed and Betty Corry purchased the property from Debbie and Tommy McClellan. They then sold it to Joe and Reba Rehberg in 1968. The motel was managed for many years by Patty and Paul Scarboro. (Courtesy of Cathey Parker Hobbs.)

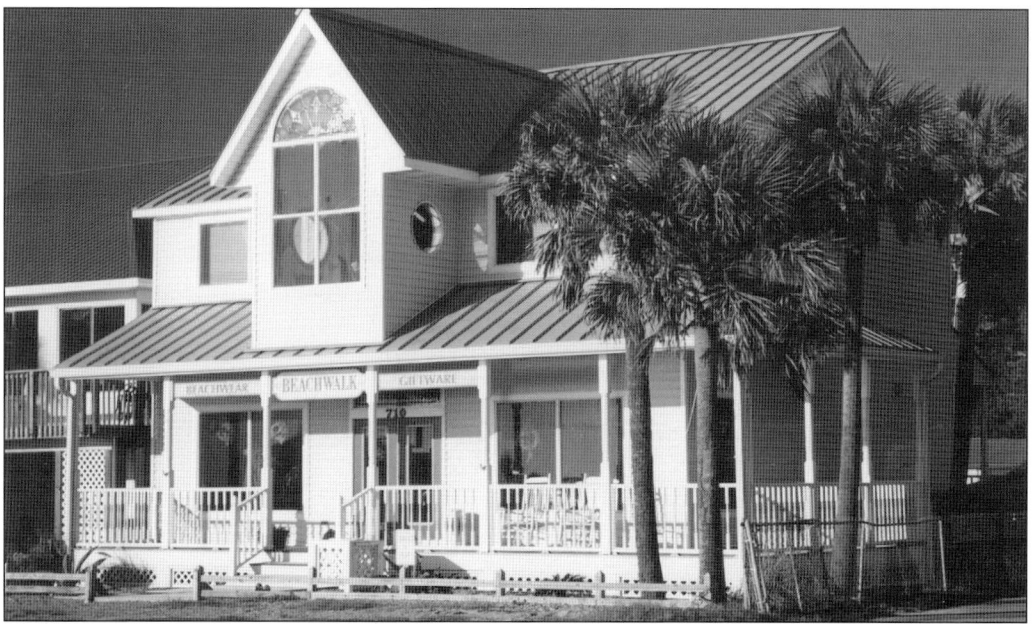

In 1994, the Beachwalk Clothing and Gift Shop was built. The shop offered name-brand men's and women's apparel, jewelry, and gifts. The building was constructed with Old Florida architecture and included large porches, stained glass, and wooden floors. Owners Joe and Sylvia Whaley and Al and Carol Cathey maintained the business for several years. In 2001, the Whaleys moved the shop to their newly remodeled Mexico Beach Grocery location. (Courtesy of Al Cathey.)

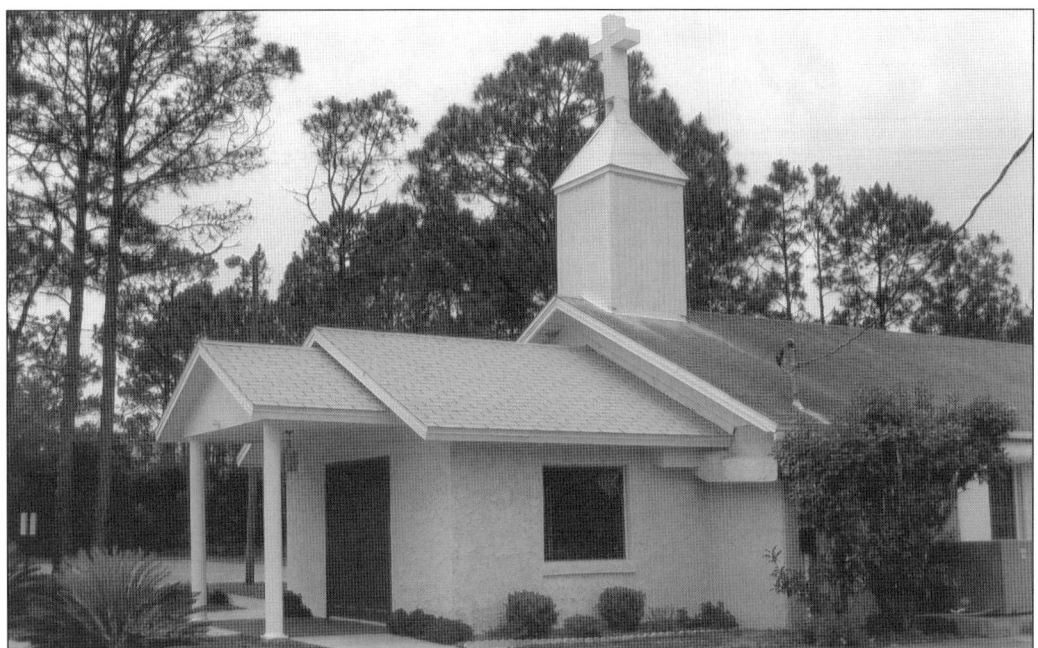

First United Methodist Church of Mexico Beach was organized on December 13, 1957. The conference suggested that the church be named Hamner Memorial in memory of Rev. John Wesley Hamner to honor Mrs. Gordon Parker, his daughter. Mrs. Parker was so modest and so Methodist that she declined, and the church became First Methodist. (Courtesy of Cathey Parker Hobbs.)

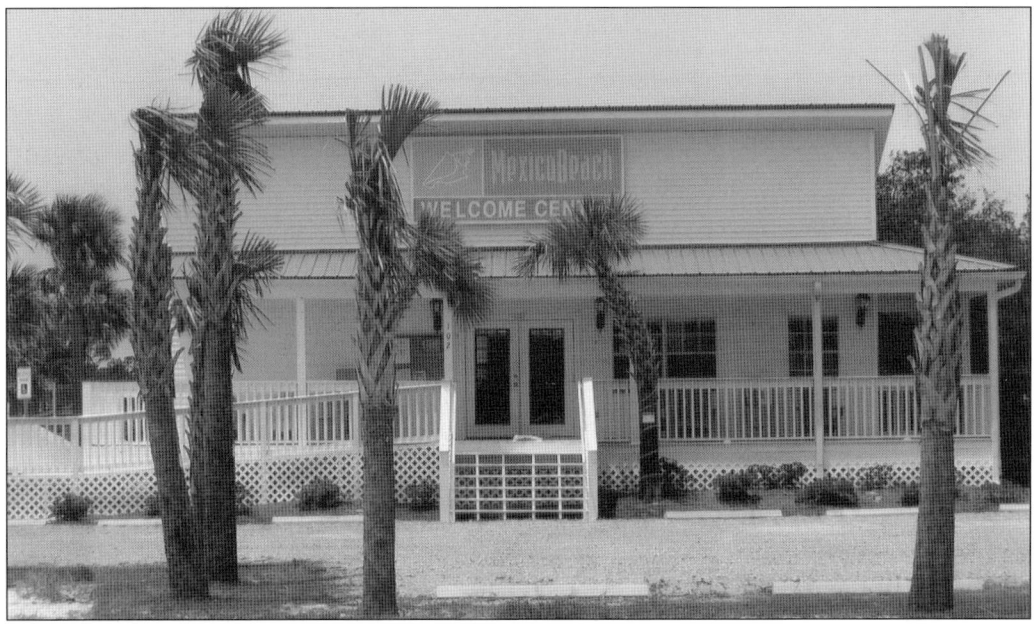

The Mexico Beach Welcome Center building was originally the ship store for Hide-A-Way Harbor Marina. The old marina store was left unusable after Hurricane Opal, and owners Jim and Kay McCullough and Sherry and Allen Pitts had the new store built. In 2003, when the property was sold for condominium construction, the new owners donated the building to the city. The structure was then moved to its current location on Canal Parkway. (Courtesy of Cathey Parker Hobbs.)

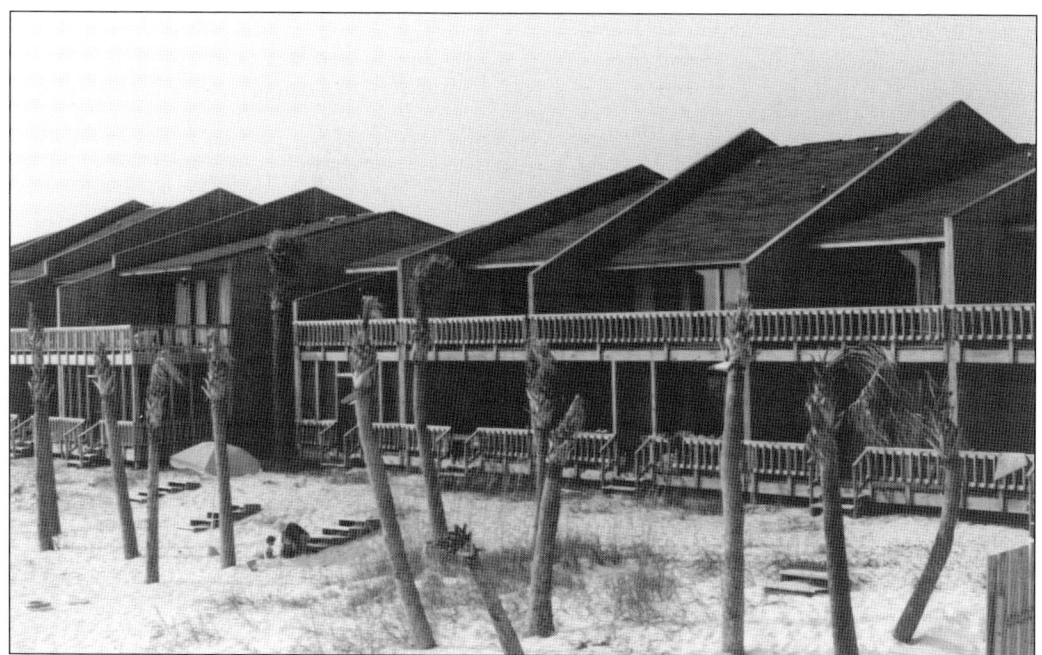

The Luxury by the Pier town houses were built in 1982 by builder James Tyson of Dothan, Alabama. They are located on the Gulf of Mexico, on both sides of Thirty-Seventh Street. Tyson introduced Mexico Beach to townhouses when he built the first ones on Thirty-second Street in 1980. (Courtesy of Cathey Parker Hobbs.)

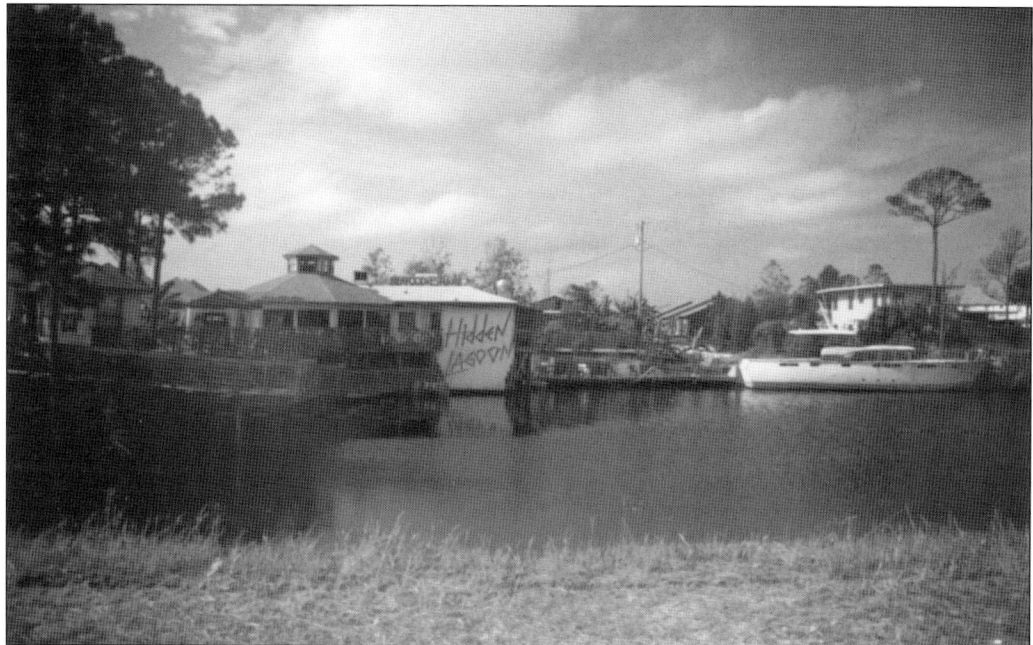

In 2000, Hidden Lagoon Restaurant owner Charlie Kent added his boat to the pond and called it his yacht club. It was later purchased by builder Thad Williams, who cleared the land and filled in the pond. Williams and Bill Beatty built the Ocean Plantation townhouses on the site in 2002. (Courtesy of Cathey Parker Hobbs.)

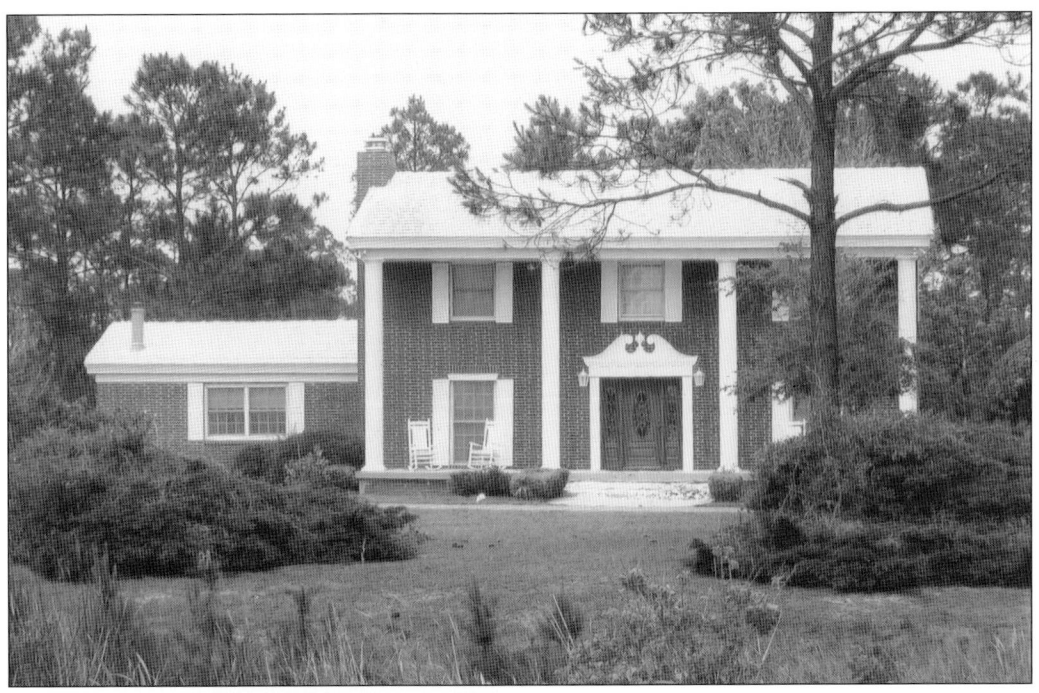

The Parker home was at 2500 Highway 98. Charlie Parker built it for his family in 1962, and they lived there for the rest of their lives. Charlie Parker died in 2003, and his wife, Inky, passed away in 2007. Many wonderful memories were created at gatherings there by the family and the community. The property was purchased by the City of Mexico Beach in July 2011 to become the new city hall. One week later, it was destroyed by a fire. (Courtesy of the Parker family.)

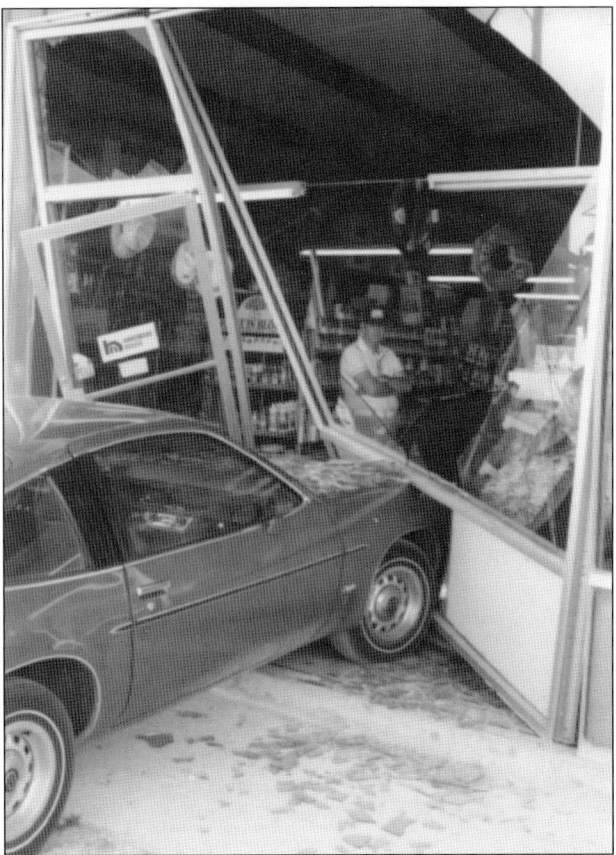

In 1975, less than a year after Cathey's Hardware and Tackle opened, this car tried turning the store into a drive-in. Here, Bubba Cathey, with a perplexed look on his face, surveys the damage. (Courtesy of Al Cathey.)

Nine
HURRICANE SEASON

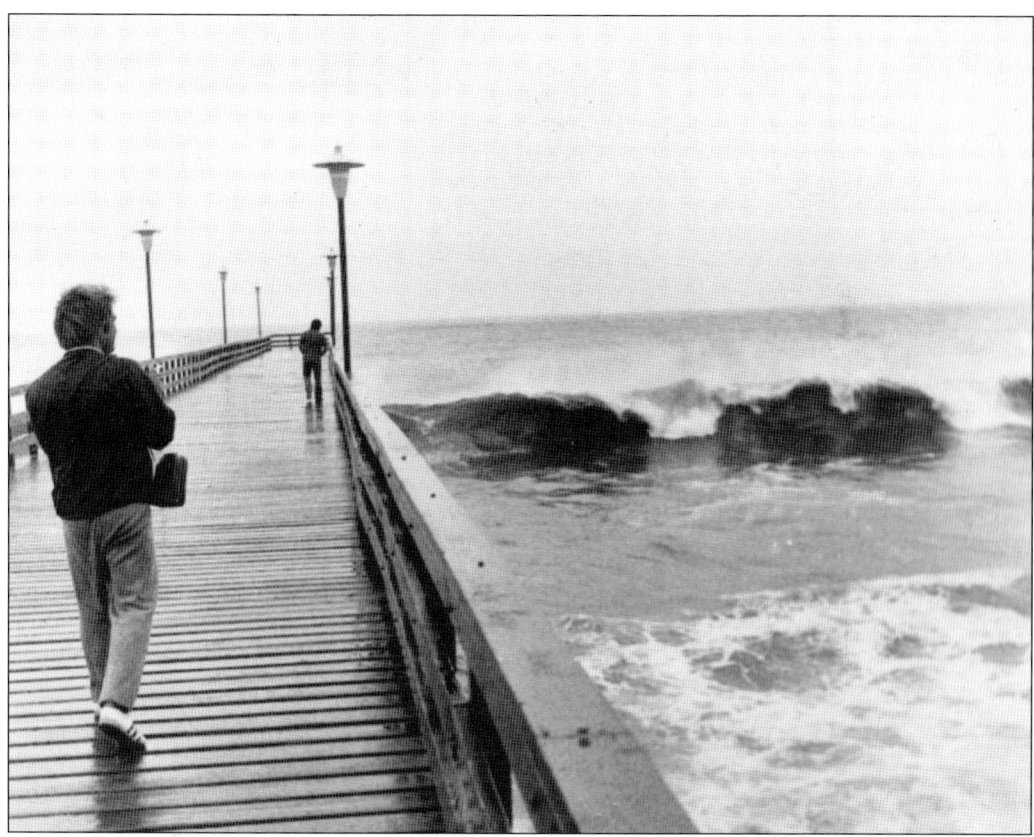

Hurricane Opal slammed into the Florida Panhandle with a fury late on Wednesday, October 6, 1995, making landfall between Pensacola and the Gulf County beaches. Mexico Beach took a major beating from the pounding surf and rising waters of the Gulf of Mexico. This brave man takes a chance standing on the pier during the storm. (Courtesy of Cathey Parker Hobbs.)

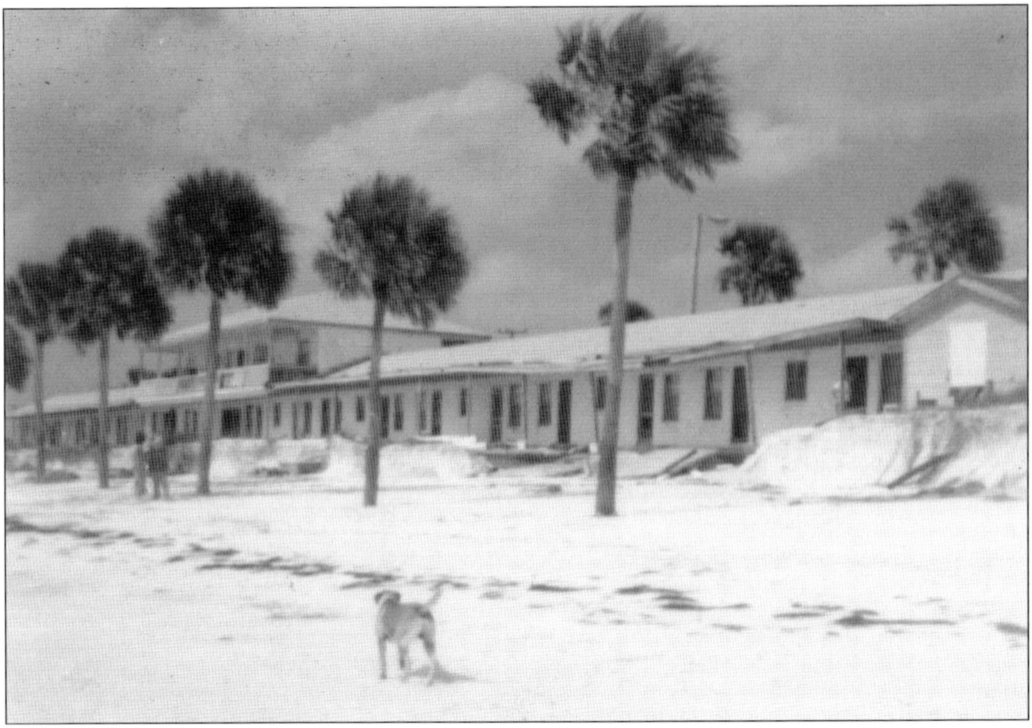

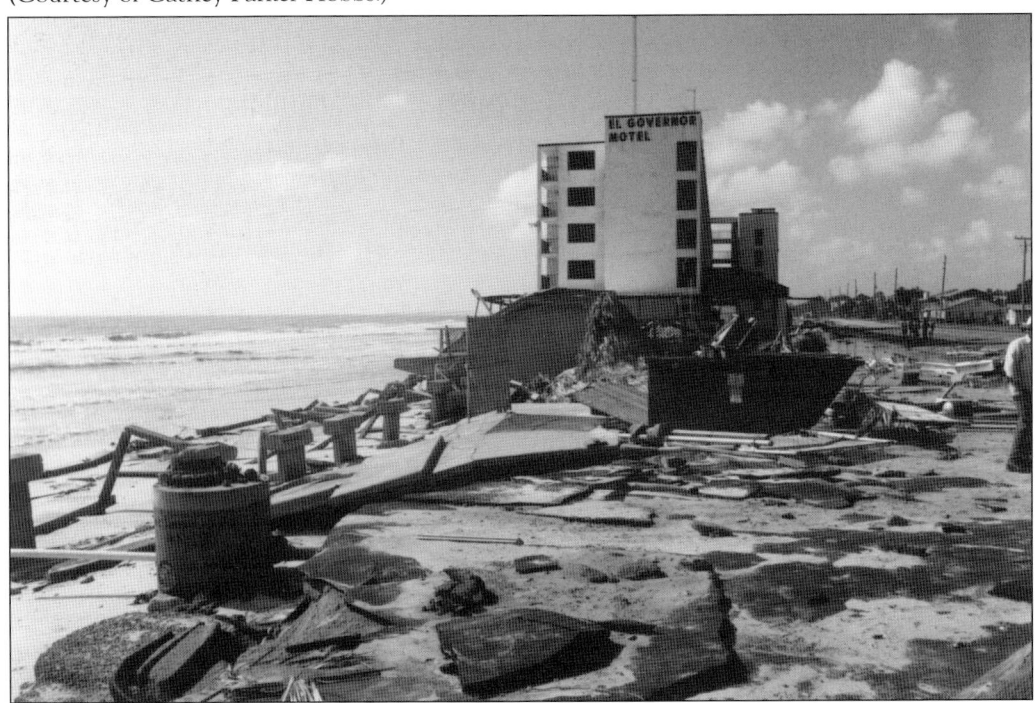

The rear of the Rainbow Motel is seen here after Hurricane Eloise on September 23, 1975. (Courtesy of Cathey Parker Hobbs.)

The El Governor Motel is seen here still standing after Hurricane Opal in 1995. (Courtesy of Cathey Parker Hobbs.)

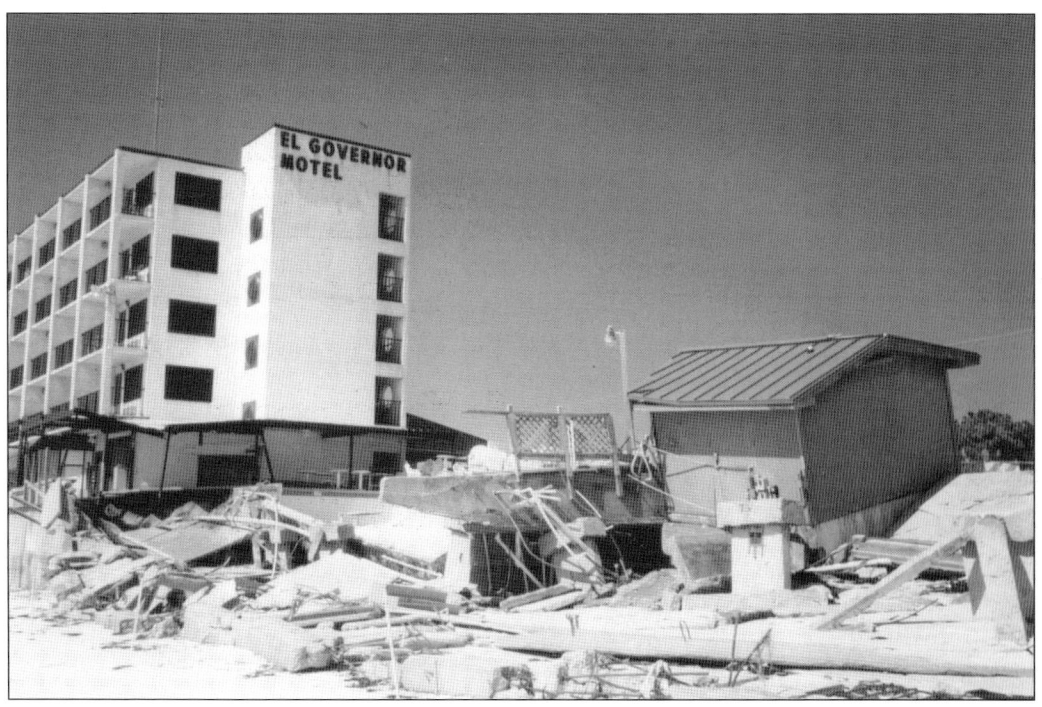

This seawall collapsed in front of the pool area of the El Governor Motel during Hurricane Opal. (Courtesy of Al Cathey.)

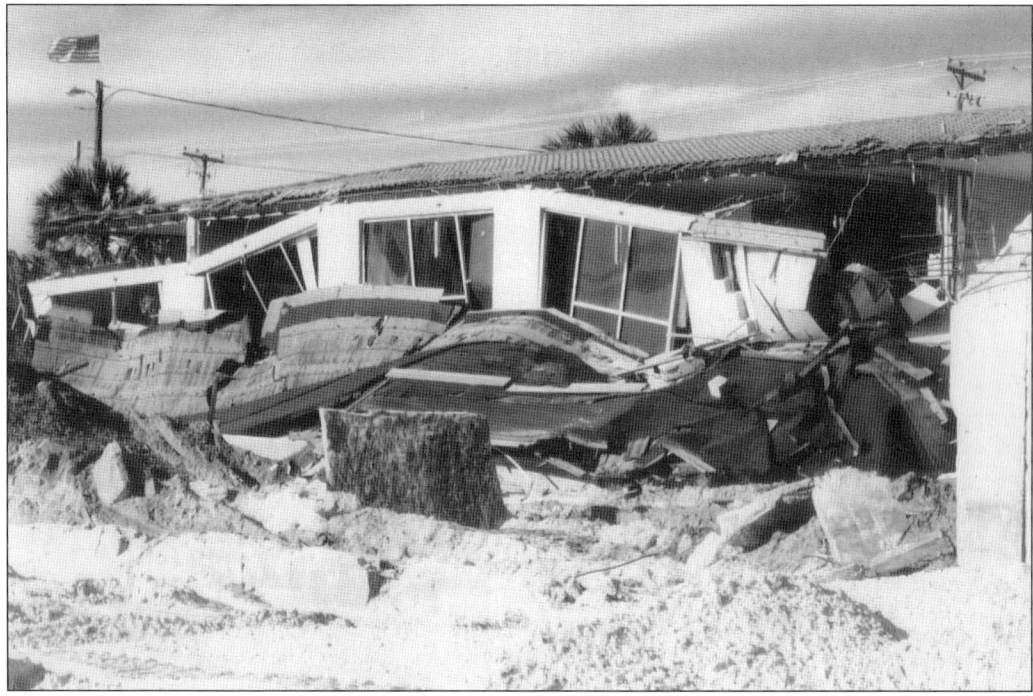

Gulf-front homes with foundations on ground level along Highway 98, between Toucan's Restaurant and the El Governor Motel, could not withstand the fury of Hurricane Opal. (Courtesy of Cathey Parker Hobbs.)

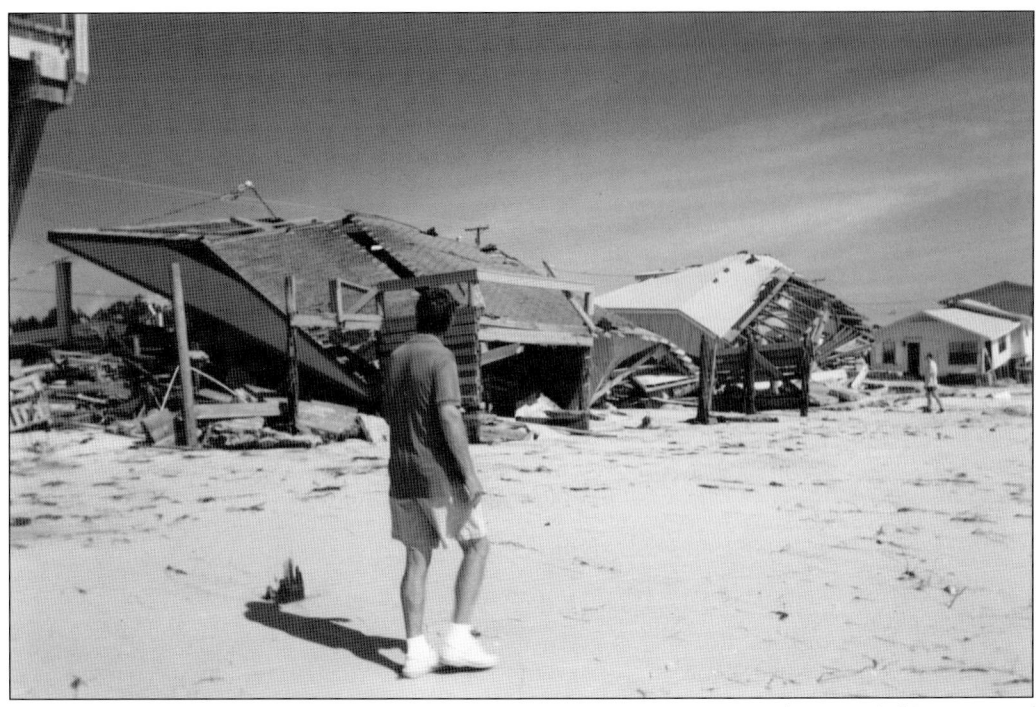
Local resident Ralph Hobbs surveys the damage after Hurricane Opal in 1995. (Courtesy of Cathey Parker Hobbs.)

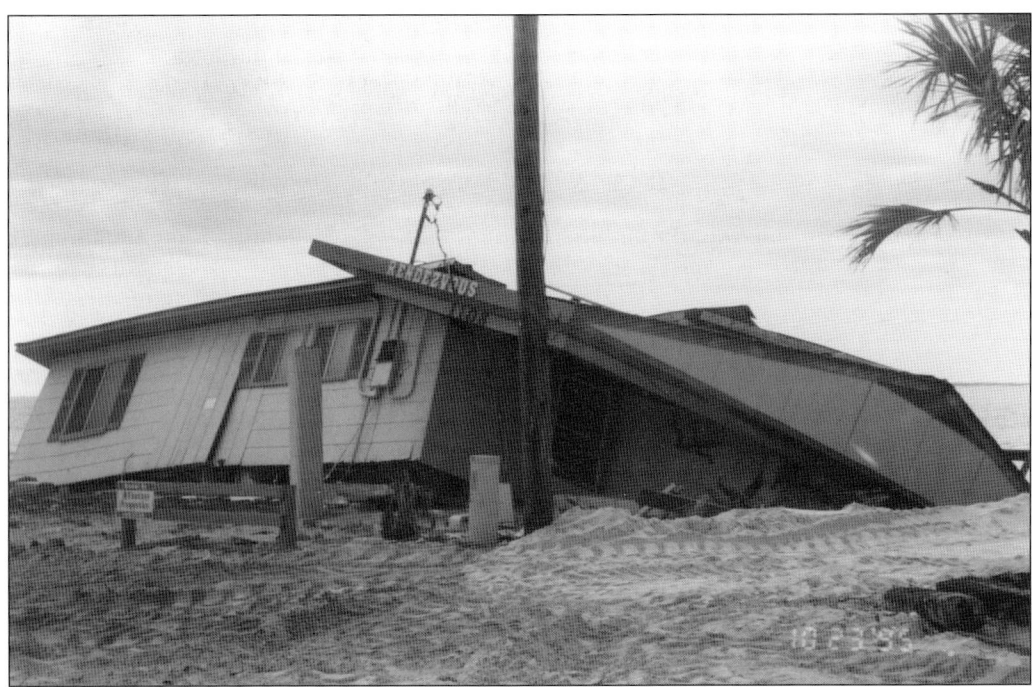
This vacation home, Rendezvous, slides into the Gulf during Opal. The owners at the time were Dr. Isadore Wexler and his wife, Rella. (Courtesy of Cathey Parker Hobbs.)

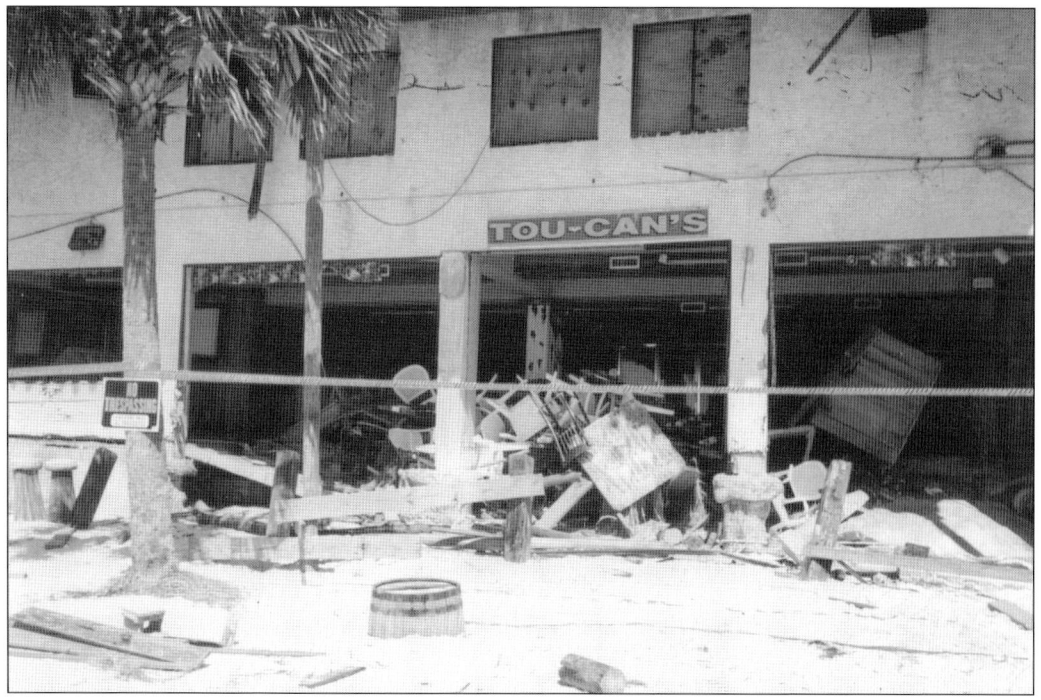
Damage caused by Hurricane Opal is seen here at Toucan's Restaurant in 1995. (Courtesy of Doris Watson.)

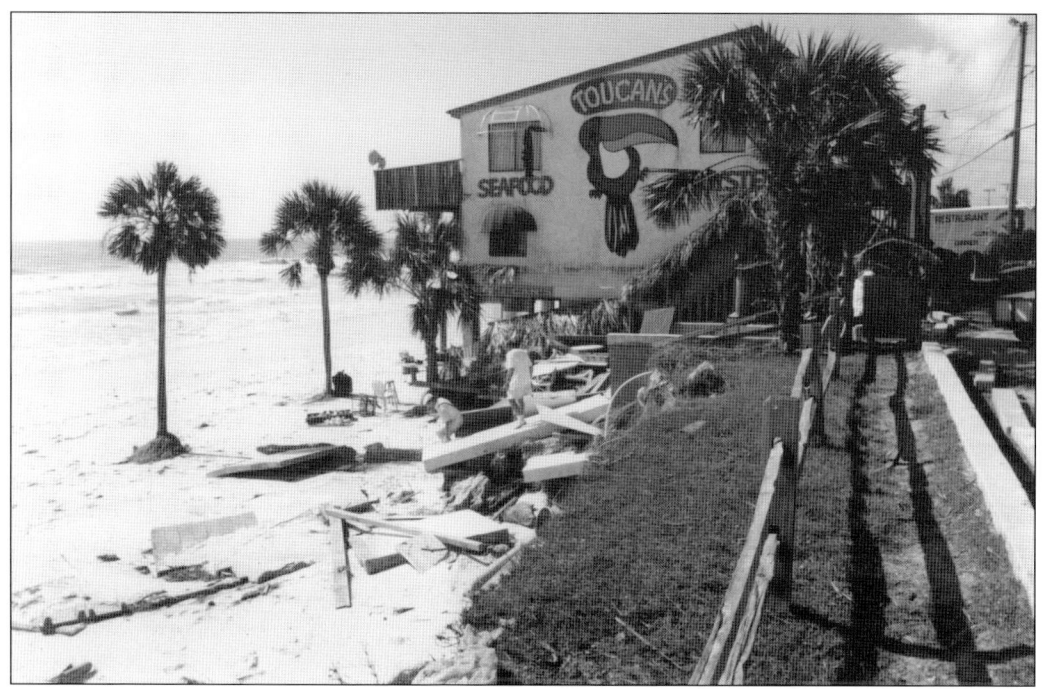
The public park area east of Toucan's was severely eroded by Opal. (Courtesy of Cathey Parker Hobbs.)

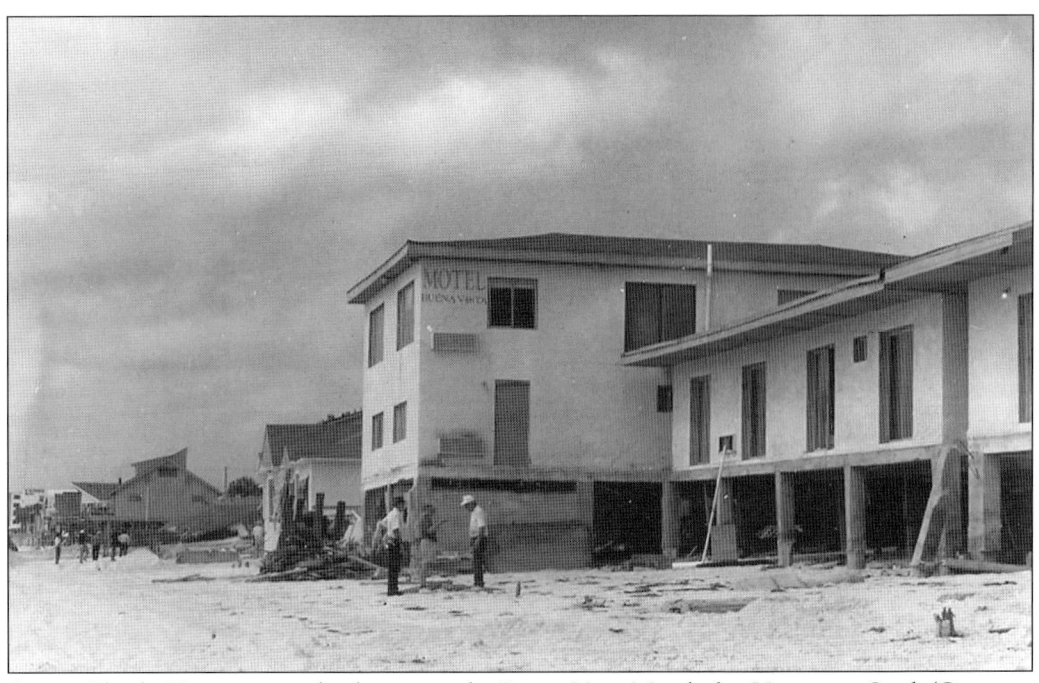
Owner Charlie Kent assesses the damage at the Buena Vista Motel after Hurricane Opal. (Courtesy of Mike Kent.)

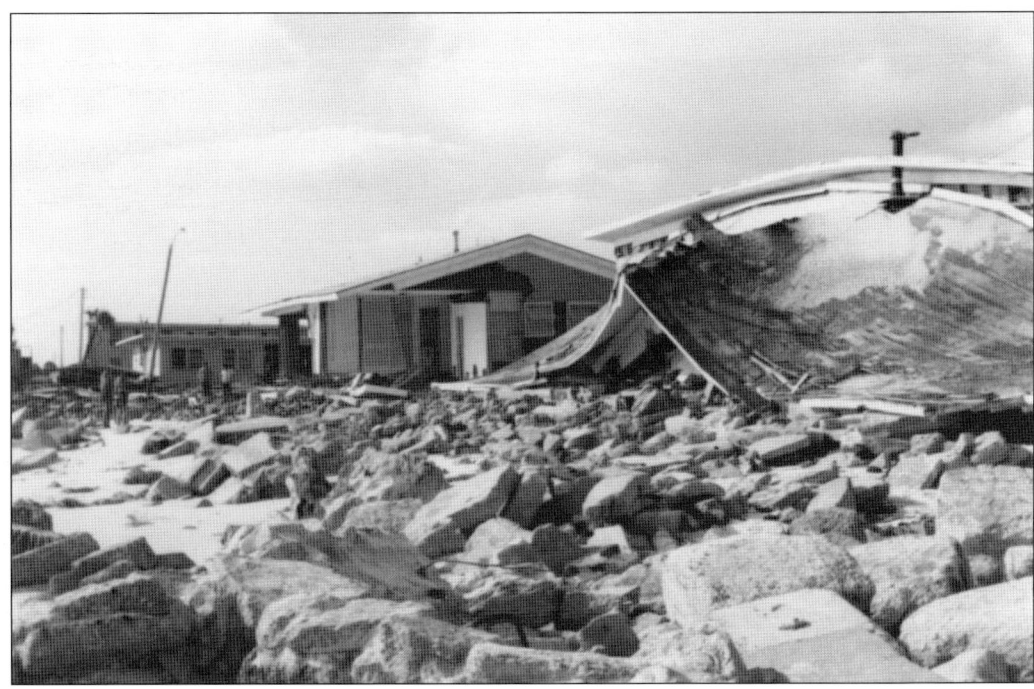
Living on the coast can be very costly. Hurricane Opal changed the landscape near Mexico Beach for many waterfront properties. (Courtesy of Al Cathey.)

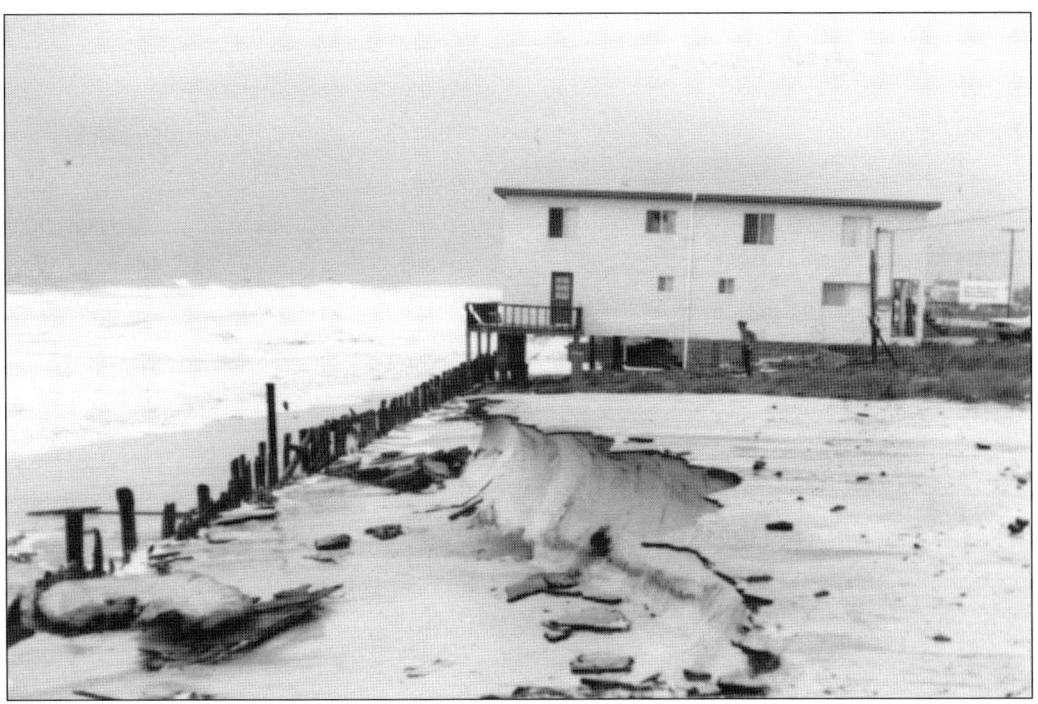
In 1975, the Surf Restaurant parking lot was washed away during Hurricane Eloise. The recently built Buena Vista Motel stood tall, however. (Courtesy of Cathey Parker Hobbs.)

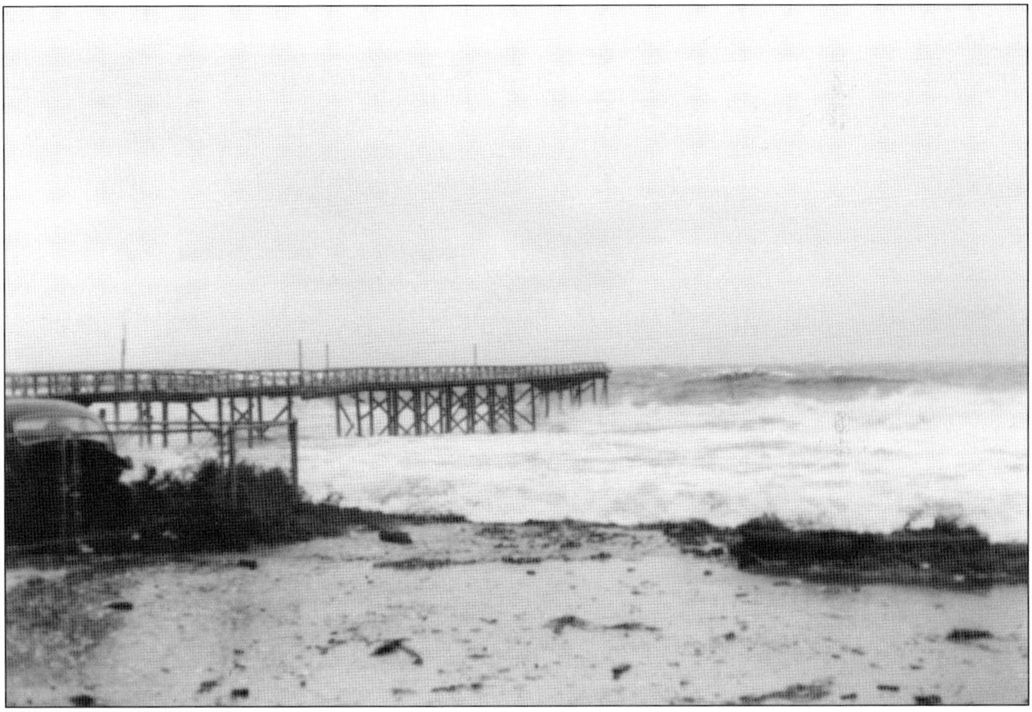

Hurricane Eloise takes aim on the Surf Pier in 1975. (Courtesy of Al Cathey.)

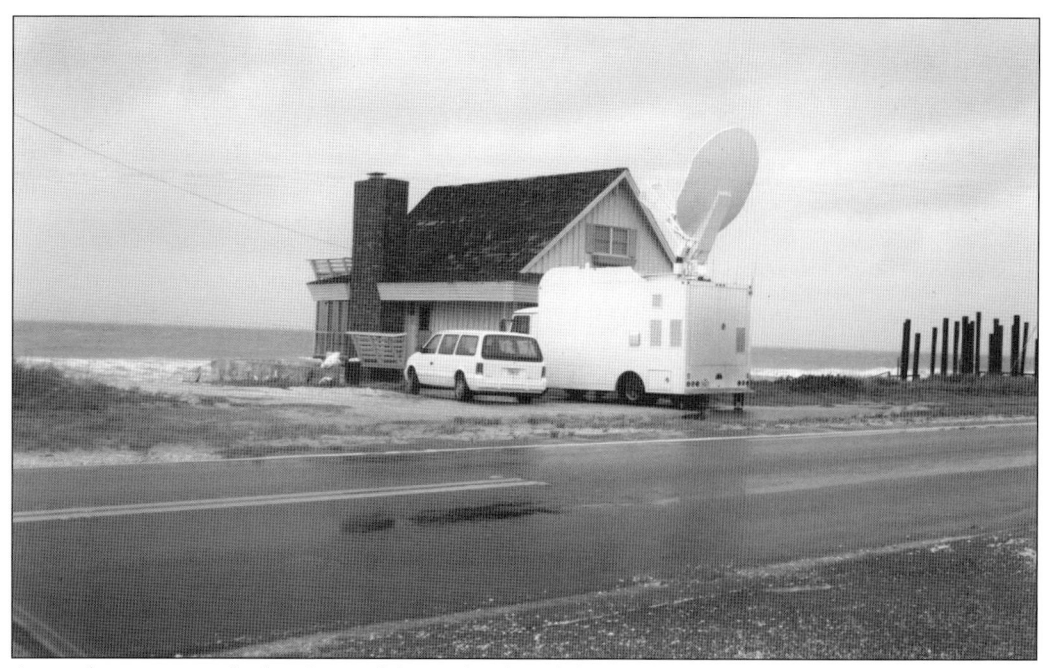
A weather van is parked in front of the Parker beach house during Tropical Storm Beryl in 1994. (Courtesy of Cathey Parker Hobbs.)

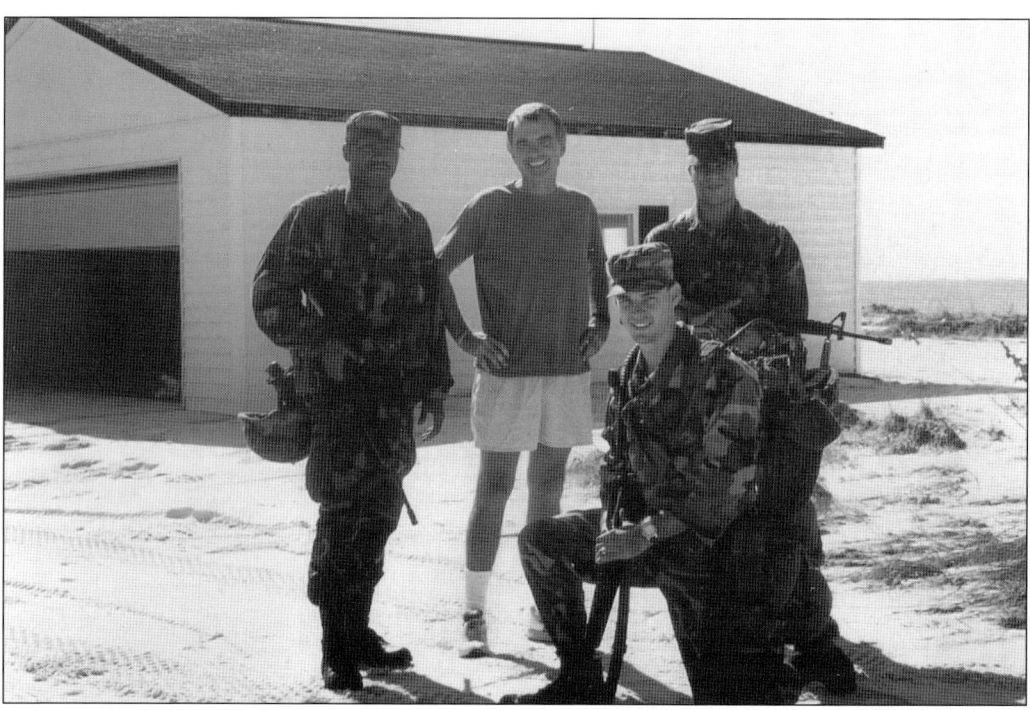
After Hurricane Opal, these National Guardsmen take a break from patrolling the beaches to share a moment with John Colton (center) at his beach house on Circle Drive. Colton resides in Nashville. (Courtesy of John Colton.)

Ten
Beacon Hill and Overstreet

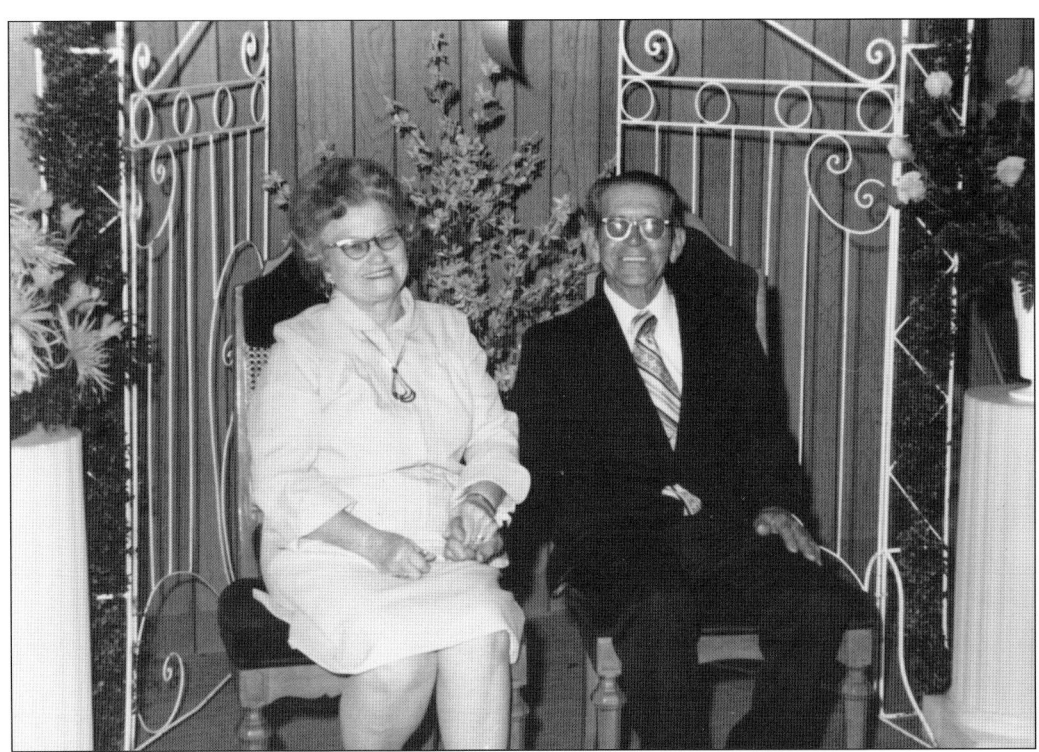

James Guilford and Gertrude Hardy were married on February 28, 1926. The Guilford family moved to Overstreet in 1933. Affectionately known as "Mom" and "Pop," the Guilfords are seen here enjoying their 50th wedding anniversary. (Courtesy of Chuck Guilford.)

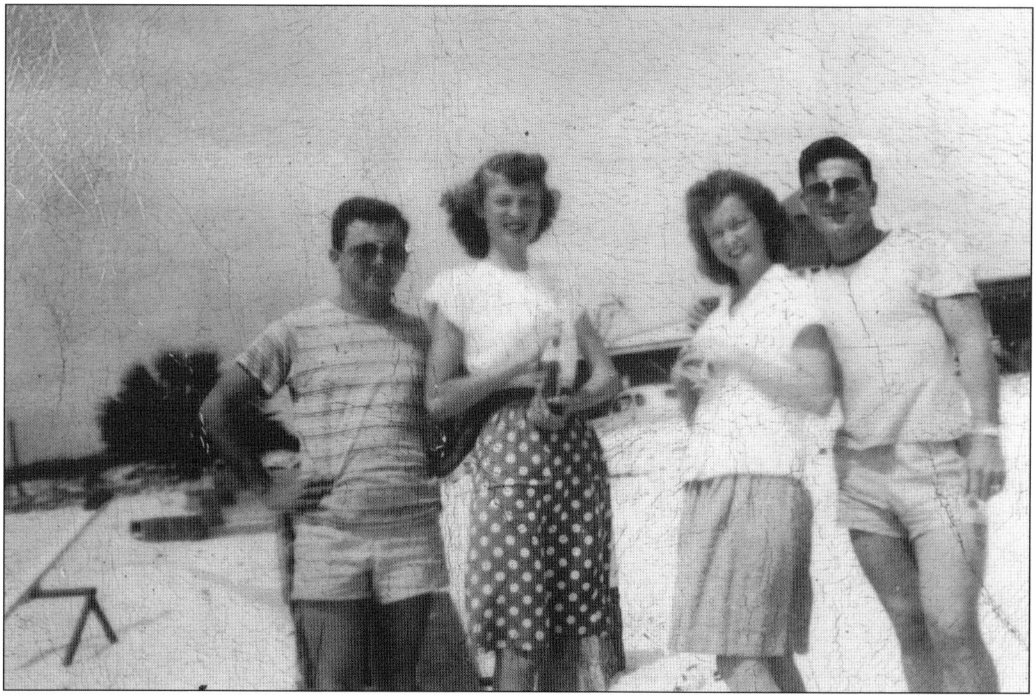

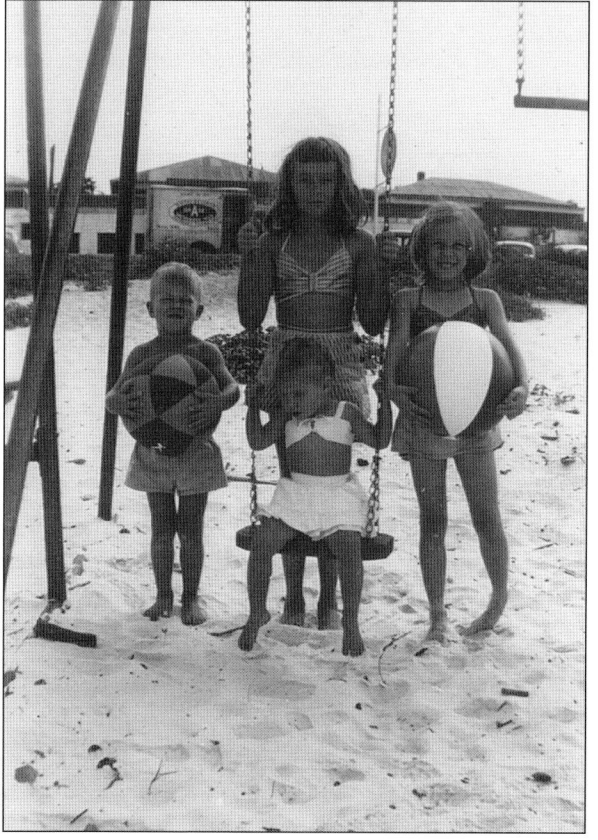

Ellis "Punk" Stevens and Terasa "Sissy" Edwards (left) stand with friends Tom and Louise Parker (right) on the beach in front of the Van Horn Restaurant and Jack's Place. In 1946, right after Tom Parker got out of the service, two men came up to them here at Beacon Hill beach, handing out flyers for G.U. Parker, who was planning a little community and naming it Mexico Beach. The flyers advertised Gulf-front lots for $200–$400. (Courtesy of Pam Parker Lawrence.)

From left to right, cousins Gordon, Joan, Terry, and Cathey Parker pose on the beach in front of the old Costin gas station in Beacon Hill around 1948. (Courtesy of Terry Parker Pope.)

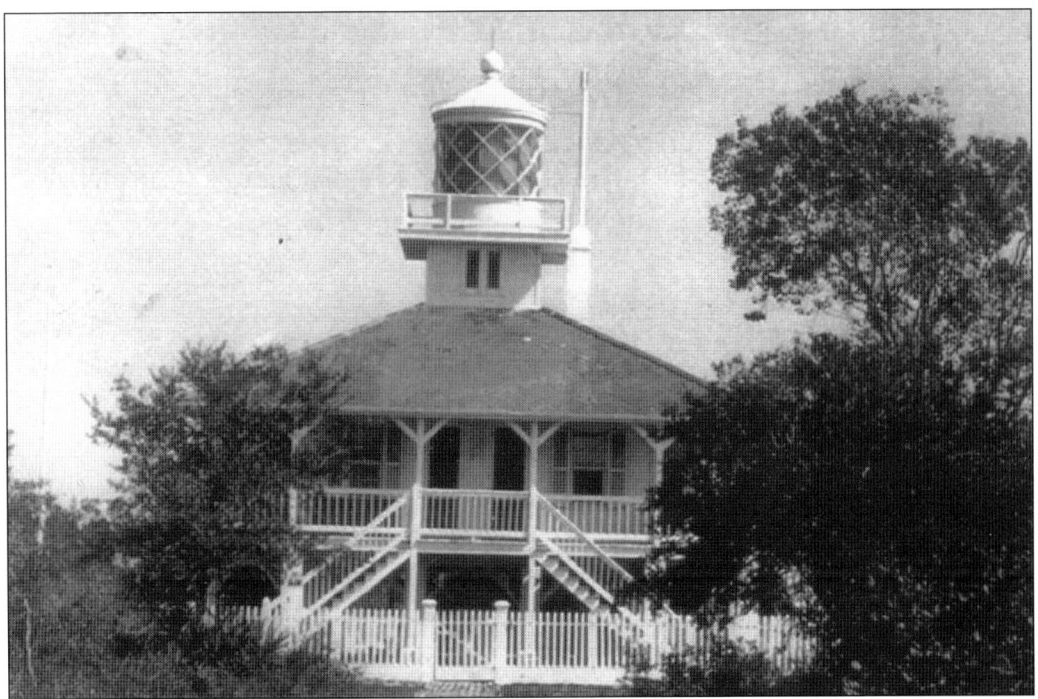

The Beacon Hill Lighthouse was built in 1902 near Port St. Joe. The first lighthouse keeper was Charles Lupton. This lighthouse was replaced in 1960 by a 78-foot-tall iron skeleton tower. In 1979, Danny Raffield of Port St. Joe moved the lighthouse to Simmons Bayou and converted it into a private home. (Courtesy of Beverly Mount Douds.)

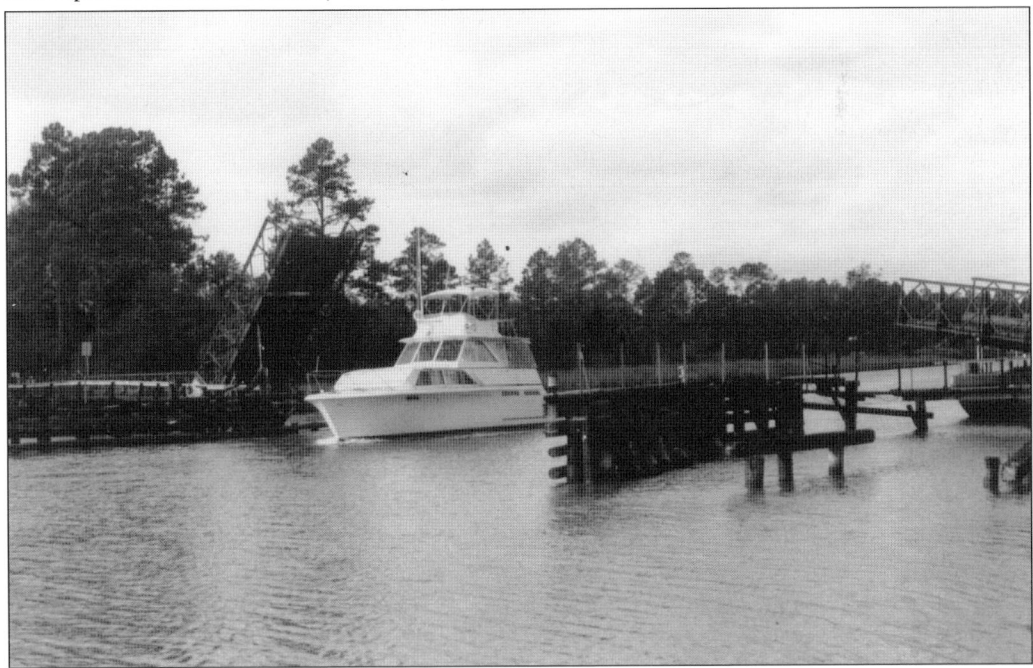

A fishing boat passes through the opened Overstreet floating bridge in the early 1980s. (Courtesy of Cathey Parker Hobbs.)

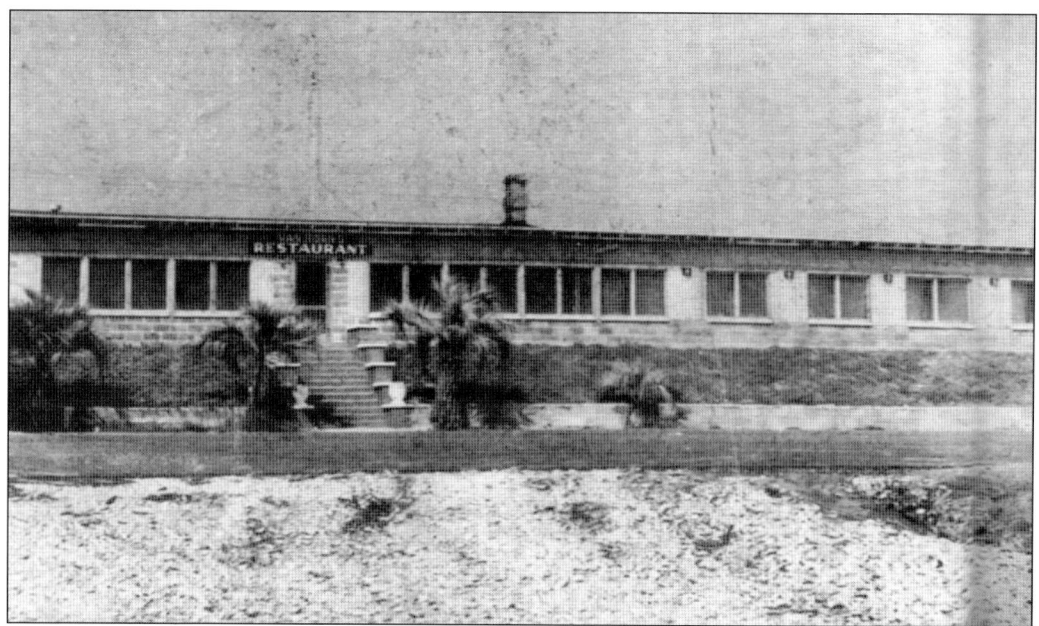

Van Horn Restaurant was located next to Jack's Place on a high terrace overlooking the Gulf of Mexico. A 1950s advertisement stated, "We have two Dining Rooms; one surrounded with jalousie windows allowing the cool Gulf breezes to blow through, a dance floor, and a large screen porch with a view of the gulf. You will enjoy the homey, quiet and friendly atmosphere." (Courtesy of Al Cathey.)

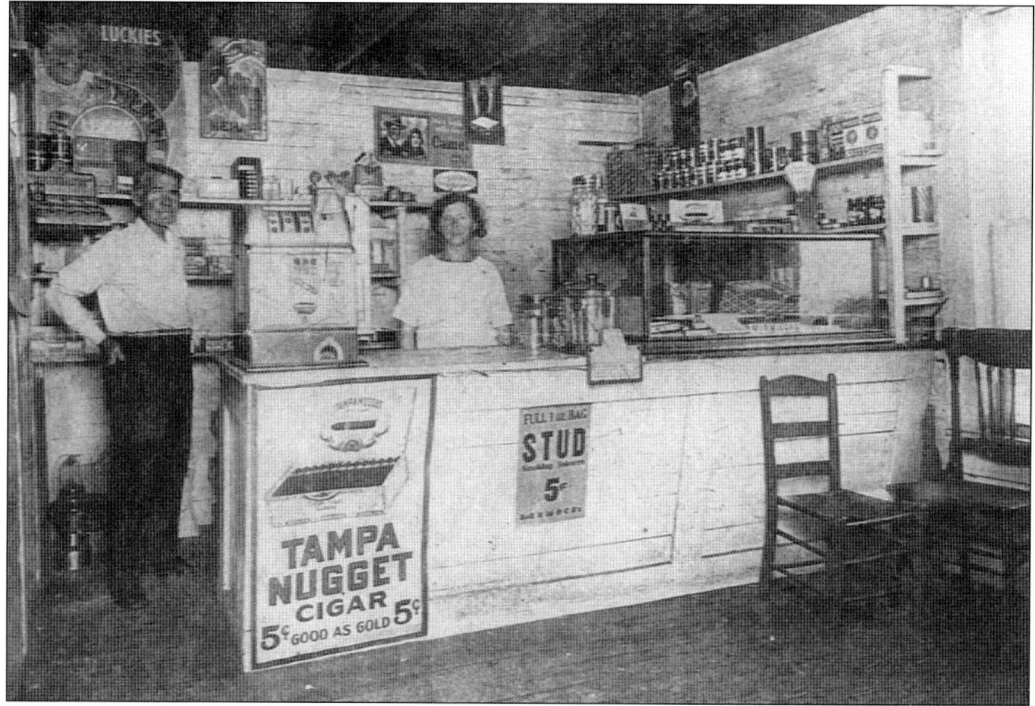

Proprietor Cornelius L. Van Horn is seen here with an unidentified woman behind the counter at Van Horn Restaurant around 1930. (Courtesy of Al Cathey.)

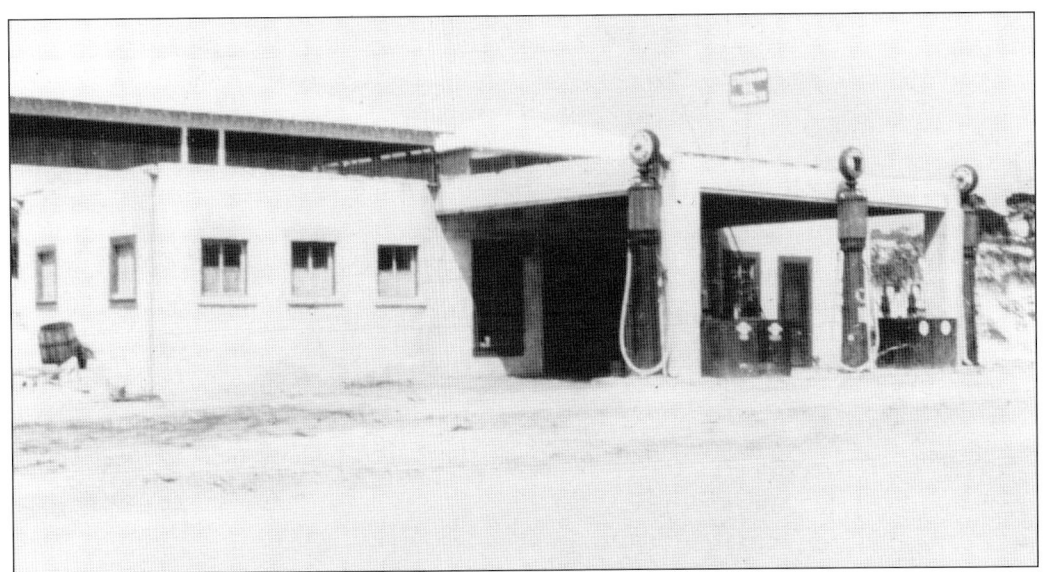

Cecil Costin Sr. built this gas station and grocery store on Highway 98 in Beacon Hill in the mid-1930s. The store sold staple goods, fresh bread, and cold drinks. Outside, there were two gravity-fed, glass-top gas pumps and a kerosene dispenser. In 1942, Costin sold the store to his brother Chauncey. With help from his wife, Marie, Chauncey operated the store until 1952, when he was appointed Port St. Joe postmaster. (Courtesy of Leonard Costin.)

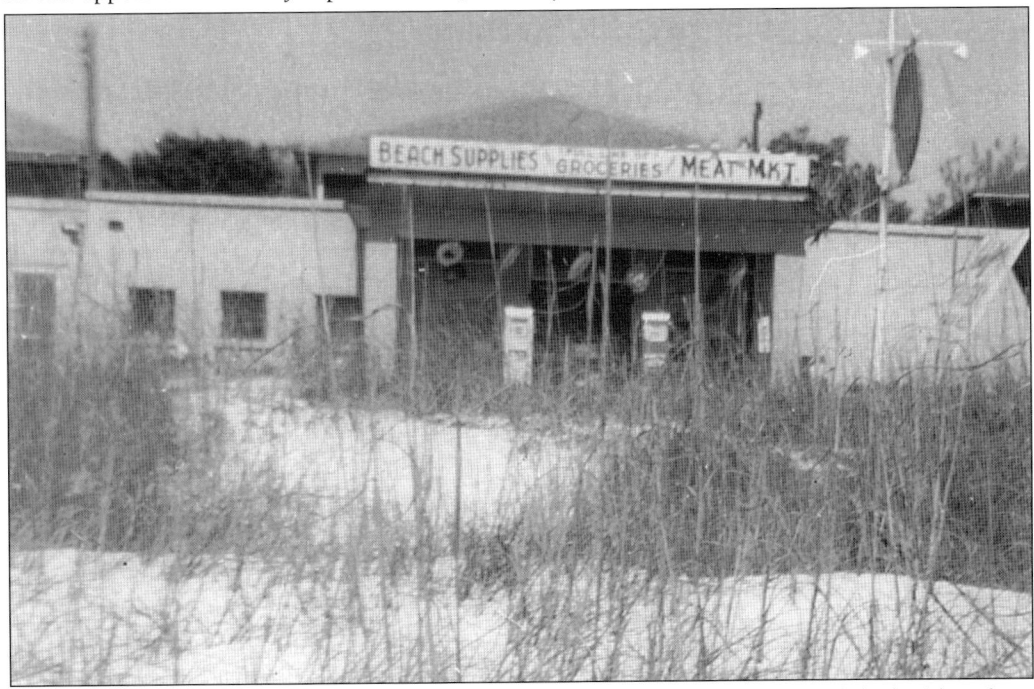

Scheffer's store in Beacon Hill is seen here. Marguerite and Foy Scheffer rented the building from Chauncey Costin from 1959 to 1988. Foy passed away in 1967. Over the next 20 years, the store was widely known simply as "Marguerite's store." It served the Beacon Hill community until 1988. Marguerite was also known as the "mayor of Beacon Hill." She was described as kindhearted, loving, funny, loud, and unique. (Courtesy of Beverly Mount Douds.)

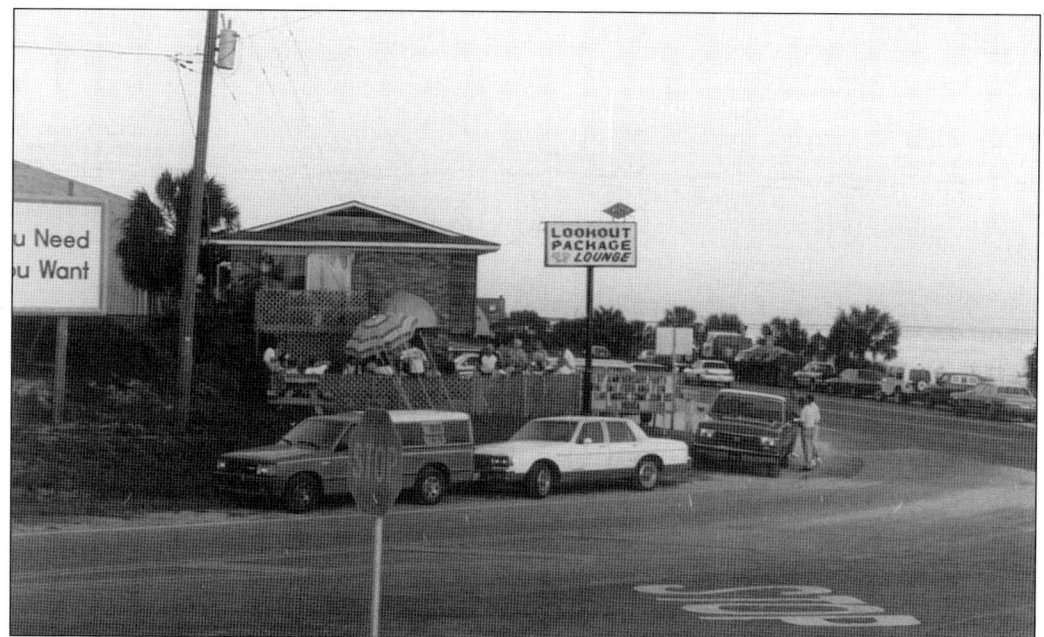

Lookout Lounge & Package Store was once a two-story home. The owner then opened a bar downstairs and later sold it to Sherry McDowell. Tony Whitfield has owned the lounge since 2005. (Courtesy of Sherry McDowell.)

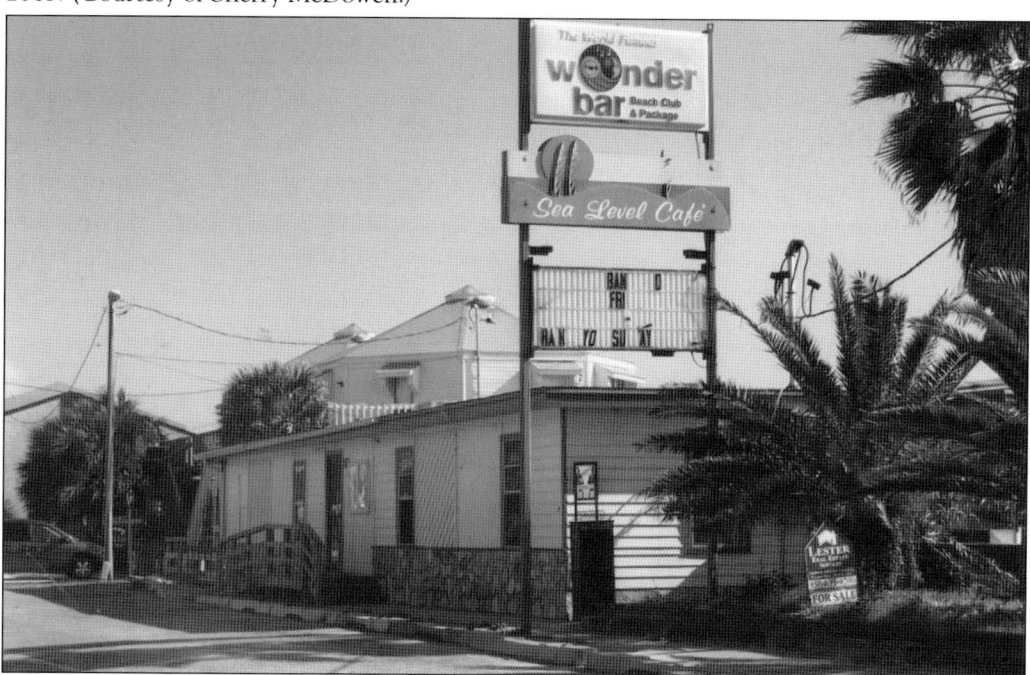

Wonder Bar, also known as Pat's Wonder Bar & Restaurant, is seen here in April 1970. It was originally owned by Elmer D. Harrell, followed by Dorothy Harrell Austin. In 2000, the bar closed its doors, and the building was torn down. The last owners were John and Joanie Hanson. For over 30 years, the Wonder Bar was one of the most popular and renowned nightspots along the Gulf beaches. (Courtesy of Cathey Parker Hobbs.)

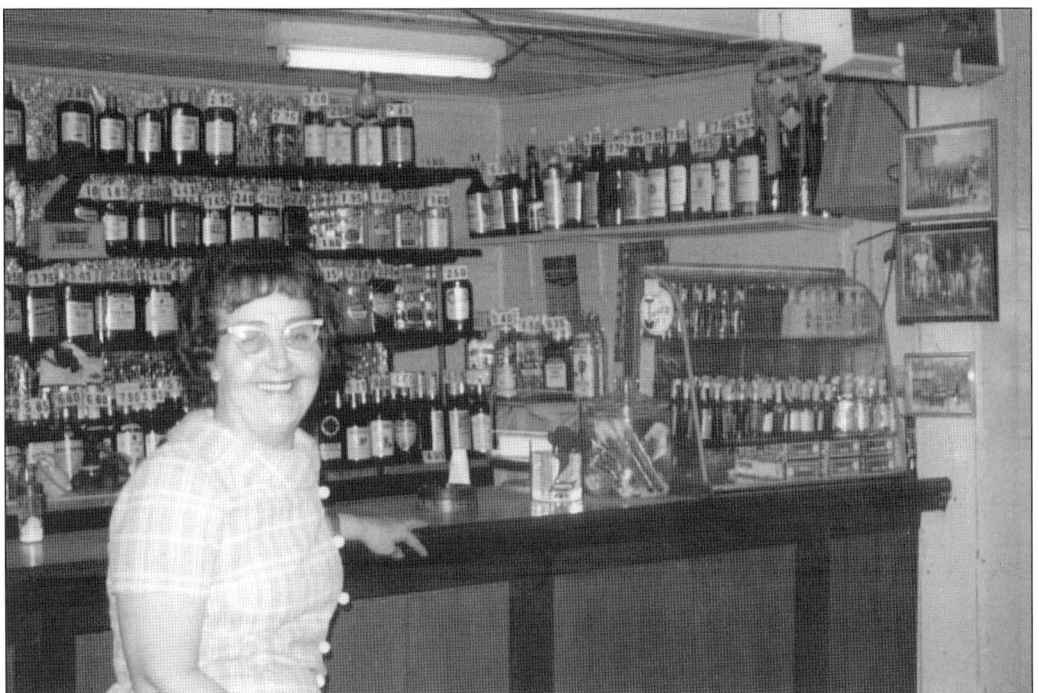

Thelma Prince was the wife of Jack Prince and the mother of Patsy, Jackie, and Ronnie Prince. She also operated the Beacon Hill business known to all as Jack's Place from the 1950s through the 1970s. (Courtesy of Ronnie Prince McDonald.)

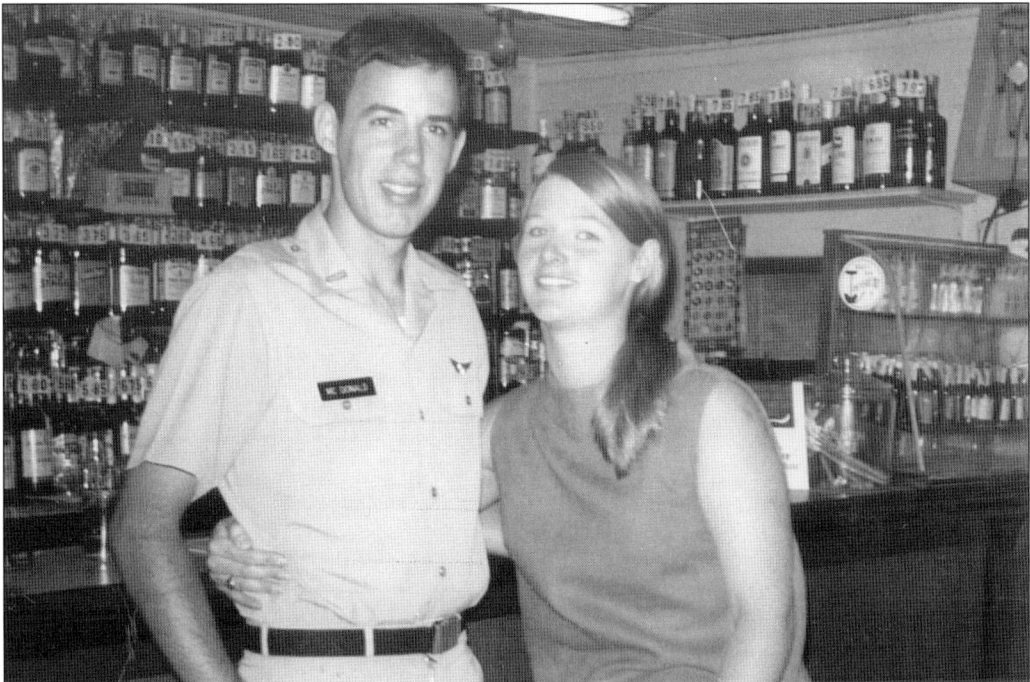

John McDonald and his wife, Ronnie (Prince) McDonald, posed for this photograph at Jack's Place just before John left for the Vietnam War in the 1970s. (Courtesy of Ronnie Prince McDonald.)

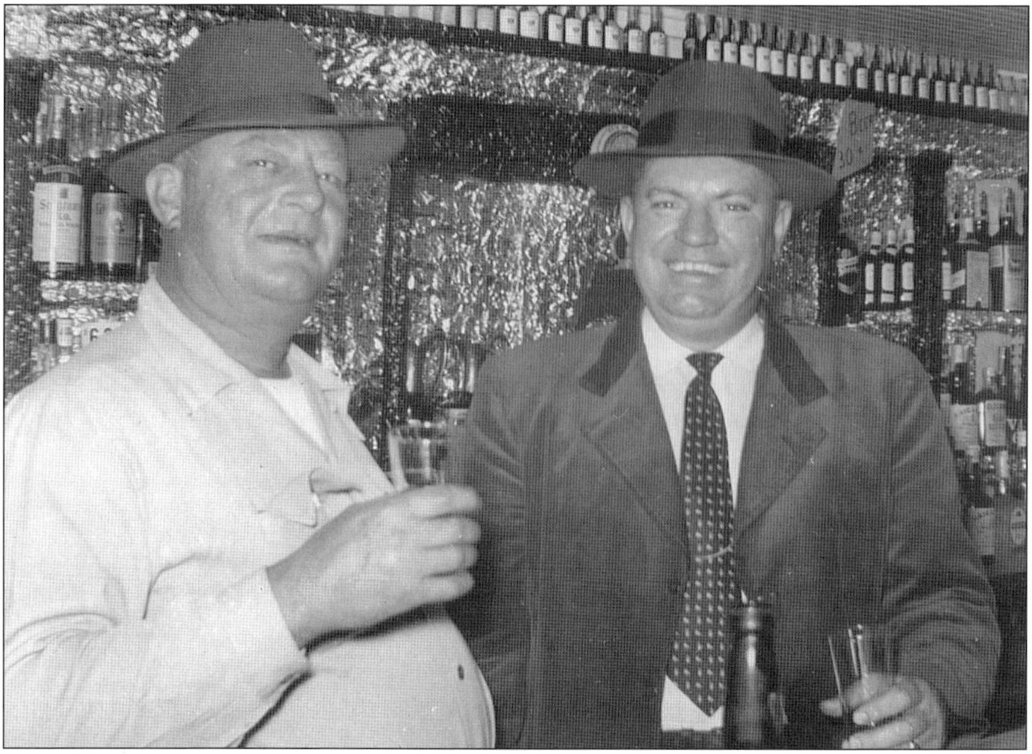

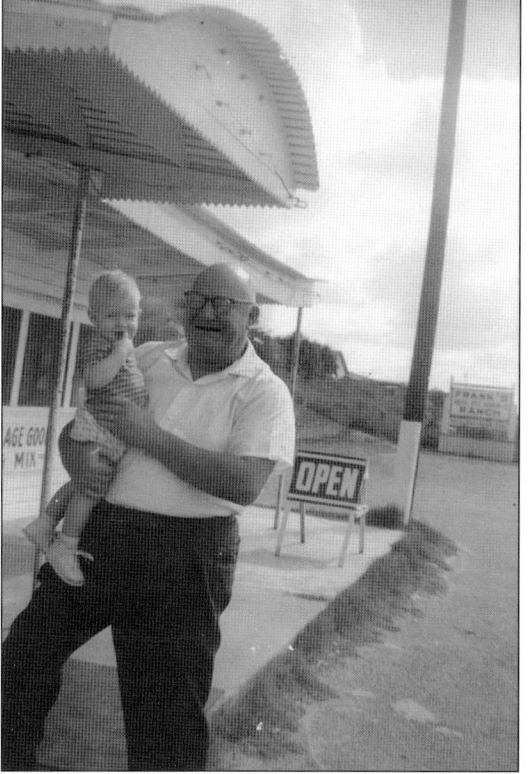

Jack Prince (left) and Mac McFalls (right) enjoy an evening together at Jack's Place in the 1950s. Prince was known to many people, and they enjoyed his company for years at Jack's Place. (Courtesy of Ronnie Prince McDonald.)

Jack Prince, the owner of Jack's Place and the father of the three Prince girls, is seen here holding little Johnny Scheffer in the 1960s. Johnny was the son of Roy and Marquette Scheffer, also of Beacon Hill. (Courtesy of Ronnie Prince McDonald.)

From left to right, Jackie, Patricia, and Ronnie Prince had their photograph taken with a friend of the family, Brezzy Winn, in Beacon Hill in the 1950s. (Courtesy of Ronnie Prince McDonald.)

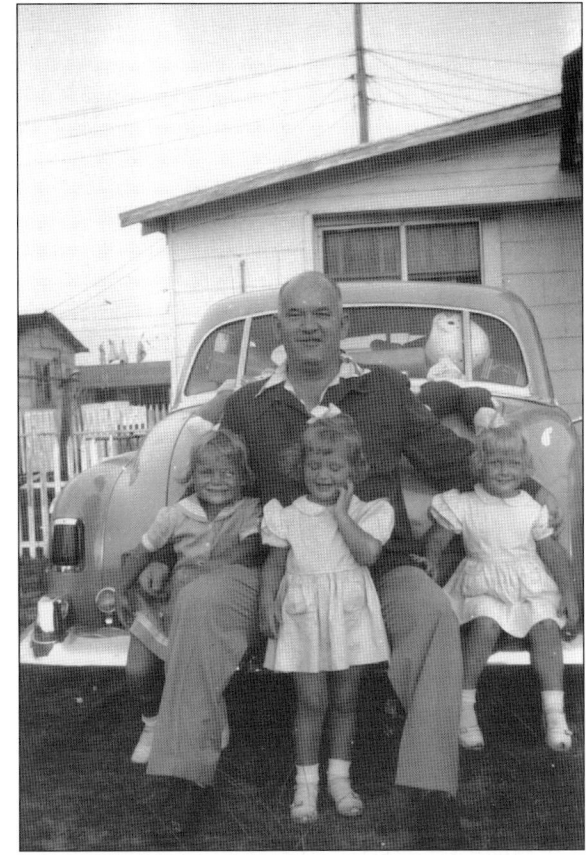

This photograph looks at the back door of the Wonder Bar on the Gulf of Mexico just before it closed in 2000. It was later torn down. (Courtesy of Cathey Parker Hobbs.)

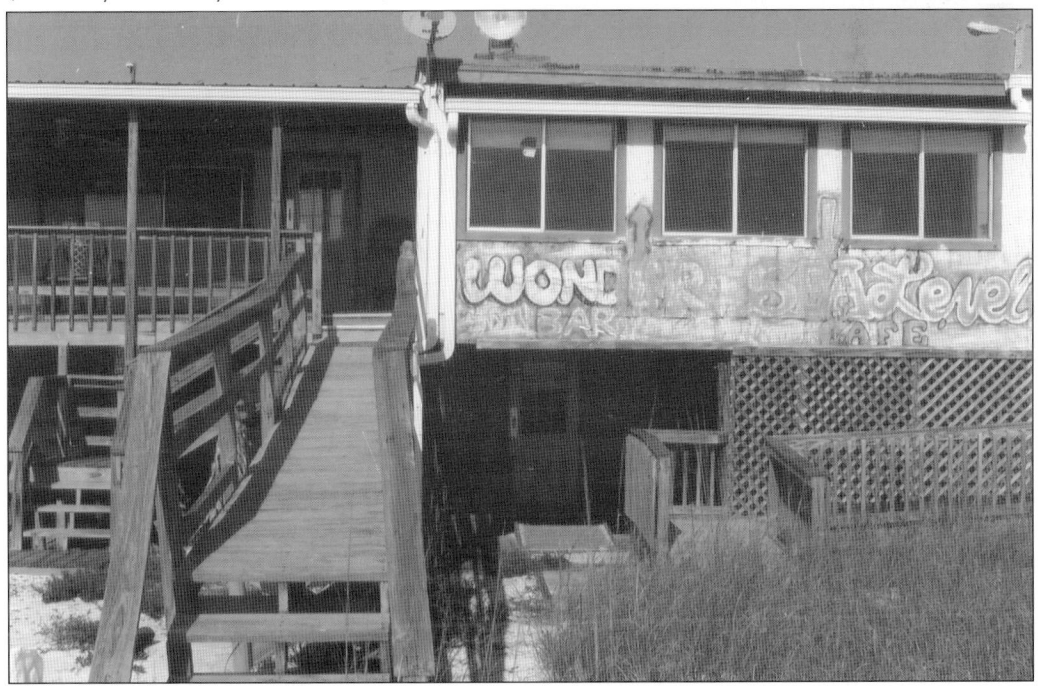

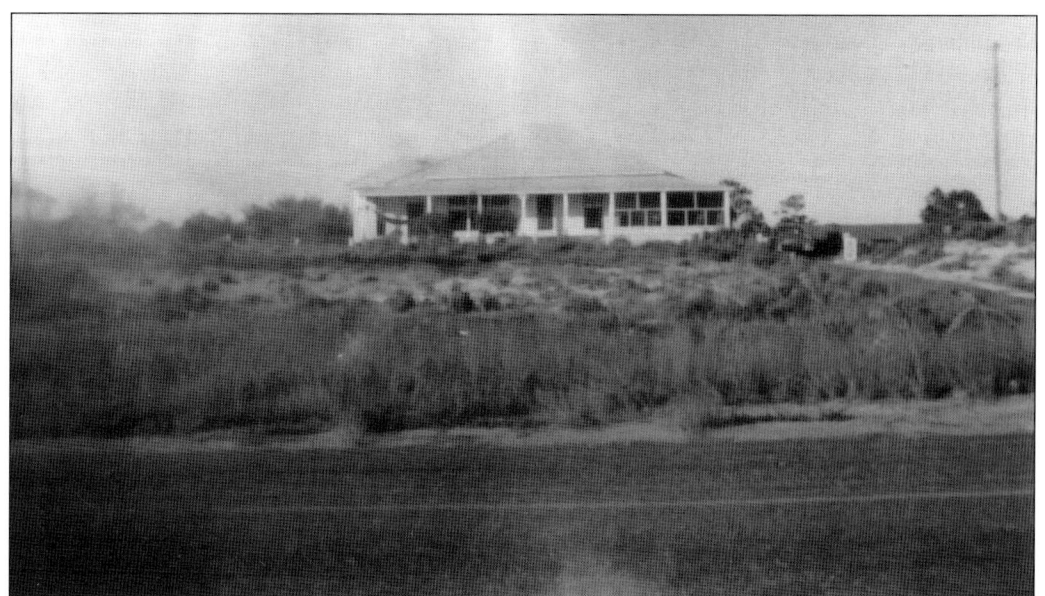

The West-Schulz cottage, located at 8956 Highway 98 in Beacon Hill is very special to many generations of folks from Jackson County and others from all over the country that were introduced to it, usually by local folks. The cottage was built in the early 1920s by Slade West's father, Dr. Theophilus West. Today, the Dr. Richard Schulz family owns the property. (Courtesy of Betty Joyce Hand.)

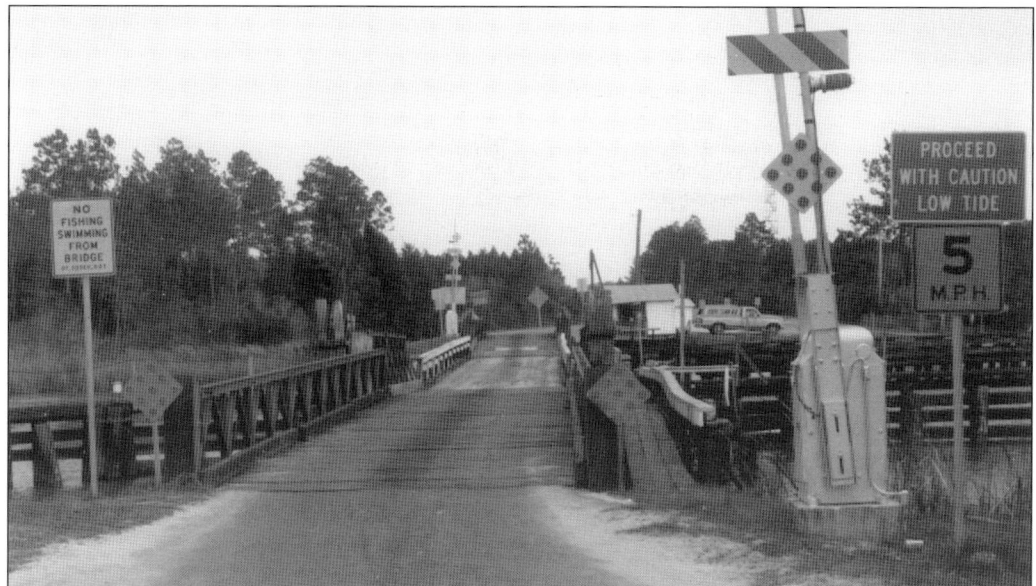

Seen here is what locals called the Overstreet floating bridge. The bridge was installed in 1932 and remained operational through 1988. For Mexico Beach residents, the shortest northern evacuation route is up Highway 386 through Overstreet. During hurricane season and storm events, the floating bridge was required to be opened to avoid damage from rising water, thus closing it to vehicular traffic. Residents seeking inland shelter from a storm would have to leave early enough to get across the Intracoastal Waterway before the bridge was opened. (Courtesy of Cathey Parker Hobbs.)

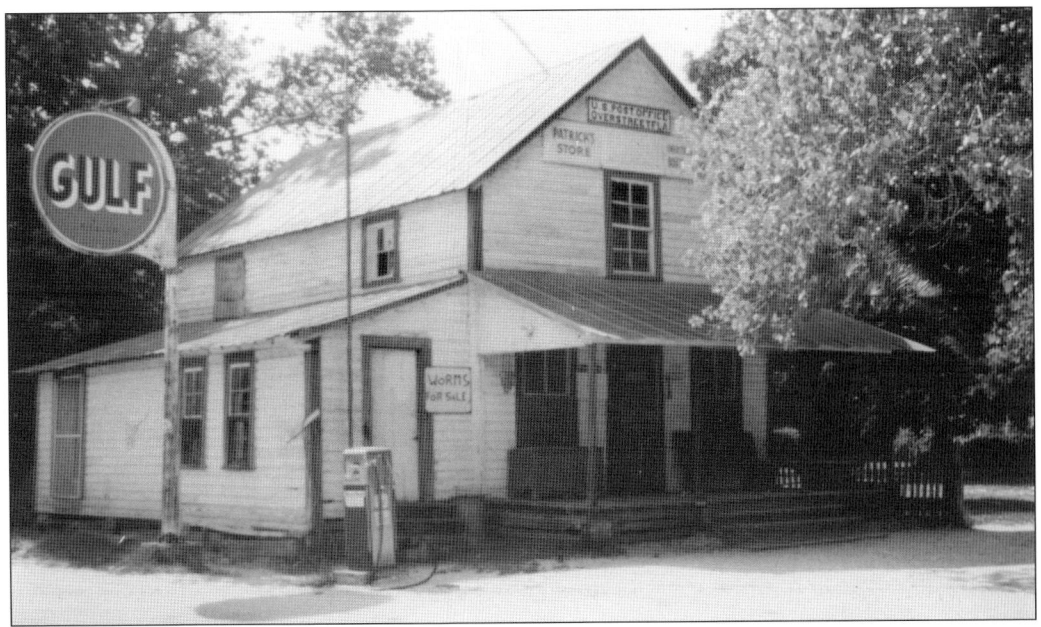

Patrick's Store was part of the Overstreet landscape from 1916 to 1991. For many years, the post office and store were operated by sisters Edna Hardy and Annie Cook. (Courtesy of Cathey Parker Hobbs.)

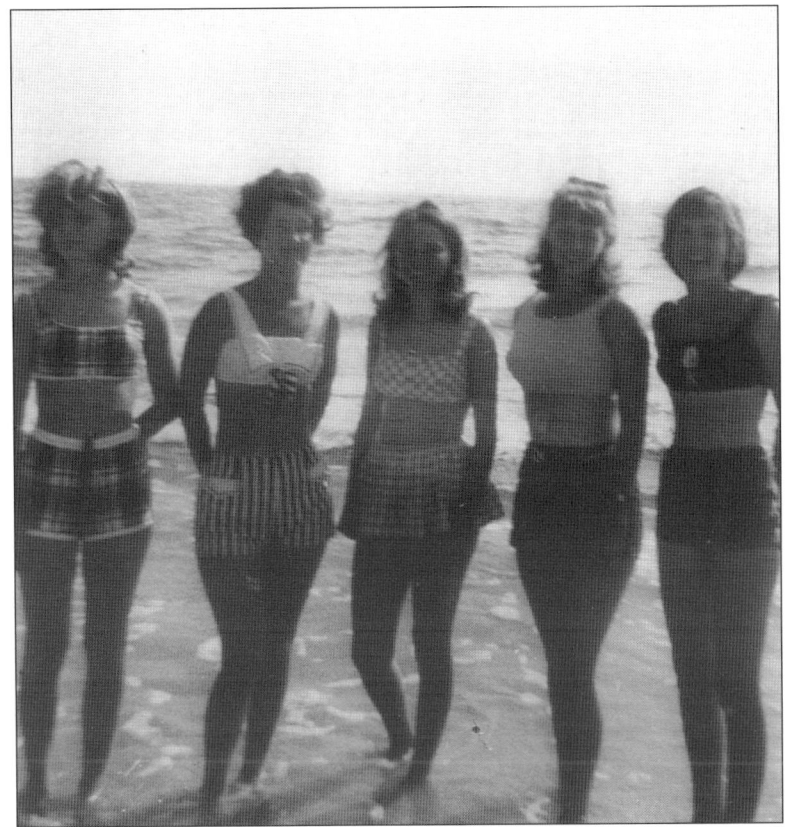

These classmates are enjoying their summer together at Beacon Hill in 1965. They are, from left to right, Rena Petty, Jackie Prince, Diane Huckeba, Ronnie Prince, and Shaleen Dunlap. (Courtesy of Ronnie Prince McDonald.)

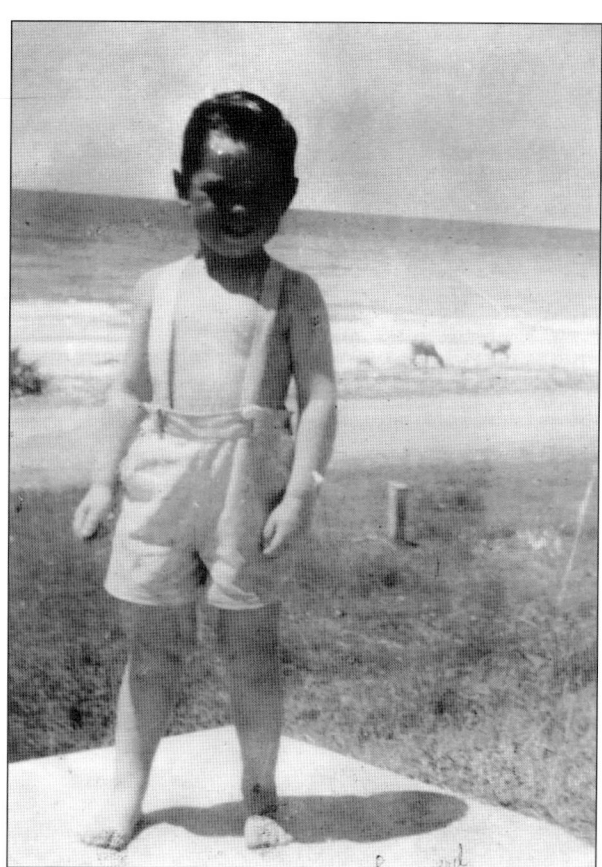
Leonard Costin is seen here as a young boy on the beaches of Beacon Hill, when cows were still allowed on the beach. (Courtesy of Leonard Costin.)

Jack's Place, which belonged to the Prince family, was located in Beacon Hill and was the first office of the Mexico Beach Corporation. This office did not last long, however, because it was too convenient to have a strong, refreshing drink. Inky Parker, a devoted Methodist, saw to it that the office was moved. (Courtesy of Ronnie Prince McDonald.)

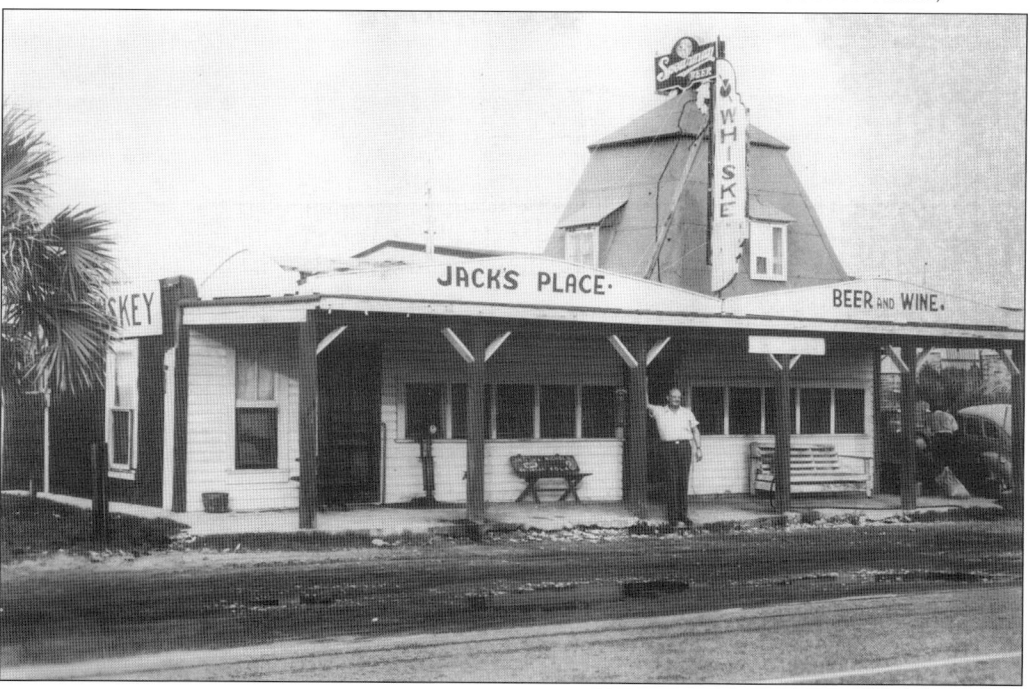

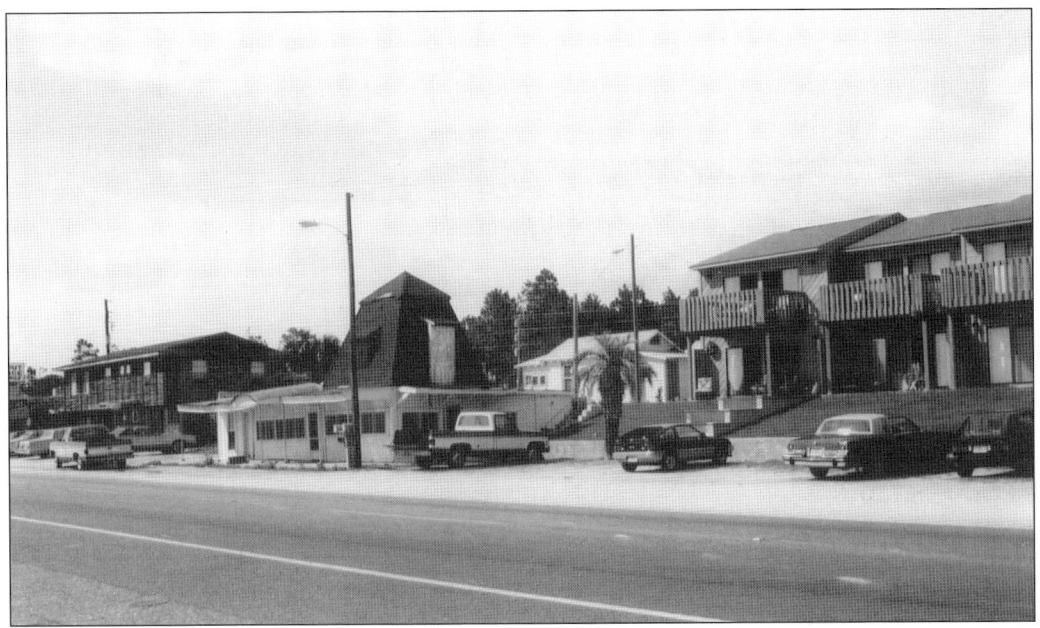

Lookout Lounge, Jack's Place, and townhouses are seen here in the 1980s, just before Jack's Place and Van Horn Restaurant closed. Townhouses were built in 1983 up on the cliff where Van Horn Restaurant was. In 1989, Ronnie Prince McDonald owned the townhouse nearest to her father's store. (Courtesy of Ronnie Prince McDonald.)

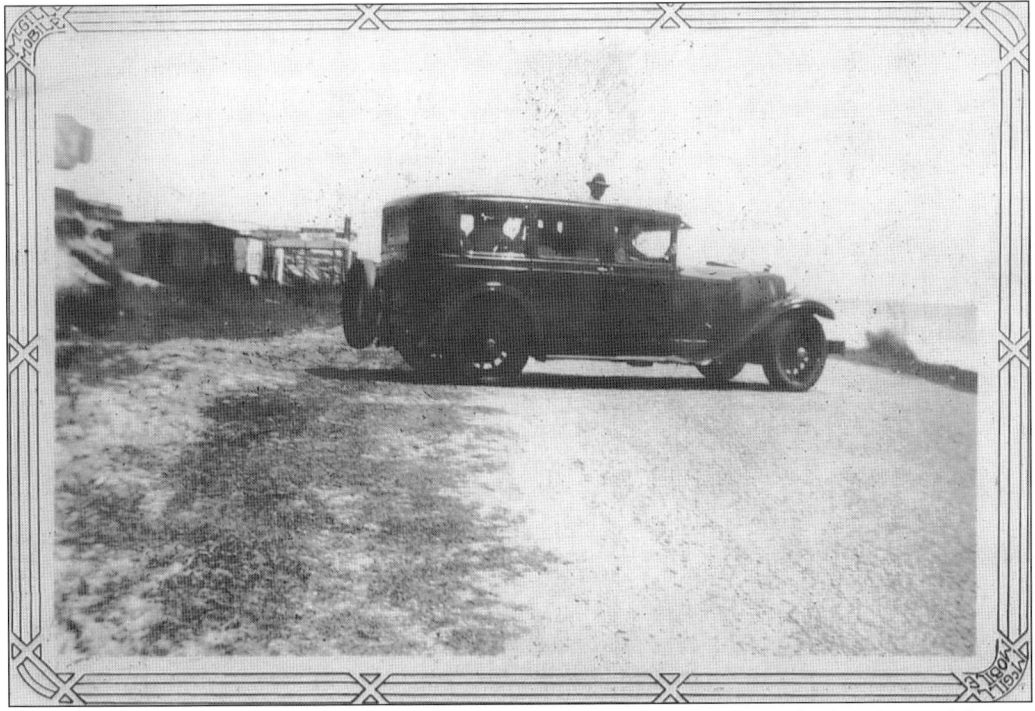

Long before Highway 98 was paved, this photograph shows an old car parked in front of the gas station that was owned by the Costin family. The photograph was taken in the late 1920s or early 1930s in Beacon Hill. (Courtesy of Tim Nelson.)

DISCOVER THOUSANDS OF LOCAL HISTORY BOOKS FEATURING MILLIONS OF VINTAGE IMAGES

Arcadia Publishing, the leading local history publisher in the United States, is committed to making history accessible and meaningful through publishing books that celebrate and preserve the heritage of America's people and places.

Find more books like this at
www.arcadiapublishing.com

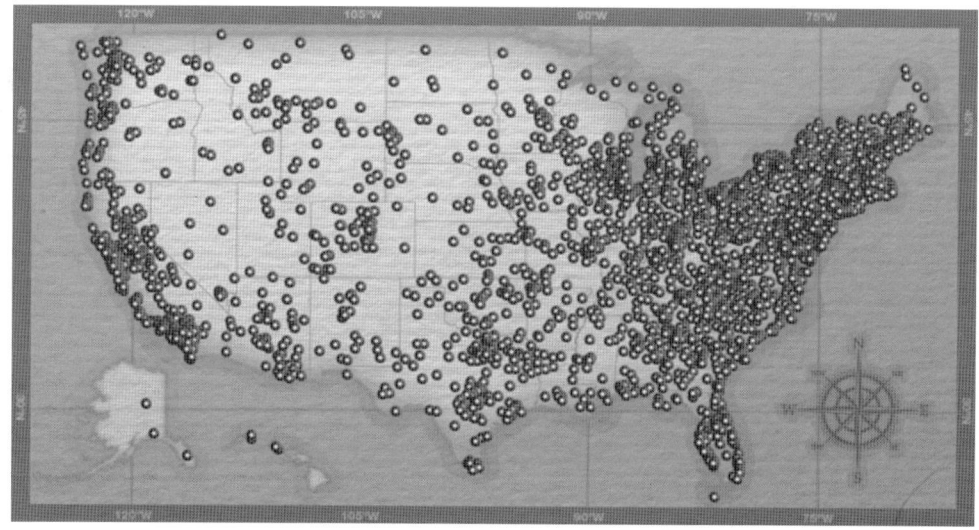

Search for your hometown history, your old stomping grounds, and even your favorite sports team.

Consistent with our mission to preserve history on a local level, this book was printed in South Carolina on American-made paper and manufactured entirely in the United States. Products carrying the accredited Forest Stewardship Council (FSC) label are printed on 100 percent FSC-certified paper.

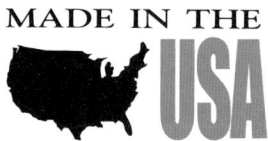